PRAISE FOR PAUL WILSON

The Little Book of Calm

"Pocket therapy."
—*Newsweek*

"Definitely a book to lend or leave around the place
to read over and over."
—Maeve Binchy, *International Express*

"Wilson's mixture of traditional meditation, alternative
therapy, positive thinking, and common sense has not only
enabled him to maintain an impressive degree of calm,
but has persuaded millions."
—*Financial Times*

Instant Calm

"One of the most comprehensive collections of relaxation
techniques ever."
—*Sydney Morning Herald*

"Wilson is a man on a mission to make the world a calmer place."
—*The Guardian*

"The most powerful anti-stress techniques conceived over
the past ten years."
—*You* magazine (UK)

"If this is what being calm is all about, I think I like it."
—*Evening Standard* (London)

PAUL WILSON is the author of *Instant Calm*, *The Calm Technique*,
and *The Little Book of Calm*. Known as "the King of Calm," he is
one of the world's leading authorities on relaxation. The chairman
of a Sydney advertising agency, he also works as a communications
consultant and serves as director of a hospital. He is a noted public
speaker and the author of two novels. He lives in Australia.

Paul Wilson

CALM AT WORK

A PLUME BOOK

PLUME
Published by the Penguin Group
Penguin Putnam Inc., 375 Hudson Street, New York, New York 10014, U.S.A.
Penguin Books Ltd, 27 Wrights Lane, London W8 5TZ, England
Penguin Books Australia Ltd, Ringwood, Victoria, Australia
Penguin Books Canada Ltd, 10 Alcorn Avenue, Toronto, Ontario, Canada M4V 3B2
Penguin Books (N.Z.) Ltd, 182–190 Wairau Road, Auckland 10, New Zealand

Penguin Books Ltd, Registered Offices: Harmondsworth, Middlesex, England

Published by Plume, a member of Penguin Putnam Inc.
Previously published by Penguin Books in Australia, 1997, and in Great Britain, 1998.

First American Printing, May, 1999
10 9 8 7 6 5 4 3 2 1

 REGISTERED TRADEMARK—MARCA REGISTRADA

LIBRARY OF CONGRESS CATALOGING-IN-PUBLICATION DATA
Wilson, Paul.
  Calm at work : breeze through your day feeling calm, relaxed
and in control / Paul Wilson.
    p. cm.
  ISBN 0-452-28042-7
  1. Job stress. 2. Stress management. 3. Relaxation. I. Title.
HF5548.85.W55   1999
155.9'042—dc21   98-52537
                                                        CIP

Printed in the United States of America
Illustrations by Monique Westermann

BOOKS ARE AVAILABLE AT QUANTITY DISCOUNTS WHEN USED TO PROMOTE PRODUCTS
OR SERVICES. FOR INFORMATION PLEASE WRITE TO PREMIUM MARKETING DIVISION,
PENGUIN PUTNAM INC., 375 HUDSON STREET, NEW YORK, NEW YORK 10014.

For Tania. And for the Calm Centre contributors whose creativity, research and tireless efforts in spreading calm and happiness deserve recognition.

CONTENTS

YOUR PORTFOLIO
OF CALM SOLUTIONS

LONGER-TERM CALM SOLUTIONS

A PERSONAL NOTE

The more confident you are that this book will change your life, the faster it *will* change your life. To earn your confidence, therefore, I am going to take the unprecedented (for me) action of commandeering a couple of pages to prove my 'calm' and 'work' credentials, to reassure you about the advice you're going to read.

My credentials for the 'calm' part of *Calm at Work* are a matter of record. I fund and maintain a calm research group, the Calm Centre (http://www.calmcentre.com), with activities covering a wide spectrum of calming arts – from teaching, to psychotherapy, to film-making, to music. At the same time I also serve on the board of a traditional hospital and medical research foundation. More visibly, perhaps, there are hundreds of thousands of my books about: *The Calm Technique* has been described as one of the world's most influential works of its type; *Instant Calm* has been translated into numerous languages and has been a best-seller in many parts of the world; and *The Little Book of Calm* is in more pockets and handbags than I would have ever dared fantasise about. As well, I have demonstrated my calming techniques on television shows from Sydney, to London, to New York (if you consider that a credential).

Yet, I could hardly expect to earn your confidence if I didn't also have sound work credentials. I've been chief executive, middle manager and office junior. In recent years I've owned my own businesses, served on the boards of public and private companies, and have advised Top 100 Corporations and governments. But I've also spent many more years as an employee – as a bank clerk (the hardest), truck driver, lathe operator and advertising copywriter, among other things.

In other words, I've learned what it means to be calm at work – from all sorts of perspectives.

A by-product of all this is that I now feel qualified to expose a centuries-old hoax: the hoax of employment. No doubt in doing this I will offend a few proprietors and managers, especially those whose employment philosophy is that 'workers should be grateful for anything they get'. Similarly, I would be disappointed if I did not offend some of the other side – the therapists, industrial advocates and various 'Blame the Boss' types who reject all do-it-yourself solutions in the belief that maintaining calm is a management responsibility, and not an individual's responsibility.

Both of these groups are guilty of perpetuating the master–slave mentality that has dogged the workplace for centuries. Both are guilty of spreading tension – not calm – in their work environments.

You would be well advised to steer clear of both of these groups as you read through *Calm at Work*, because this book was not designed to work for management, Human Resources departments, unions or legislators – but for you.

Just you.

If you are the only person to profit from my research – whether you're the trainee or the CEO – I will have succeeded.

Then both of us can be calm.

Paul

http://www.calmcentre.com

THE FIRST STEPS
TO CALM

HOW TO USE THIS BOOK

Calm at Work has been written for one purpose: to be a simple handbook you can open at any time

> *Calm at Work* will give you all the tools you need to breeze through your work day feeling calm, positive and fulfilled.

to help you stay calm through your working day.

It is not a textbook. Nor is it intended to be a detailed treatise on the problems of stress in the workplace – I'll leave that to the psychology industry, which is fixated with problems. No, this is simply a handbook of calm solutions.

These are not all my solutions; many were developed with the assistance of others at the Calm Centre. Here, developing calm solutions is our only interest; we research them, test them wherever possible, and pass them on to you with our best wishes.

Approached in the right spirit, *any* of the solutions in this book can work for you. As you read them you will intuitively know which ones will work best. Sometimes the psychological or physiological reasoning for their effectiveness may not be apparent, but this is not as important as the fact that they do work. In other words, don't get hung up on the question, 'Why am I feeling calm?', just enjoy feeling calm.

To find the solutions faster, I've used an office metaphor throughout. It relates to notepaper and filing cabinets. With index cards, files and folders.

Look for these calm solutions:
Breathing Calm .... page 103
Life Priorities Calculator .... page 91
The Art of Being Heard .... page 255

At the end of each section, you'll see an 'index card' icon like the one above, containing information on where to look for related solutions throughout the book.

TAKE AN EASYGOING BREAK

Each solution is highlighted by a paper clip icon.

And all of these solutions are contained within one large filing area – your Portfolio of Calm Solutions, starting on page 91.

One more thing before you go ...

You're probably thinking you could go straight to the Portfolio section, choose the solutions that appeal to you, and ignore the rest of this book.

You could. But I recommend against it for one very good reason. There is a lot of confusion that surrounds stress and anxiety; sufferers tend to excuse or to blame their problems on a variety of different factors – most of which have little to do with what really causes the problems.

This is why I urge you to read *Calm at Work* right through from the beginning. You will know soon enough which is the area you should concentrate on. That area will then direct you to the appropriate solution, or solutions, in the Portfolio section.

WOULD SOMEBODY PLEASE TELL ME WHAT HAPPENED?

THIS WAS SUPPOSED to be the age when our biggest problem each day would be finding ways of occupying all the additional leisure time at our dis-

> The thrust of *Calm at Work* is not about problems, it is about solutions. It is not about criticising conditions in the workplace, it is about feeling good about what you do for a living.

posal. With technology removing all the drudge from work, our lives were supposed to feature shorter working days and weeks, and longer weekends. All this extra time available meant we should be able to enrich our lives through education, leisure, absorbing and uplifting work, and personal and cultural development.

I remember reading about this fantasy when I was a teenager, and if I recall correctly I may even have added to it myself when I started writing in my twenties. The reality, however, has turned out to be far from idyllic.

In recent years, in an orgy of self-analysis and comparison, businesses and organisations have begun to reinvent themselves in the name of efficiency. Achievement began to be measured in terms of savings rather than growth. Managers confused 'downsizing' with progress, while 'rationalisation' was mistaken as some sort of productive ideal. Organisational restructuring ruined lives and careers, and ripped the soul out of many enterprises.

Accountancy became more prized than creativity, cutting costs more important than adding value, and the quest for competitiveness outweighed the values of either relationships or tradition.

That was organisational change.

Changes were also happening on the personal front. On the one hand we were pressured to specialise, while on the other we kept hearing of the need for 'de-skilling' and 'multiskilling'. When we thought we'd reached the stage where we could feel secure about our jobs, we learned of the financial and structural benefits of 'outsourcing'. When we finally thought we'd reached a position of trust, we entered a new era of 'accountability' and measurement of our efforts. And when we believed we'd invested so much of our lives in our jobs that we could begin to ease off and enjoy the fruits of our labours, we learned that anyone over forty-five was on limited tenure.

That was not the end of it. When we thought we were seeing the last of the mind-numbing nature of the assembly line, we were in fact seeing the beginning of the mind-numbing nature of data entry. While we were admiring the new efficiency levels that technology now allows us, we overlooked the rampant dehumanisation of many aspects of our workplaces. While we were planning what we'd do with all the newfound riches the new world was going to deliver, we saw the chasm widen between the Haves and the Have-nots. And, as we looked forward to the enlightenment that would come from unbounded information, we realised the knowledge we (as individuals) had already accumulated now amounted to very little.

Will somebody please tell me what happened?

The bottom line to all this is that many *organisations* are, at least technically, more efficient than they used to be – that is, they produce what they're meant to produce at a lower cost. (And if they're not, they're out of business, which more or less explains the high rate of business failure.) In addition, many *individuals* have become more productive – that is, they produce more of what they used to for the same or reduced cost.

But the rewards we were promised have, in many cases, failed to materialise. Instead of being blessed with all that extra leisure time, we've been burdened by extra work. Instead of becoming more interesting, many of our jobs have become more predictable and humdrum. Now we're doing more, with less help, and with decreased resources. Instead of handing over more responsibility to technology, we've had to take on responsibility for the technology itself. Instead of learning more and more, we discover the things we've already learned are fast becoming obsolescent. Today, most of us are working harder, longer and more intensely than ever before. With increased scrutiny and accountability, combined with decreased job security. And, even more alarming, we've been told that we're going to have to work harder still, become even more productive and accountable – because international competition will force us onto the industrial scrap heap unless we maintain the pain.

And they tell us the change has only just begun!

Then there's the fear

While I have little respect for the way many corporations and their executives chase ideals that they don't understand the social ramifications of, I am aware of the fear under which they now operate. (I write of corporations, but the same phenomenon exists in most large organisations – political, public service, medical, religious.)

'Fear?' you scoff. 'With all those bonuses, BMWs and business-class travel?'

But today, fear is one of the dominant motivators among the executive ranks of large organisations – more so than greed, altruism or adventurism, and possibly even more so than personal ambition.

(In my brief forays into the world of Motivation, I found that greed, personal ambition and altruism were by far the easiest forces to work with, because from a managerial point of view they were 'positive' and forward-directed; you knew where the individual was coming from and where they wanted to go. Fear, on the other hand, was invariably negative and often subversive; while it was the easiest emotion to activate, it had the least potential for turning into success.)

In a way, you can understand it. The job-life expectancy for the average chief executive of a public company these days is three to five years (slightly more or less depending on the country), so there is little job security in being a CEO. But fear is even more pronounced in the lower executive ranks. Whether it is fear of failure, of reproach, of legislation, of unions or other interest groups, of discovery, of competition, or simply of the unknown, it bubbles away in large organisations: seething, festering, sometimes influencing the psyche of the entire place. Moreover, this negative energy has an osmotic effect, causing problems not only through the corporation, but often throughout entire industries.

Of course, not everyone works for a large corporation or organisation. This has much to commend it, because smaller enterprises (in my observation) are generally happier and less fearful than large ones. But when these are governed by fear, it is closer to the heart of every employee.

What a mess.

A change is *not* as good as a holiday

In human terms, the cost of this decade's change has been immense. Not only in stress-related illnesses and absenteeism, but in more permanent conditions such as those that arise from hypertension, depleted immune systems and depression.

In addition to this we're seeing a comparatively new phenomenon described as 'burnout', whose overriding symptom is a desire to leave or walk out on your job, to give up, throw it all in.

Ironically, the result of all these changes – remembering they were brought about because of industry's quest for increased efficiency and productivity – is *de*creased efficiency and productivity. Yes, *de*creased. Researchers are now beginning to discover that some of the old-fashioned people-powered procedures were actually more efficient than the new technologically-oriented ones that replaced them. They are also beginning to discover many of those 'outmoded' people-intensive activities actually result in a more contented, and more efficient, workplace.

So now what do we do? Start again?

Nope, just keep reading

Fortunately, you've opened this book at exactly the right time.

There is no time like this very moment to turn all the world's turmoil to *your* advantage. There is no time like right now to discover a sense of calm that occupational therapists theorise about and stressed employees fantasise over. There is no time like this very instant to transform your job – whatever it is – into a fascinating, fulfilling occupation.

It can be done.

Moreover, by the end of *Calm at Work*, you will be able to do it easily. You will have all the resources you need to shrug off the unfortunate by-products of change, and to concentrate instead on the benefits.

After you have read this book, you will have the tools you need to breeze through your work day feeling calm, positive and fulfilled, approaching every day with a wide-eyed sense of adventure that many of us have not experienced since childhood.

HOW SUSCEPTIBLE ARE YOU?

To REITERATE, THE focus of *Calm at Work* is solutions, rather than problems. Before we embark on our solution-gathering journey, however, it may help to isolate exactly what the problem is.

> No matter how much emphasis is placed on competitiveness, downsizing or increased productivity in your place of employment, you can be calm, contented and totally fulfilled by what you do.

You may think that every stressed person would know this, but there are times when this may not be so, especially when the stress levels are chronic or excessive. Someone under extreme pressure is seldom in an orderly frame of mind, and instead of recognising the condition that ails them, will blame any number of external influences: their job, their employer, the government, their spouse, the traffic, the society they live in – anything but their own attitude or behaviour.

Isolating the causes of your discomfort, therefore, may involve a degree of self-analysis. I do not advocate too much introspection, but it may be worth exploring the personality types, industries and situations that are most susceptible to the stressful feelings you want to overcome.

Who has most reason to complain?

The two questions about stress I encounter most are: 'What are the most stressful occupations?' and 'Who are the most stressed people?'

The former is a difficult question for me to answer accurately since research statistics vary between the countries in which this book is published. Nevertheless, by taking a general approach to the various surveys, I can at least highlight the similarities.

One thing common to all countries surveyed is the view that some occupations are more stressful than others. It's difficult to be specific because no-one can agree on what defines a stressful occupation. Should it be evaluated according to the number of lost work days, employee turnover or burnout? Or according to behavioural problems, such as alcoholism? Or should it be evaluated according to what employees believe is the case (that is, how they feel, morale and so on)?

The most revealing area is the latter. After all, if people *believe* they're suffering from stress-related problems, then you can be sure they are suffering – lost work days and other problems are simply the next stages in the decline. So what are the occupations where workers believe they are suffering most?

Predictably, the larger the organisation, the more common is the reporting of stress-related problems. These increase in direct proportion to the perceived oppressiveness of the organisation's management.

The industries most susceptible to stress-related complaints and absenteeism include education, health, transport, the public sector and communications, with retail, small business and construction coming further down the ladder.

Regardless of the industry or the occupation, the one thing certain is that stress-related complaints are on the rise. Whether the organisation is shrinking or expanding, failing or succeeding, the problems seem similar.

But the comforting news is that you do not have to be part of this suffering or unrest. The content of this book will enable you to avoid these tensions with only a minimum of effort. No matter how much emphasis is placed on competitiveness, downsizing or increased productivity in your place of employment, you can be calm, contented and totally fulfilled by what you do.

Because you will know the secret of being calm at work.

What does it mean to be 'stressed'?

The stress-relief industry is a huge, multi-billion-dollar industry with a vested interest in having you believe that it is abnormal to feel stressed at work. But it's not! Everyone feels under pressure at one time or another, perhaps several times a day. That's life in the workplace.

It's not ideal. It's not productive. And it's not necessary. But it *is* normal, and accepting that fact is the first step in ensuring that so-called 'stress conditions' are not debilitating and do not become habitual.

So, where do you fit into all this? Do you suffer from specific symptoms of stress? Is it habitual or occasional? Are you the stressful type (if there is such a thing)? What are the causes of your tension? Do you recognise them?

Psychologists sometimes refer to the Theory of Self-Perception, which says we generally make the same errors in assessing our own behaviour and personality as we do when we try to assess others. In other words, we're not very good at working out what drives us, or what causes our individual problems.

Blaming this Theory of Self-Perception, however, will not make you feel better. You need to determine the areas where you are most at risk and, if necessary, to take corrective action. Fortunately, there are well-defined warning signs, most of which are easy to recognise.

Here are several ways of recognising these signs. Try them and see what you discover about yourself in going through the following steps:

(i)   On Charts 1 and 2, place a tick beside the feelings and reactions that best describe your own.

(ii) Add up your points from each column and total them.

(iii) On Chart 3, in the right-hand column, list the points that relate to you, and total them.

(iv) Add together the totals from Charts 1, 2 and 3.

(v)   Now, *subtract* the points from Chart 4, deducting seven points for each description that applies to you.

Please don't make too much of this analysis – it's here to highlight your propensity for feeling tense and under pressure, nothing more. Have a bit of fun with it.

CHART 1 Do you experience these physical symptoms?

SYMPTOM	DAILY (3 points)	WEEKLY (2 points)	SOMETIMES (1 point)	SELDOM (0 points)
Breathing difficulties				
Butterflies in the stomach				
Chest pain				
Clenched fingers				
Cold hands or fingers				
Cold sweats				
Constipation				
Diarrhoea				
Dry mouth				
Feeling faint				
Fidgeting				
Grinding teeth				
Headache				
Impotence				
Indigestion				
Insomnia				
Loss of appetite				
Lower back pain				
Need to urinate frequently				
Oversleeping				
Palpitations				
Rapid pulse				
Sick in the stomach				
Skin rashes				
Speeded-up conversation				
Stiff neck or shoulders				
Tenseness				
Tightness in stomach or chest wall				
Tiredness				
Trembling hands				
COLUMN TOTALS				

TOTAL _____

CHART 2 Do you experience these feelings or tendencies?

SYMPTOM	DAILY (3 points)	WEEKLY (2 points)	SOMETIMES (1 point)	SELDOM (0 points)
Anger				
Confusion				
Drug or alcohol abuse				
Easily bored				
Fear				
Fear of open spaces				
Feeling something is about to go wrong				
Frustrated by detail				
Hysteria				
Impatience				
Inability to concentrate				
Intolerance of people				
Irrationality				
Irritability				
Low tolerance of noise				
Negative attitude				
Overeating				
Overreaction to events				
Oversleeping				
Pessimism				
Poor memory				
Reduced sex drive				
Short temper				
Sleep disorders				
Smoking				
Suspiciousness				
'There's never enough time'				
'This can't be happening to me'				
Emotional states				
Worries about the future				
COLUMN TOTALS				

TOTAL _____

CHART 3	Which of these events have occurred recently or are likely to occur?		
A death in the immediate family	30	
Diagnosed with a life-threatening illness	29	
Divorce	28	
Separation	27	
Retrenchment	26	
Dismissed from job	26	
Serious illness	26	
Problems with a child at home	23	
Changed job	22	
Changed job function	21	
Threats of dismissal	20	
Pregnancy	19	
Relationship problems (out of work)	18	
Relationship problems (at work)	18	
Change in nature of employment	15	
Merger of employer and other organisation	15	
Change in financial state	14	
Financial problems	14	
Spouse begins or stops work	10	
Outstanding achievement	10	
Change of living arrangements	10	
Giving up smoking	9	
Threat of legal action	7	
Regular enforced overtime	7	
Employer financial problems	6	
Christmas	5	
Threats from boss/board/shareholders	4	
Intimidating superior	4	
Uncooperative staff	4	
Changes to your industry	3	
	TOTAL _____	

CHART 4 Which of these attributes apply to you?	
SYMPTOM	SUBTRACT 7 POINTS
I look after my diet	
I exercise regularly	
I spend at least 30 minutes a day doing nothing	
I meditate often	
I drink less than three cups of coffee a day	
I am comfortable with silence	
I allow time between appointments	
I plan my day	
I admire others' success	
I help others whenever I can	
I have a happy home life	
I work in a job I like	
My efforts are recognised by my superiors	
I get on well with workmates	
I have minimal debt	
My job is for my benefit, no-one else's	
I get satisfaction from my work	
I take regular holidays	
I leave my work worries at work	
I expect change in life and work	
Becoming calm is *my* responsibility	
I am seldom bored	
I listen to others' points of view	
I have some 'positive stress' in my life	
I am assertive in my work and personal life	
I have at least 30 minutes a day to myself	
I have a pet	
I have an active social life	
My work is varied	
I can see the positive side of change	
TOTAL _____	

Ideally, your total score will be as low as possible. If your score is very low (0 to 35), you're one of the more fortunate people in the workforce, and you're probably reading this book out of curiosity.

Conversely, if your total is high, your need is likely to be every bit as pressing as you suspected.

If you fall somewhere in between, you're in good company, because that's where most people find themselves. This is considered 'normal' in the workforce. While it may be normal, it's far from natural and, with a little effort, this feeling can be significantly improved upon.

Which group of words best describes your behaviour and language?		
A	B	C
Reason	Fight	Retreat
Calm voice	Loud!	Quiet
Open expression	Challenging look	Downcast eyes
Relaxed posture	Folded arms	Fidgeting fingers
Conversational gestures	Staccato gestures	Clenched hands
'I . . .'	'You should . . .'	'Maybe . . .'
'I want . . .'	'Do it!'	'Do you think . . .?'
'I did . . .'	'You should have . . .'	'I should have . . .'
'I feel . . .'	'That's the way it is!'	'Sorry if I . . .'
'Let's . . .'	'Hurry up . . .'	'Do you mind terribly if . . .'
'I see what you mean.'	'You're wrong!'	'I don't know . . .'
'How can we work this out?'	'Why can't you . . .'	'I don't mean to . . .'

If you identify more with the words in group A, rather than group B or C, then you are probably what's known as an 'assertive type'. This is considered the ideal personality trait to help you get what you want out of your work and, as a result, to remain calm.

If you identify more with the words in the B category, then chances are you're more of an 'aggressive type'. Aggressive personalities often mistake their aggressiveness for assertiveness – and this leads to frustration when they fail to get their own way (which is often). And, contrary to popular opinion, aggressive behaviour does not expend stress – it increases it, just as it increases the tendency towards even more aggressive behaviour.

If you see more of yourself in the C category, then you are almost certainly aware of your 'submissive' or 'passive' tendencies. While this may not be a direct source of stress, it can certainly lead to it.

The good news is that both submissive and aggressive personalities can use the same techniques to channel their leanings into more assertive – and more rewarding – behaviour.

Which group of characteristics best describes you?						
A						B
	POINTS					
	5	4	3	2	1	
Create your own stress						Have stress created for you
Are achievement oriented						Are interested in 'living', not 'having'
Are highly competitive						If ambitious, are not overcompetitive
See yourself as assertive						Are fairly easygoing
Set yourself difficult targets						Are realistic about what is achievable
Set yourself unrealistic deadlines						Set reasonable deadlines, or none at all
Never late for appointments						Relaxed about appointments
Attempt several things at once						Approach tasks methodically
Push yourself to the limit						Know your limits
Are always in a hurry						Are less driven, less obsessive
Are impatient, easily bored						Can find interest in most things
Use clipped, aggressive speech						Speak slower, communicate better
Anticipate others' conversations (such as completing sentences)						Listen well
Breathe faster and shallower						Breathe slower and deeper
Display tense body language						Display relaxed body language
Eat, speak, move quickly						Take things slowly
Are self-centred						Are more outgoing
Conceal feelings						Express feelings
Always feel responsible						Share responsibility
Delegate reluctantly						Delegate willingly
Precise, obsessed about detail, yet . . .						Do not feel obliged to be precise, yet . . .

A						B
	POINTS					
	5	4	3	2	1	
Forget details, make mistakes						Are organised, make fewer mistakes
Consume too much coffee						Consume modestly
Feel guilty about relaxing						Relish the opportunity to unwind
Crave recognition for own efforts						Concerned with satisfying others
Must get things finished once started						Don't mind leaving things temporarily
Always working (weekends, home)						Work is only one part of life
Few interests outside work						Work is one of many interests
Obsessed with quantifying things						Not overly concerned with how much, how often or how many

If you see more of yourself in group A than in group B, you are demonstrating the classic 'Type A' behaviour patterns you have probably read about. Conversely, if you see more of yourself in B, you demonstrate more 'Type B' behaviours.

According to the stereotypes – and these *are* stereotypes that ignore the fact that each person is an individual – Type A people suffer from more self-induced stress than Type B people. To exacerbate matters, Type A people often believe they are more in control of themselves and situations than other types of people – which means they are less likely to seek help for their problems.

If you want to see how you fit into this equation, and you want to play the game, simply rate yourself from 5 to 1 using the above scale for each of the given attributes. Then, add up those figures, and see where you're placed.

How you fared

120–150 By all appearances, you exhibit classic Type A1 behaviour habits. For the sake of your well-being, you would be wise to absorb the advice in this book – quickly.

90–120 While these (Type A2) behaviour patterns are not as severe or as intense as the above, they probably warrant an active, ongoing effort towards adding calm habits to your life.

60–90 Many people fall into this (AB) category, a balance of both A and B behaviour types. My observation is that when such people vary their behaviour patterns, they are more inclined to move towards A.

30–60 According to statistics, you should be fairly relaxed and able to deal with stressful situations. Of course, life is never that neat and you may very well suffer from stressful situations in the workplace.

0–30 A classic B1. Your behaviour expresses few of the characteristics that we normally associate with stress. If you feel under pressure, then that pressure is likely to be coming from places other than yourself.

Naturally, all of the above are generalisations. Type A people do not all suffer stress problems, and Type B people are not all immune to stress. Wherever you saw yourself on this table, it is nothing more than a guide, something to accept or reject according to your fancy. If you feel calm, then chances are that you are calm. Conversely, if you feel stressed then, regardless of how you fared on the above table, you need this book. So don't waste a page, read on!

In the cause of political correctness

Today, it's considered politically incorrect to try to stereotype people. This applies as much to psychological stereotypes as it does to occupational or racial stereotypes.

For the sake of any delicate sensibilities among my readers, I will refrain from using the words Type A and Type B wherever possible.

So, for the rest of this book, whenever you read my *new* stereotype 'Driven', feel free to mentally substitute 'Type A' instead. And where you read 'Easygoing', feel free to substitute 'Type B'.

Driven = Type A

Easygoing = Type B

PUTTING THE FUN BACK INTO WORK

'BILLIONS WASTED ON Stress Leave in Workplace.' 'Stress Epidemic.' 'The Plague of the 90s.' 'Stress Greatest Killer.' 'Millions of Lost Days Due to Stress.'

> The one attribute that differentiates my work from that of so many 'stress managers' is my determination to take the angst out of the topic of stress. And to inject a bit of fun into it.

No matter where you are in the world, you'll be exposed to similar headlines. And, if you can believe the press, stress problems in the workplace are out of control.

I'll tell you what *is* getting out of control: media hysteria and stress clichés. How can you be exposed to such bleakness and exaggerations without feeling stressed? How can you absorb all the discussion of stress problems without taking on – at least subconsciously – some of the symptoms? It is a sad fact of life, for example, that the suicide rate increases whenever there is significant reportage of suicides in the media. There is evidence to suggest that workplace stress also increases when it is featured in the media. The more we talk about a problem, the more we contribute to it; the more we discuss certain symptoms, the more prevalent they become.

The thrust of *Calm at Work* is not about criticising conditions in the workplace, it is about feeling good about what you do for a living. If we highlight a particular problem – and we will highlight many – it is only so that the ideal solution can be directed towards it.

What's fun got to do with working?

Have you ever noticed how difficult it is to feel stressed or worried while you're having fun? One cancels out the other. As well, you can overcome many of the long-term effects of stress in this way.

It's an old-fashioned concept, I admit, but I believe work should not only be satisfying but enjoyable. Fun even. This applies whether you're an actor, accounts clerk or an ambulance driver.

I can hear you scoffing. You know very well that the biggest challenges to your enjoyment usually surface when you're at work. Somehow, it seems that those eight to ten hours a day have been specially contrived to wring any semblance of fun from your existence, and to fill your day with so many pressures and anxieties that your next day will continue to be as burdensome.

But you won't have to feel that way much longer. The techniques in this book will help you instil calm and enjoyment into your work life – whether it is on the factory floor or in the office.

The techniques are the product of 'coalface' experience and nous. I have developed and refined them in the high stress industries in which I have worked over the years – both as worker, manager and employer. Many of these techniques were formulated with the help of psychologists and other therapists, and most have at least been road-tested by people in various positions, in different industries.

If you approach these techniques with an open mind, you will discover that some will work wonderfully for you.

Which will work best? Only you can tell. Trust your intuition, and it will guide you to the right ones. Because it is *you* who has the most powerful influence on how you feel at work. (Which is just as well, because you are the person reading this book.)

Invest in calm

Look at the people who've attained the professional status you most admire and, in the majority of cases, you'll see a relaxed person. Usually, they will exhibit a calmness under pressure – you might even describe it as steadfastness – that others come to depend on.

For people like this, calm is an investment. And it can be an investment for every person in every organisation.

Personal investment

Why aren't you calm at work? Do you have too many duties to perform? Do you put in too many hours at the office, then feel guilty about how little time you spend with your family? Is someone else taking the credit for the good work you do? Is your workplace too noisy? Does your boss treat you unfairly? Is work unrewarding? Do you feel unappreciated or unfulfilled?

Chances are there will be no single issue that's the source of your tensions, they're caused by a combination. If this is the case, your health will be affected as well as your work, so you'll have a vested interest in becoming calm.

Learn how to become calm – at will – and you'll get through each work day feeling useful and in control. You'll perform your duties better and gain more satisfaction from your work. And no matter what circumstances or workmates do to test your patience, no matter how much doom and gloom the newspapers preach, no matter where the economy is taking your income, you'll still feel good about your work. You'll cope better, you'll enjoy a zest for life that stressed people only fantasise about, and you'll look forward to going to work each day with a childlike enthusiasm.

That's what I call a great personal investment.

Business investment

As companies struggle to compete in a frenetically changing marketplace (and they will continue to do so), the pressures on the workforce increase.

From a managerial or corporate point of view, therefore, a calm workforce would be one of the best commercial investments. It means fewer industrial problems, more work completed each hour and the reduced turnover of staff. Not only does calm add stability and motivation to an organisation, but the harmony it evokes creates a powerful dynamism that will be necessary in the days ahead.

It is in the area of productivity that being calm at work pays its greatest dividend. A calm, enthusiastic employee generates higher output, makes fewer mistakes and is more efficient overall.

But it's not just your employers who profit from improved efficiency and enjoyment of your work – it's you.

And that has to be something worth pursuing.

Discount the silly excuses

The first step towards becoming calm in the workplace is to dispense with the silly excuses that stressed employees often resort to in an effort to rationalise their discomforts.

Following is a list of the more popular excuses. You'll probably recognise a few.

'I can't do anything about it.' Nonsense. Soon you'll wonder why it's taken you so long to discover how much you really can do about it.

'It's too hard.' See above.

'I thrive on stress.' In the self-honesty stakes, 'I thrive on stress' rates about as highly as 'I love smoking'. It's an excuse, mainly used by the addicted or the foolhardy. And, while you should feel free to use these justifications on whoever will listen, you should be wary about using them on yourself. Because *no-one* thrives on stress.

Thrive on being calm, and you will achieve much more.

'I need stress to do my work/meet deadlines.' Many depend on stress to provide the adrenalin, fear and panic they need to complete their work (this is particularly evident in the insecure world of arts and communications), but it is nothing more than a poor work practice – one that inhibits achievement and reduces your long-term effectiveness. The older you get, the more dangerous and career-shortening this practice becomes. People who work this way invariably burn out early in life, and require ever-increasing quantities of stimulants, such as alcohol or conflict, to maintain the drive.

If you are calm you will achieve these higher levels of achievement, and keep on achieving them throughout life.

'Stressed people are the hardest workers.' Ironically, this might be true. Stressed people often create extra work for themselves because of the inefficiencies brought about by being in that state. So, while they may be the hardest workers, they are not necessarily the best workers.

'The best workers work the longest hours.' Having spent many years closely associated with two industries that pride themselves on the long hours they work, I now appreciate that some people who work a solid eight hours a day often produce more than others who work twelve. Working smarter (that is, at your most efficient) is usually more productive than working longer.

Try it. And think of all the positive things you can do with the extra time you'll have.

'I don't have time to change.' Self-pity is not an attractive characteristic. Besides, positive change is an attitudinal issue, not a time issue.

'To get ahead, you have to worry about your work.' To get ahead, you have to perform your work to your capacity. Your capacity increases when you're calm.

'I'm in a lowly position, there's nothing I can do about it.' Whatever your position, you are the most influential person in choosing the way you feel. Use this influence to help yourself feel calmer and better.

'The system is at fault.' These are the world's most overused buck-passing words. 'The system' is easy to blame because most people don't really know what 'the system' is; for many, it's everything they can't understand or relate to.

If you want to blame the system or management for your stress, go ahead. But please remember that there is

only one person responsible for making you feel better.
Yes, it's you.

'Without stress I'd be bored.' One of the more common justifications for feeling stressed. Even though the media and advertising would have us believe that enjoyment can only come from excitement, it is a shallow argument.

You can enjoy and derive pleasure from everything you do *without* stimulation and excitement. Be calm and appreciate life more.

'Work is meant to be a chore.' Says who? Even if it were true, wouldn't you still be inclined to try to make your work a pleasure? It's easy. Just keep reading.

'I've tried, but I can't change things.' Striving is the nature of most improvement in life. Be comforted, though, in the knowledge that many of the techniques in this book are easier to apply than others you might have tried.

'Stress goes as soon as you've had a holiday.' While it is true that holidays work wonders for the relief of stress, the relief is only temporary. One or two holidays a year will not overcome most of the problems that arise in the workplace. The reason for this is that stress is not a black-and-white condition like flu or acne, but something that encompasses a myriad of specific problems – from conflict in work relationships, to frustration at having no control over what you do – that will still be unresolved when you return from your holiday.

'Stress is more prevalent today than at any other time in history.' You hear this excuse a lot these days. Yet, it's hard to believe you're worse off today than you would have been when you stood a 50 percent chance of dying of smallpox, or when the norm was working twelve hours a day, seven days a week.

The difference today is that we hear much more about the prevalence of stressful conditions and read about the symptoms others are meant to be suffering.

The media have a lot to answer for.

'It's not fair that the proprietors make all the profits, and we do all the work.' This complaint has only one outcome: it causes further dissatisfaction for the employee. In most cases, it is not an issue of fairness at all, but one of self-righteousness. In any event, it is an argument that has minimal effect on the proprietor.

'How do we know if we're stressed?' This is usually the first question raised by journalists. My feeling has always been that if you stop and think about how you feel, you'll know sure enough. But, if you're uncertain, there's a couple of questionnaires on pages 16–17. Try them, you might be calmer than you think.

'It's not easy becoming calm.' Sorry, but it's incredibly easy. By the end of this book, you'll agree.

'All stress is bad.' Contrary to what many believe, all stress is not all bad. There is positive stress and there is negative stress.

Positive stress is fun and life-enriching. It's the stress you feel when you get a pay rise or a promotion, or when you achieve something outstanding. It's the stress you feel when the lift doors open and there stands the most attractive person you've ever laid eyes on. This is positive stress – it enriches your life, and keeps you feeling young and alive.

Negative stress, on the other hand, is something you can well do without.

The ideal combination is some positive stress – without it life would be dull and less effective – with as little negative stress as you can achieve.

But enough of the excuses, let's get to work on helping you to feel calm at work.

1 TAKE THIS FIRST STEP

THIS IS THE most impor-
tant section of the book.
Taking the first step to
calm requires no study
and no effort.

> The first step is easy. Decide that
> you're going to become calm, and
> you're well on the way to becoming
> calm.

All you have to do is pause for 60 seconds and make
a single decision. Decide that you will adopt a minimum
of three or four suggestions from this book – even though
you haven't read them yet – and pursue them with vigour.

That's all you have to do. The
first step towards becoming calm is
simply *deciding that you're going to
become calm*. Did you ever suspect
it would be as simple as that? I have
a surprise for you: it's always been
that simple.

Now, please devote the next 60
seconds to making that decision.

2 LIFE-CHANGING CHOICES

Isn't it curious how you automatically begin to feel more comfortable, the moment you realise you have choices?

> Slavish commitment to vague or even abstract masters (such as corporations) and ideals is seldom in your best interest.

It may be difficult to accept this while you're locked into a strict work routine, but you always have choices – especially when it comes to feeling calm and satisfied about your work.

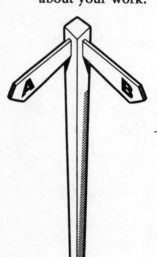

Here are two ways these choices can change the way you look at work and your life – and so become calm.

1. Your life priorities

Most reasonable people believe that work (that is, having a job) is a basic human right, one which is essential not only for their material needs, but also for their self-esteem.

Then philosophy creeps into the equation.

At one end of the spectrum you have the Hindu belief that says work is the purest form of devotion to God (a concept shared by many religions). Further along is a more familiar belief system you'd probably describe as the Work Ethic. The philosophers among you may challenge my oversimplification here, but at the core of this Ethic is a pair of understandings:

(i) Work is noble.

(ii) The harder the work, the more noble it is.

This could be a sensible, productive philosophy for most people to follow as they work their way through life. Unfortunately, you will often find this ideal is accompanied by a rigid set of embellishments. I call these the *Extended* Work Ethic. They will probably be familiar to you:

(i) The more discomfort involved, the more noble the work is.

(ii) Leisure is an inferior, perhaps virtueless, activity.

(iii) The employer (individual, corporation or state) warrants obeisance simply because of its status as employer.

Clearly, this is an unhealthy corruption of the original philosophy. It is a paternalistic, employer-serving construct that encourages a slavish commitment to harder work and longer hours. Worse, this dronelike behaviour is rampant throughout the workplace – especially among those known as 'good workers'.

Calculate your commitment to the (Extended) Work Ethic

Answer each of the following with a True or False:

	TRUE	FALSE
I like others to know how hard I work.	☐	☐
People who work long hours are better workers.	☐	☐
I feel awkward in the presence of my boss.	☐	☐
Even if I've got nothing to do, I wouldn't go home early.	☐	☐
I have no sympathy for the unemployed.	☐	☐
I hate wasting time.	☐	☐
I'd rather get a mention in the staff newsletter than a letter from a friend.	☐	☐
I find it difficult to relax on the weekends.	☐	☐
I'm suspicious of workmates who take too many holidays.	☐	☐
I never take sick days, even when I'm feeling bad.	☐	☐
My work owes me holidays.	☐	☐
I'd miss my child's concert if my boss needed my help.	☐	☐
If I wake early, I'll go to work in preference to reading a magazine.	☐	☐
I don't approve of people who waste time at work.	☐	☐
I feel embarrassed about discussing my salary.	☐	☐
There's something satisfying about feeling sore and dirty at the end of the day.	☐	☐

If you complete the questionnaire, don't bother counting your answers. While this is only an indication, chances are the more times you answered True, the more committed you would be to the Extended Work Ethic.

Most of us who live by this Ethic do so without ever having thought about what it entails, or the damage it may wreak. You probably won't be surprised to read that stress levels in the workplace increase in direct proportion to the level of commitment to this corrupted ideal!

You'd think there must be an upside. Surely this commitment would result in increased job satisfaction? Quite the opposite.

I have to confess that in my capacity as an employer, I have a degree of affection for the Extended Work Ethic:

it makes committed employees, it gets things done and it's good for business. But as an advocate of calm, I have to caution you about it.

Slavish commitment to vague or abstract masters (such as corporations) and ideals is not necessarily in your best interest. Especially if you have a tendency to worry about work and to take it too seriously. Far better to challenge what you believe in and what you believe you want from your work, *then* to make your commitments. When you are working towards goals that *you* define and believe in, you will be more calm about your work.

This is where your choices come to the fore. If you want to feel calm and contented about the work you do, first you have to determine your life's priorities. Is your work so important to your self-worth? Are your relationships more important than your work? Do you want to rise to the top in your occupation? Do you want to meet people? Do you want to save enough to go travelling for the rest of your days?

Most people spend a great part of their lives trying to come to grips with these priorities. To make it easier, I have devised the Life Priorities Calculator on page 92.

This simple technique will help you put into order the important things in your life. You may discover that work priorities – money, position, success – are at the top of your list. If so, you can make the choice that you're going to succeed in your work at all costs, determined that only failure will cause you stress.

Conversely, you may decide that family or relationship priorities are at the top of your list. Then you won't lose sleep over petty things that happen during your day. The Life Priorities Calculator will help you make that decision.

2. Your circumstances

At the risk of oversimplifying, you have two choices when it comes to stressful conditions or circumstances:

(i) you can change the things that cause you stress; or

(ii) you can change the way you look at them.

Many of the practitioners in the stress-management industry concentrate on trying to change the workplace: modifying management attitudes, redefining work responsibilities, empowering employees. While these are fine ideals, they are limited by the fact that they are ideals. They advocate structural changes that may be impossible or very slow for you to implement.

Changing the circumstances that cause you stress is seldom easy. You can't easily replace your boss. You may not want to transfer to another city. You might find it difficult to become a computer programmer when you've been trained as a typist. It may not be wise to walk out on a well-paying job because your immediate superior doesn't like you.

Your most practical choice is not to try to change the circumstances, but to change the way you view them.

I will not pretend it is easy to change long-standing habits and attitudes, but you can transform yourself from a victim of stress into a calm person – not by trying to change the stressors in your work life, but changing how you perceive them.

> **Look for these calm solutions:**
>
> Creative Long-Range Planner.....page 171
>
> The Unconscious Planner ....page 177
>
> Permission to Reject Success....page 214

3 EMPLOYERS TO CHOOSE FROM

YOU'VE PROBABLY BEEN trained to think your employer chooses you for your job, rather than you choosing your employer.

> Whatever your role or occupation, you are a powerful individual. When you perform your duties well, your role is extremely valuable to your employer.

Employers love it when you think this way. It perpetuates the master–slave relationship.

But there is no need for you to think this way.

Whatever your role, whatever your occupation, you are a powerful individual. You contribute to your employer's wealth, power, position and career advancement. When you perform your duties well, your role is extremely valuable to them.

Let me repeat that: the role you play is *extremely* valuable! As a rule of thumb, in a well-run enterprise, your contribution to your employer's fortunes will be worth several times the total of what you cost. Probably more so. Did you get that? *Several times your cost.* By any conventional measure, you are more valuable to your employer than your employer is to you – at least on a day-to-day basis.

This is theoretical, of course. But, from this moment forward, you are well within your rights to assume you're in your job because *you* did the choosing.

Even if you had only one employer to choose from, look upon this as you choosing your employer – not the other way around. If you can view your job this way, you are already on the way to dictating whether you'll be calm or not in your workplace.

How to choose your employer

Most employers fall into, or between, one of three categories. These descriptions apply equally to private and public enterprises. They also apply to enterprises that manufacture, repair, sell, advise, service or clean up afterwards – in other words, they apply to all workplaces.

I define the three employer categories as Creators, Cutters and Undecideds. These categories are the product of the attitudes of shareholders, boards of directors and managers. Ultimately, they define the spirit of the organisation itself.

Creators

Creators think: 'People are my greatest asset. I will cultivate that asset to achieve greater things – for them as well as me.' Creators say, 'How can we improve things?'

Creators strive to improve their world (and, as a result, *your* world) by externally-focused, growth-oriented activities. This does not necessarily mean expansion, such as increasing in size or even increasing profit: all it means is that the organisation is devoted to improvement – in output as well as employment, learning and personal growth opportunities. This is *not* idealism or 'New Age' fantasising; it is the hallmark of every employer or manager who hopes to make a difference through their work. And, even more importantly, it is the hallmark of virtually every business and organisation that is making an impact in the world today.

Creators are the positive force in business, public service, education, medicine, religion and politics. They deserve our respect. They deserve your support.

My personal policy is to own or work only for businesses that can be described as Creators. This description has nothing to do with the function of these enterprises, but all to do with their attitude – the commitment to make a difference to those who work for them as much as for those they work for. It makes good business sense to be, and to work for, Creators.

People are my greatest asset. I will cultivate that asset to achieve greater things – for them as well as me.

Cutters

Cutters think: 'People are my greatest overhead. I can reduce that overhead easily by cutting people, or by cutting what they earn. This will mean an improved bottom line – for the time being.'

Cutters are easy to recognise. You will hear them describing themselves as pragmatists, and speaking endlessly about efficiency and productivity. Although their MBA tutors had hoped to provide a broader focus, they usually excel in non-producing functions such as accountancy or internal management.

People are my greatest overhead. I can reduce that overhead easily by cutting people, or cutting what they earn. This will mean an improved bottom line – for the time being.

I suspect most of the Cutters were intoxicated by the rush of Economic Rationalist thinking of the early 1990s. They were thrilled to discover how much easier it was to influence the bottom line – at least in the short term – by cutting rather than creating. They often have a slavish commitment to downsizing, and they love to tell you that 'a dollar saved is worth three earned'. Their obsession is *cheaper, faster, leaner*. And, most alarming of all, their short-term tactics increasingly become long-term strategies.

Although they will probably be insulted by my assessment, Cutters are the negative force among employers. They usually run introverted, restless organisations, and they are *never* great long-term successes.

You may think I am being unnecessarily harsh on a well-intentioned section of the working community, but I have observed the misery this negative philosophy has been responsible for: the decimation of middle-management, the ostracism of older employees, the trimming of employment conditions and, most insidious of all, the spread of fear and uncertainty in the workplace.

All this in the name of efficiency!

Fortunately, there is now a substantial body of evidence that highlights the failure of the negative strategies of Cutters. A study of 700 negatively-oriented American companies showed that over a five-year period, most suffered serious falls in their share prices. (Paradoxically, the one move guaranteed to make an immediate improvement in a corporation's share price – in the short term – is massive shedding of staff.) Another study showed that employee stress levels in companies of this type – compared with employee stress levels in companies you'd describe as Creators – were markedly more pronounced. And, most damning of all, yet another study has shown that fewer than 50 percent of these negatively-oriented companies have managed to achieve the one goal they were philosophically driven to achieve: to improve their levels of productivity.

Yet, in spite of this frightening record, the Cutters still exist. Scary, isn't it?

Undecideds

Undecideds are exactly as their name implies – indifferent, unmotivated, unable or unwilling to decide whether they should be a Creator or a Cutter.

There is nothing inherently negative about the Undecideds approach (if they have an approach), but there is nothing inherently positive about it either. Although they may leave a bit to be desired from a leadership or a managerial point of view, Undecideds may still be good employers.

Who should you work for?

Generally speaking, Creators create positive, outward-looking workplace environments, while Cutters are more negative and inwardly-focused.

If you have the choice, and you are not seeking to take over the organisation, you will probably derive most satisfaction and least stress by choosing a Creator as your employer (all other things being equal).

Conversely, you will probably derive least satisfaction and most stress if you work for a Cutter.

Even during the tough times, Creators are better to work for. During the last recession, an industry in which I was working fell upon hard times. Most of our competitors were shedding staff in a series of very public bloodlettings. Income opportunities were shrinking. The conventional Cutter 'wisdom' was to shed staff. Instead, our business employed a Creator tactic – it asked every employee to commit an extra 5 percent of their time to exploring new opportunities for the company, however small or irrelevant this may have seemed. The result? Every employee of that business breezed through a very difficult period feeling useful, optimistic, and not overly stressed by the turmoil in their industry. The shared goals and outward orientation both stimulated and satisfied them in their work. And through their efforts, our company was one of the few businesses in a decimated industry to be actually recruiting rather than firing.

Not every organisation has the luxury of being able to choose such a course. Turnaround times in large organisations, for example, demand that tough Cutter-like decisions are made early. And decisively. There is no room or call for sentiment in these situations: employees who cannot be afforded, cannot be afforded; it is weak business practice to assume otherwise. However, once the hard decisions are made, Creators immediately resume their positive, externally-oriented course – while Cutters go back for more.

Life is not always as clear-cut as this. Often employers will fall somewhere between the two extremes, demonstrating some Creator and some Cutter attributes. Nevertheless, the *spirit* of an organisation usually skews one way or the other. And if you want my advice, and if you want to be calm, choose the one that skews towards Creators.

4 SANITY-SAVING UNDERSTANDINGS

Having been involved with the management of many businesses and enterprises, I always thought certain fundamentals of commerce and industry

> Even the most mundane task has its value – if you're prepared to search for it. When you find this value, you'll find work satisfaction. And when you find satisfaction, calm will not be far behind.

were appreciated by all those involved. Yet, I am regularly surprised at how little is known of these basic understandings.

1. The shared nature of work

Theoretically, all work is a shared enterprise between the employer (principals or shareholders), managers and employees. If any one group fails in its responsibilities, the enterprise eventually fails. If the opposite happens, and the enterprise succeeds, then each of the groups theoretically succeeds.

The calmest workplaces are those where individuals believe there is a sense of shared endeavour, a social contract, between each of these groups.

The converse of this is the 'Them and Us' sentiment that exists in many workplaces. At its most extreme, you have workers believing the basic nature of management is to be overdemanding and greedy, and management believing that the basic nature of workers is to be indolent and greedy. Thankfully, these sentiments are becoming less common in enlightened work environments, but wherever they exist they are accompanied by an atmosphere of distrust and tension. In addition, in many organisations, increasing globalisation and technological change has meant a great straining, or at least distance, in the social contract between worker and employer; this is not easily overcome, especially in large multinational corporations.

However, that is taking an abstract or corporate view of 'employer'. Mostly you would consider your employer to be one or two people: the person or persons who hired you, or those you report to. In this case, it is easier for you to view your work as a shared enterprise between you and your 'employer'.

When you approach your work this way, it is so much easier to feel contented, satisfied and calm about what you do.

2. The nature of business

To be satisfied in any endeavour, it helps to know why you are doing it. Why is what I do so important? Why do I come to work each day? What is the net benefit of my contribution?

If you work for the government, charity or the church, you will probably have a fair idea of the answer (if you believe your purpose is to serve the community). Most of us, however, do not work for the government, charity or the church. We work for businesses. For us, it is important to understand one simple business fundamental.

In the main, businesses do not exist to provide

employment, for the amusement of proprietors, or to make tax losses. *The nature of business is to manufacture something, or to perform a service, then to sell it for a profit –* that is, sell it for more than it costs to produce. Regardless of where those profits ultimately go, this principle applies to all commercial enterprises, be it a hosiery retailer, a hot dog manufacturer, or a private hospital.

It may seem obvious, it may not be particularly idealistic, and it may not even appeal to you as a reason for going to work each day, but it is a commercial reality, and recognising it is critical to finding peace and satisfaction in what you do – if you choose to work for a business.

3. The purpose of employment

Many people in the workforce have only a hazy concept of why they are there, other than the need to earn an income. In light of this, it is worth outlining the third understanding of working for a living.

Ultimately, you work in your job for your benefit – not your boss's, the government's, or the company's.

You'll have to go a long way before you'll find a boss or a manager who will publicly agree to this proposition, but if you think about it, there can be no other reason for working – except altruism.

All this may seem obvious, but you'd be surprised at how many employees lose sight of this simple understanding, and how much stress is caused when they do.

Once you acknowledge this fundamental, you can work towards preserving a calm state of mind, secure in the knowledge that *you* are the one who benefits most from your work.

4. The power of the individual

If you are to find peace and satisfaction in what you do, the most important understanding is of your rights as a working individual.

Second to that is your responsibilities.

Whether it is out of fear, insecurity, gratitude or a misplaced sense of duty, we occasionally lose sight of these basic *rights*. Among them are:

(i)   your right to ask for what you want;
(ii) your right to make your own decisions within the parameters of your brief or job description;
(iii) your right to adequate compensation for your efforts;
(iv) your right to privacy;
(v)   your right to say no, or to withdraw your services.

These are not only legal rights; they are core moral rights; in a democratic society, they cannot be denied, withdrawn or abrogated. Having said that, it is equally as important for you to recognise your *responsibilities* as a working individual (foremost among these is your responsibility to recognise the rights of others).

Your responsibilities

The difference between suffering and satisfaction in your work is, in most cases, what *you* do rather than what somebody else does. As comforting as it may be to feel someone else is always responsible, when it comes to feeling good about yourself and what you do, only one person is responsible. You.

Every position, every job, every task can be as meaningful and fulfilling as you allow it to be. *As long as you assume the responsibility for making it so.*

To help you get the most out of your work – whatever you choose to do or are obliged to do – use The 100

Percent Effort on page 159. Follow this procedure faithfully, and not only will you derive maximum satisfaction from what you do, but you'll find that the work itself helps you to become calm and relaxed.

5 LIFE-ENRICHING PIECES OF ADVICE

Generally, I shy away from dispensing advice. On this occasion, however, I have included these little gems because they are so simple, yet they can

> Your boss or your job may be responsible for making you feel stressed, but they are *not* responsible for making you feel calm and contented. You are.

have a great impact on helping you to feel calm at work.

1. Look on the bright side

You are already well on the way to becoming calm – simply because you've taken the hardest and most positive step: You've made the decision to become calm. Keep thinking positively and you will continue on this course.

2. Assume responsibility for yourself

It never ceases to amaze me when I conduct workshops, or deliver advisory programs on radio, just how widespread is the belief that 'it's the boss's responsibility', that 'how I feel is a management issue, not a personal one'.

When you hear it said, it sounds kind of plausible. But when you see it written down like this, it starts to look ridiculous, doesn't it? Yet, this is one of the most commonly held workplace perceptions. It is also one of the main reasons there is so much stress and anxiety about.

The argument is that good managers alleviate stressful problems while bad managers create them. Often this is true. But so what? Are you in the position to have managers replaced? Even if you are, are you in the position to find better ones? In many cases, you cannot.

Your boss or your job *may* be responsible for making you feel stressed, but they are not responsible for making you feel calm and contented, or for making you feel good about yourself.

That is *your* responsibility.

When you take into account the understanding that you work in your job for your benefit – not your boss's, not the government's, not the company's – you will see a certain degree of fairness in what I suggest.

You can blame whoever you like for your stresses and anxieties, but you must assume responsibility for overcoming them yourself. The more enthusiastically you do so, the more profound will be the result.

3. Do your own job first

We all like to be well thought of. Even me. And the surest way to be well thought of is to do everything that everyone asks, right?

Well, that's the perception.

This problem is exacerbated by a certain personality type – the type who invariably ends up taking on more than they can sensibly handle.

You might wonder why they do this. Are they bad

planners? Do they overestimate their capabilities? Or perhaps they take pleasure in being able to claim they are overworked?

The reason may include several of these factors, but often it will be the simple inability to say 'no'. You can't say no to extra workloads. You can't say no to invitations. You can't say no to requests for favours or assistance.

Learn to say 'no' when necessary, and not only will you feel more contented because you're more in control, but you'll be much more efficient for having taken this action.

Look for these calm solutions:

The Power of No ....page 143
The Nice Way to No ....page 145
Allocating Time for Calm ....page 138
Know Your Limits ....page 147
Self Time............................page 153
Work One Day at a Time ....page 156

4. Have a life

Don't tell the boss I said this, but there is more to life than work.

Even if you want to be top of the ladder, the most valuable employee, the perfect leader, the most wealthy proprietor, you cannot do it by being a single-dimension person.

Make time for yourself outside of work, and you'll enjoy your work more.

Look for these calm solutions:

Work One Day at a Time ....page 156
Have Fun............................page 317
Look for a Little Stress...........page 217

5. Learn to breathe

The single most important skill in learning to relax is learning how to breathe properly.

'Breathe properly,' you gasp, 'I've been doing that since the first seconds of my birth. I'm an expert at breathing.'

Chances are you're not an expert. Chances are also that your poor breathing habits not only fail to help you feel calm, but actually contribute to feelings of tension.

Read the section on breathing (pages 95–104), get to know it, make its advice a part of your life – and you will know more about becoming calm than 99 percent of the world.

6 AREAS WHERE YOU CAN MAKE A DIFFERENCE

THERE ARE SIX major areas where you can easily make a difference to the way you feel at work.

> Whatever your workplace, most of your stresses will arise in the same place – in your mind.

Make a meaningful improvement in any one of these areas – preferably all of them – and you will help yourself to become calm.

1. Behaviour

The way you behave at work is a major influence on the way you feel at work. Indulge in stress-producing behaviour and it follows that you will feel stressed.

So, what are some of these stress-producing behaviours?

Leave everything you have to do to the last moment and your anxiety levels will always have something to feed on. Mix with your really tense workmates, and you'll end up feeling really tense (unless you can help them to become calm). Chain-smoke and drink fifteen cups of coffee a day, and you can be sure of feeling on edge even if everything else runs smoothly.

Conversely, adopt some of the calm behaviour

characteristics mentioned later in this book, and guess how you'll end up feeling ...

Look for these calm solutions:

How Susceptible Are You?........page 12

Depressurising Deadlines.........page 137

2. Attitude

No matter where the workplace or whatever the industry, most of your stresses will arise in the same place, or from the same source.

The place is your mind. Its most troublesome attribute is your attitudes.

Many of the techniques that follow work towards addressing the imbalances that occur in your attitudes. It is nothing short of amazing how even minor adjustments in this area can produce major improvements in the way you feel.

Look for these calm solutions:

A Positive Word ....page 184

Positive Contributions ....page 186

The Positive Picture ....page 188

Search for the Upside ....page 190

The Plus and Minus Method .....page 198

Worry about the BIG Things .....page 201

3. Circumstance

Work in a noisy factory and you will probably feel on edge as a result. Work in overcrowded surroundings and you'll feel under pressure. Sit on an uncomfortable chair all day and you'll soon be feeling tense. Wear a necktie and you'll feel a sense of constriction and inhibition as a result. There are certain physical aspects of your workplace or work habits that will have a noticeable impact on your state of mind.

Many of these elements will be outside your control. But even if you can't control the elements, you can always control the way you respond to them.

Look for these calm solutions:

Create Your Own Space .... page 278
The Sound of Calm .... page 280
The Scent of Calm .... page 282
The Calm Space .... page 287

4. Procedure

It's often said that poor managers create stressful workplaces. So do poor work practices and procedures.

To cover, or even address, all of these issues is beyond the scope of a book like this. However, there is one blanket piece of advice that covers them all: if you can't change the procedure, change the way you look at it.

Becoming calm can be as easy as that.

Look for these calm solutions:

The Calm Agenda .... page 180
Idling .... page 216
Consort with the Calm .... page 262

5. Planning

Time management. Goal setting. Targeting. Planning. Volumes are written, courses are held, and MBA programs have been preoccupied with these topics.

In running large organisations, planning often means the difference between success and failure. For individuals, it can also mean the difference in how you cope with work.

People who know where they're going find it easier to stay calm on the way there. People who know how to plan can plan ways of overcoming their anxieties. People who educate themselves, who take courses and strive to know more, can learn the ways to a fulfilling and stress-free job. And, most importantly, organised people suffer less from the pressures of time.

Plan to be calm.

6. Decision-making

Many people who search for solutions to a problem never actually make the decision to solve the problem. They have the solutions, but don't use them. They see the doctor, buy the book, study the latest aerobics tape, plan to take up yoga, read the recipes – but they don't actually take the one step that's necessary to solving the problem: that is, making the decision to solve the problem.

Failing to make decisions is a feature of failures and procrastinators. Making a decision has nothing to do with willpower or determination. It is merely making a decision.

At the risk of becoming repetitive, it is now time to make that decision to become calm. Once you have done that, all you have to do is implement the solutions in this book.

7 CAUSES OF STRESS IN THE WORKPLACE

INVARIABLY, THE THINGS that cause workplace stress fall into one of three categories: physical, emotional and behavioural.

> To determine the best solutions to feeling calm at work, we need to explore the seven major areas of workplace stress: time, control, self, social, change, physical and lifestyle.

Physical causes can range from illness, to uncomfortable shoes, to environmental conditions such as noise, cold or dust. Emotional (psychological) stressors are those that originate in your mind, and are the most prominent and complex of them all. Behavioural stressors (mostly a combination of physical and emotional conditions) range from procrastination, to inefficient work habits, to drug and alcohol abuse.

These are the categories common to all workplace stress. The *issues* that cause this stress, however, are different.

Most stress problems tend to arise from the same issues. Primarily, these relate to change, time, control, other people (social) and workload.

Some occupational stress therapists insist that workplace problems are dominated by a combination of maximum work pressure and minimal control, while others say more problems evolve from the sense of insecurity produced by change. (Studies done ten or more years ago barely mention 'change' as a primary cause of stress; yet today it is uppermost in our minds.) Few studies ever highlight 'self' or 'lifestyle and habits' as major causes, which clearly they must be.

The following graph highlights the main areas of workplace stress. The ratios between the stress areas vary according to the industry, country and era.

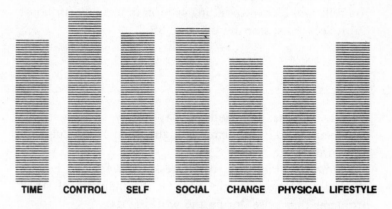

Then there's another belief that says stressful feelings in the workplace are often not products of the workplace at all! Here you have another major factor coming into play: concerns about personal and family life. With such a high proportion of working parents (singles and couples), combined with the financial and social insecurity that seems so prevalent these days, this is hardly surprising.

These outside concerns can encompass all of life's problems – from poor health, to troubled relationships, financial problems, worries about families, baldness, overeating, undereating, or practically anything you care to name – and they are too many to attempt to solve in a book. Indeed, it is not my intention to analyse any of these causes in great depth – as stated before, we are interested in the solutions rather than the problems. However, in order to determine the best solutions to help you feel calm and relaxed in the workplace, we will need to explore, at least briefly, each of the workplace stressors shown in the graph.

If you can recognise the causes, you will be able to take them into account before they can do too much damage.

For each of the seven major causes of workplace stress, you will find a corresponding section in Your Portfolio of Calm Solutions, starting on page 89.

1. Time

If you examine the niggling, day-to-day stresses in the workplace, you'll find Time is highlighted as the culprit – time after time.

Time is behind the work pressures we know best of all. Indeed, time is at the root of the majority of stress problems that arise during the working day.

'Time. is money.' 'Time and tide wait for nobody.' 'Procrastination is the thief of time.' Looming deadlines, time running out, so much to do with not enough time to do it, nowhere near enough hours in the day. For some of us, these pressures never seem to ease. And just when you think you've got on top of them, the whole process starts over again the next morning.

Have you ever wondered why this is so? When I ask why modern people feel under such great time pressure, almost everyone has the same response. They talk of the pace of modern life; of the need to do and achieve more and more each day; of the pressures that constant bombardment of advertising messages add to this mix; of the seemingly unending array of entertainment opportunities.

I know I'm in the minority when I say this, but I believe those factors are only a small part of why time causes such pressure in our lives. My belief is this so-called 'time pressure' is something drilled into each and every one of us at the earliest possible age. You listen to any parent–child dialogue. I guarantee that even in the most enlightened families, one of the most common exhortations you will hear is, 'Hurry up' (or, 'Come on, Eliza; get a move on'; or 'Quickly, Oliver!'). Listen and you'll be astounded at how many times a child is subjected to these expressions in the average day. Is it any wonder we are such victims of time pressure?

Whatever the reason, time is seen as one of the most common stressors in the workplace. And, as productivity expectations increase so too will this time pressure.

Or will it?

The entire notion of time is an abstract concept. Time itself is not the culprit, it is your *attitude* to time, your *perceptions* of it. In other words, heads create time pressures, not clocks.

Deadlines

Deadlines and your perception of time – or how much time you believe you have at your disposal – are directly related to one another.

For many of us, if a deadline has been set, a problem has been created. This is particularly so for certain personality types and industries. Look at any deadline-oriented occupation, or any deadline-oriented person, and you will find a host of stress-related problems. Tensions rise as the deadline nears.

On the other hand, some people work better, and with a greater sense of security, only when a deadline is set.

Why do deadlines threaten one group, yet provide

comfort for another?
Once again, the answer
lies in your perception of
time, closely followed by
your skills in time
management.

Workload

If you survey all people in the workforce and ask what
causes their stress, you will find one cause mentioned more
often than any other (though not necessarily always as the
main cause of stress).

That cause is overwork.

This is particularly so in the post-recession nineties,
where increased productivity demands have meant that
more and more of us are now having to work harder. Are
we really overworked? Have workloads really increased
that much? In many cases,
the answer is a resounding
yes. However, in just as
many cases, the *perception*
that we are overworked is
just as problematical as
the reality.

Information overload

In the executive ranks, a new problem has surfaced. It's
called 'information overload'. I have seen surveys where,
in some industries, up to 40 percent of executive respon-
dents (and around 25 percent of non-executives) blamed
information overload for their longer hours and some or
all of their work problems.

Surveys of three years ago hardly mentioned this category at all. Now up to 40 percent of executives are complaining of information overload. What has been going on?

It's not difficult to see where it's coming from. We're told the world's knowledge doubles every couple of years, and that more information is contained in a single issue of the *New York Times* than your great-grandparents would have encountered in their entire lives. The Internet exposes you to so much information that older brains simply cannot, or refuse to, comprehend. On any given topic, therefore, the amount of information at any executive's disposal is simply mind-boggling. (Hard to justify the level of ignorance being peddled in some quarters, then, isn't it!)

Faced with all these gigabytes of information, you could justifiably wonder how you were meant to absorb it all. Even the speediest speedreader wouldn't make a dent in the amount of information that crosses some executives' desks on an average day. So, is ignorance the only solution?

Thankfully not. Selectivity and discipline are the answers.

> **Look for these calm solutions:**
> Information Emancipation ....page 144
> Life Priorities Calculator .... page 91

Procrastination

Why do I list procrastination as a 'time' issue rather than a 'behaviour' or 'work practice' issue?

The main reason is that procrastination is a misuse of your time. Postponing things that you know have to be done only adds to the pressure in your life. Moreover, the things you postpone are invariably the things you enjoy doing least, so you have all these unpleasantries banking up for some distant, but getting-closer-every-minute, occasion.

Look for these calm solutions:
The 100 Percent Effort ....page 159

2. Control

Generally, the impact of stressful situations is governed by three factors: being able to predict the stressful event and its outcome; being able to exert some control over it; and having the emotional support of others in the face of these events.

Occupational psychologists say that lack of control over your work is one of the major contributors to workplace stress. The less control you exert over your work and your world, the more likely you are to suffer some degree of stress, fear, anxiety or anger in relation to it. (What they really mean is the amount of control you *feel* you exert over it.)

The solution they have begun to promote is a policy of 'empowerment' – creating a workplace environment where employees or subordinates can be given a degree of autonomy, and can exercise a degree of control over their work and output. According to the theory, this results in a reduction in the stressful feelings that normally accompany lack of control. It does work. However, while the concept of empowerment is admirable in principle, it is unfortunately another 'leave it to the boss' ideal, and of little interest to the general thrust of this book. If you have to depend on management to overcome your feelings of pressure and tension in your job, you're in a very vulnerable position.

Real empowerment comes from within. When you choose to exercise control over those aspects of your job that it is possible for you to control – however small or insignificant they may appear initially – you are empowered.

What can you do then?

We know that stress is caused by monotonous, repetitive tasks; we know it is caused by incommunicative, authoritarian supervision; and we know that it is caused by frustration due to workload, position, lack of information and inadequate job description. We also know that the less control you *feel* you have, the more likely you are to feel under pressure. Indeed, some research shows that stress-related illnesses can increase in direct proportion to the level of impotence someone feels in their work. Because if you're not in control of the things that are going on in your world, then you are a victim of them; you cannot steer or dictate timing, you can only respond. This is no way to become calm.

(You might think that the people who enjoy the greatest level of control in their jobs are the managers – after all, aren't they the ones giving the orders, making all the decisions, dictating the timing of events? If this were so, then it follows that most people in management would feel in total control of their lives and destinies. This is far from the case. Managers, like all other members of the workforce, suffer from these same feelings of not being able to control the events of their lives – only the scale and the detail varies.)

Just as stressful as the belief that you can't control anything in your life, is the belief that you *must* control everything in your life. No doubt you've heard the pejorative 'control freak' – typically, someone who is driven to control all people and events they come into contact with. This type of person will always be under pressure, because nothing in life ever follows the script they write for it. And when they cannot control, they are frustrated or maddened beyond the norm.

So, on one hand we have people who perhaps could take control, but don't; and on the other we have people who insist on exerting control, but can't.

In both cases, one simple understanding could be the solution to their problems: the only thing in life you can really count on controlling is yourself. Your actions, your attitudes, your perceptions. Bring them into line, and you'll be surprised at just how much in control it is possible for you to feel.

Waiting

If you don't know what to expect, or when to expect it, waiting can be stressful.

When you've been warned that the boss is angry and wants to speak to you, and you don't know when you're going to get the call, a half hour of waiting can be more distressing than the reprimand.

Yet someone else might find that half an hour to be relaxing instead of distressing, they might engross themselves in chatting to the receptionist or reading a magazine.

Your challenge is to turn unscheduled waiting time into something more productive. Then you can be calm.

Look for these calm solutions:
An End to Boredom .... page 164
The 100 Percent Effort .... page 159

Boredom

Boredom is often accompanied by a sense of restlessness and impotence – this is why we search for distraction when we are bored. As much stress is caused by boredom as is caused by overwork. In addition to this, if you suffer the ill effects of stress, then you'll be more prone to feeling bored.

The big question: is boredom the result of stress, or is stress the result of boredom?

It doesn't really matter. Boredom has to be dealt with if you're to feel fulfilled, and if you seek to reduce the negative effects of stress in your life.

Frustration

You're caught in traffic, stuck in the lift, cornered by the world's greatest bore, impeded by an assistant who will never learn, or desperate to be heard by the head of your department – in themselves these issues may be relatively minor inconveniences but, to many of us, they are the pinnacles of frustration.

Frustration leads to negative stress. Conversely, the greater your general stress level, the greater will be your disposition to frustration. By treating one, you treat the other.

You'll be pleased to know, though, that frustration, like boredom, is easily overcome.

Look for these calm solutions:
The 100 Percent Effort .... page 159
An End to Boredom .... page 164
The Joy of Repetition............ page 161

Divided responsibilities

The last area of 'control' – or, more precisely, lack of control – is the divided responsibilities that arise when you combine work and family life.

According to one survey, up to 40 percent of the working population take personal and family problems into the workplace at any given time. While many of those problems relate to temporary events like arguments or financial issues, often they will reflect the changing nature of the household unit.

In another era, you had breadwinners, homemakers and children, with minimal variation in the family unit. Today, most two-parent families require two income earners. Many families do not have two live-in parents at all, but one. Most sole-parent families struggle, many are financially deprived. Most sole-parent families cannot afford adequate child-minding or domestic assistance. Most sole parents travel further to work, yet can afford less time to do so. So it is not surprising that many sole-parent families carry disproportionate burdens.

This changed family unit affects more than just families. Many adults now live in single-adult dwellings. There are more single people than couples. There are more divorced people, more widows and widowers, than at any other time in history. The impact of all these changed households has a pronounced effect on lifestyles and attitudes – which are then carried into the workplace.

When you have conflicts of responsibility, you have stress.

Look for these calm solutions:
Life Priorities Calculator .... page 91
Undividing Responsibilities .... page 161
The Power of No .... page 143
The Get Stuffed Fund .... page 224

3. Self

By far the greatest cause of disharmony in the workplace is not time, change or lack of control. It's you. The way you think. The type of personality you have. The things you believe. How you reason. *What's inside your head.*

I could devote an entire book to this one problem area and still hardly touch the surface. However, the solutions can be well covered in just a few pages.

The comforting aspect of knowing that problems

flourish within the confines of your head, is knowing that the solutions reside in the same place – for you, one of the most readily accessible places at your disposal.

By focusing on your perceptions and attitudes, and the way you respond to work problems, you can help to eliminate those problems and be well on your way to achieving a state of calm.

Personality

The question must be asked: are some people naturally predisposed towards feeling tense and anxious? Are some more vulnerable to worry and nervousness than others?

Though some of my academic colleagues might cringe at the crudeness of my terminology, there are people who could only be classified as 'worriers'. I know this condition well: I am inclined to be that way myself.

In addition, there is a whole range of personality types who, by virtue of their make-up, are susceptible to the problems of negative stress.

The majority of readers of *Calm at Work* will probably display Driven behavioural characteristics. According to the stereotype, Driven people suffer from more self-induced stress problems than Easygoing people. One of the characteristics of Driven behaviour is impatience, so the Driven reader will be inclined to flick through the pages, snatching a few paragraphs here and there, before shifting their attention to something else.

A second characteristic of Driven people is the belief that they are more in control – of themselves and situations – than other behavioural types.

Anxiety

I've heard dozens of theories about why people suffer from anxiety. These range from the exotic – repressed memory syndrome, biochemical or neurochemical imbalances, cultural perspectives – to environmental factors such as home, social or workplace conditions. The theory I give most credence to is one that says that anxiety is the second phase of stress degeneration – first comes a succession of stressful incidents or behaviour, then comes generalised feelings of anxiety (the third phase is loss of emotional control).

It hardly matters which of these theories you accept, the anxiety persists. Because anxiety is a 'result', not a 'cause'. Indeed, you might never be aware of the cause of your anxieties.

Ask most sufferers what causes their anxiety, and they will have no idea. 'I just feel anxious.' These feelings are commonplace and so familiar to most of us, that it may come as a surprise to learn they are not as vague or as generalised as they may appear.

The feelings of apprehension that we know as 'anxiety' are quite specific: they are always a product of the imagination, always relate to time, and almost always relate to the future (even if those features are not obvious to the sufferer). 'What if ... ?', 'What will I ... ?', 'Who will ... ?' and so on. They can express themselves in a variety of ways: concerns about financial or health matters, disquiet about accountability, fear of authority or failure, or they could be just generalised feelings of dread and unease.

All these concerns have two things in common: they usually lack substance and they relate to the future. Whether this is the foreseeable future – say, 30 minutes ahead – or for the distant future, is irrelevant; the fact is you're concerned about something that at this moment does not exist. At the present moment, the future is nothing more than an abstract concept. Our efforts to endow it with some form of reality (even with words like 'foreseeable future' and 'distant future'), along with our efforts to treat it as something that can be controlled or manipulated, exacerbate, if not cause, these feelings of anxiety.

If you could analyse the likelihood of your worry becoming a reality, you would probably conclude that it was very unlikely. You would therefore have nothing to worry about, no reason to feel anxious.

Of course, few of us have the objectivity to analyse our anxieties in this way. That is why I have developed a number of techniques to overcome these pressures through relaxed, sometimes even fun, approaches.

Ambition

You would think that ambitious people should enjoy some sort of work advantage over those who lack ambition; after all, they know what they want and are usually motivated to devote whatever concentration and effort is required to getting it – and that includes being in control of work's many stressors. Or, at least, that's how the theory goes.

In reality, ambitious people are just as likely to suffer the ill effects of negative stress as others; perhaps even more so. The pressures that arise from being ambitious are closely related to those that arise from being deadline-oriented: you set yourself an objective, then you pressure

73

yourself until you achieve that objective. As a result of such drive, there will be a lot of highly ambitious people reading this book.

The fact that ambition drives you to achieve certain goals does not become a stressor in itself; indeed, many people are enriched and invigorated by the challenge. For some, ambition gives work life direction and purpose. Certainly as people grow older, ambition can become a powerful, life-extending force. But when ambition is coupled with unclear goals, you have a dangerous cocktail. Because you have all of the drive, but none of the satisfaction that comes from achievement. Hence, vaguely-defined goals like 'I want to be rich', or 'I want to be famous' – especially if these are beyond your capabilities, or beyond the time limit you allow yourself – create their own pressure.

The best way to achieve peace and satisfaction from your ambition is to establish clear objectives for yourself. As someone who has spent many years working as a strategic planner, I have learned that the most relaxed (and efficient) organisations are those that fully understand where they are headed; in other words, those who have plans. I have also discovered that the soundest plans emanate from calm frames of mind – neither influenced by uncontrolled ambition, nor panic.

Look for these calm solutions:
Life Priorities Calculator .... page 91
The Worry Eliminator .... page 192
The Three Laws of Time and Effort Management .... page 134

Fear

Fear is one of the most ferocious stressors in the workplace. If you exclude the way it galvanises your resources to defend against threat or adversity, its physiological effects are almost entirely negative. Indeed, fear is sometimes considered to be the most damaging emotional stressor of all. And, for some reason, it tends to breed in the workplace.

Fear is seldom rational. You fear that the comment you made in the lunch room is going to get back to your supervisor – even though commonsense tells you it is unlikely. You fear that the environmental recklessness of your competitors is going to destroy the planet. You fear that someone else is going to get the position you covet. You fear that the tax inspector is going to hound you over those deductions you claimed last year. Even more debilitating than any of those is when you are unaware of what specific issue is causing your fear – you just know you are feeling uneasy, afraid that something *might* happen.

Workplace fears are usually as irrational as feelings of anxiety – concerns that are centred on something that is not actually happening at that moment and, in many cases, is not likely to happen in the future. In these cases, your fear would be about what *might* happen.

Clearly, these feelings are as counterproductive as they are irritating. Fortunately, they are countered by the very thing that causes them: your subconscious – a resource we will be using more and more throughout this book.

> **Look for these calm solutions:**
> The Plus and Minus Method .....page 198
> A Positive Word ....page 184
> The Positive Picture ....page 188

Guilt

As unlikely as it may appear, feelings of guilt are another major cause of stress in the workplace. Whether inspired by your own insecurities, or pressures placed upon you by external influences, or even an overactive sense of duty, the results are equally as negative.

Generally, guilt falls into two categories:

(i) what you think of yourself (such as the type of person you are, the things you've done or intend doing, or aspects of yourself you've been conditioned to think are bad or unattractive); and

(ii) what others try to make you feel or do (such as being responsible for *their* moods or conditions, or making you feel guilty about things you do at work).

Thankfully, the calmer you are, the less prone you are to suffering from feelings of guilt. And vice versa.

Ego

How much pain is caused, not by what you think of yourself, but by what you believe other people may think of you? It hurts to discover someone else thinks you're inefficient, unprofessional or unreliable. It hurts to discover you're unliked or unrespected.

This is not always a case of vanity or conceit which, as negative emotions, are other causes of negative stress in the workplace. It will usually be the result of people thinking (so you believe) certain things about you that conflict with the image you hold of yourself. When this dissonance exists you feel hurt, wronged, distressed.

One way around this is to have a reasonable, objective image of yourself – knowing your strengths and weaknesses, and accepting them for what they are.

Psychologists tell us, however, that it is difficult for us to formulate an accurate assessment of our individual personalities without the assistance of another party. While I can hardly dispute the existence of this limitation, I totally reject the notion that it should limit the way we *view* ourselves. We are, after all, products of our own thoughts and self-images. That being the case, what is to stop us creating the thoughts and self-images that will help us achieve the things we want to achieve? What is to stop us creating mental images of ourselves as calm, confident, capable people? What is to stop us creating images of ourselves as winners, achievers or successful human beings?

Not a thing.

All you need to know is how to do it.

Look for these calm solutions:
Basic Visualisation Template .....page 118
Set Your Own Benchmarks.......page 213
Life Priorities Calculator ....page 91
Permission to Reject Success....page 214
The 100 Percent Effort ....page 159

Insecurity

Insecurity deserves a special mention. It is ubiquitous. And, as the world changes, it becomes more pronounced.

In today's workplace, insecurities tend to grow with the passing of time. There comes a stage in most employees' lives when they realise they are no longer the pick of the crop, that they are no longer indispensable, that there are better-equipped people for their jobs. This knowledge is intensified by the realisation that their expertise is diminishing. Their knowledge base is not so much being eroded, as being outclassed – by a data base, a young graduate, or a street-wise young salesperson.

Whatever your accomplishments or position, there is an understandable tendency to feel insecure when these things occur. But, with an element of planning, these feelings can be easily overcome.

Look for these calm solutions:
Assume You're Secure ....page 222
Say You're Secure ....page 223
The Get Stuffed Fund.............page 224
The Scent of Calm................page 282

Focus

The textbooks tend to ignore this last category, yet it is one of the great causes of personal negative stress in the workplace.

It is to do with focus or, more precisely, the *lack* of focus.

You will have seen and heard sports commentators speak of 'focus' in awed tones. Personality profiles in the business press use the same word – 'a highly focused chief executive' or 'a focused organisation'. In both instances this attribute is associated with success or accomplishment.

You seldom read anything complimentary about the reverse, the *un*focused. An unfocused person is never sure where they are heading from one moment to the next. The unfocused individual takes longer to do things, does them less competently and suffers more frustration in the process. Similarly, the unfocused leader spreads stress and disharmony, and the unfocused organisation is a sorry place to work.

You may not have any influence over the focus of the organisation you work for, but you are still in a powerful position: if you, as an individual, know how to become focused, and how to retain that focus, you are well on the way to being calm and in control of how you feel about your work.

You may be thinking at this stage that my talk of focus relates to the higher ideals of success and achievement. This is, after all, one of the qualities most attributed to high achievers. But all I am referring to is a

Look for these calm solutions:
The 100 Percent Effort ....page 159
Creative Long-Range
Planner...........................page 171
A 30-Second Course in
Marketing ....page 237
The Unconscious Planner ....page 177
Undividing Responsibilities ....page 166

way of using focus to make your work easier and more satisfying, whether you choose to excel at it or not.

Being focused is a calming technique in itself. More about this later.

4. Social

We know the main causes of negative stress in the workplace relate to time pressures, lack of control over what you do, and lack of social support in what you do.

This last cause – lack of social support in the workplace – is a many-headed monster. It ranges from lack of respect for you as a person, to lack of acknowledgment of your contributions, to everyday conflicts that arise involving people you work with and work for, customers, and remote sources such as the board or regulatory authorities.

Competitiveness

The increasing emphasis on competition and competitiveness by government and industry fuels the social tensions in the workplace. This quest for competitiveness is only just starting to warm up and will increase manifold. Will competition take all the enjoyment out of life? Will competition force the weaker of us into early retirement or redundancy? Will we be forced to become more competitive or to perish?

Competition is, of its very nature, stressful.

Many 'great competitors' have taught themselves to transform the related stress into a positive force – helping them to push themselves that little bit further, or to strive for increasingly difficult goals. For such people, the stress of competition may fall into the area of positive stress (see page 218) which is both invigorating and life-enriching.

On the other hand, many of us respond to competition in quite the opposite way. Instead of finding it stimulating and enriching, we find it debilitating or vulgar. Those of us who have not been raised in a competitive environment may find it intimidating. And those who are plagued by feelings of insecurity or self-doubt will be affected most of all.

Why? Because we would rather not be compared. We dislike the feeling of being constantly under challenge. We find it distasteful that someone else should earn their rewards (or gratification) by measuring their performance against ours, or expecting ours to be measured against theirs.

I am convinced the majority of people in the workplace fall into the latter category: those who find competitiveness to be a negative stress rather than a positive one. If you are in this category, all you probably want from your job is to put in a solid day's work and to be suitably rewarded for having done so. The thought of having your contribution evaluated and compared against that of your workmates, or workers in Korea, Sweden or the Czech Republic, may seem offensive to you. All of which adds up to more stress.

The secret for achieving a calm, fulfilling work day in such an atmosphere is to approach your work with a purpose, and to work to the best of your abilities. On the surface that might appear idealistic, but you will discover it is both a satisfying and effortless way to spend your day.

Look for these calm solutions:

How Susceptible Are You .... page 12

Set Your Own Benchmarks....... page 213

Permission to Reject Success....page 214

A 30-Second Course in Marketing .... page 237

Anger

The physiological effects of anger are similar to those of fear (or other states of arousal): increased heart rate, speeded-up breathing, dilated pupils, blood diverted from the stomach and intestines to the brain and muscles, increased blood-sugar levels and so on.

While it is well known that anger is frequently a by-product of stress, it can also have the converse effect and exacerbate your stress. The reason for this is simple. The natural response of human beings is to dispense the effects of their anger by either physically running away from or attacking (physically, verbally) the source of their frustration. Physical attacks are generally frowned upon in nice workplaces, and verbal attacks do not always come out your way, so we don't often have the luxury of such releases. Similarly, physically running away from the source of your frustration is not a popular way to advance your career. Added to this, the source of your frustration at work will often be vague, outside your control or perhaps even unknown. So all you can do is let your anger transmute into more and more stress. Hardly a great way to spend your life.

Anger is an emotion that you have to deal with. It is equally as life-shortening if you give into it or bottle it up. You will be pleased to know, however, that there are a couple of simple techniques you can employ to overcome the negative effects of this emotion.

> **Look for these calm solutions:**
> Diffusing Anger .... page 230
> Park It .... page 220

Envy

One of the more noticeable traits in private enterprise is, for want of a better word, greed. Closely related to this is envy, which usually relates to feelings about another's position, possessions or accomplishments. Both result in stressful feelings.

Because envy is often accompanied by high levels of expectation (a cause of stress), it can also lead to frustration (another cause of stress) if left unfulfilled. It also has the capacity to soften the logic and to blind normally well-balanced people to acts of folly and insensitivity.

The important thing to recognise about envy is its mere existence. Being aware of it, and its drawbacks, is usually the first step towards overcoming it. From then on, any of the techniques in this book that relate to planning or positivity will complete the process.

Look for these calm solutions:
Life Priorities Calculator .... page 91
A Positive Word .... page 184
Have Fun .... page 317

Relationships

How do you handle an overbearing boss, an unreasonable supervisor, an unresponsive underling? How do you get on with someone who is spiteful or dishonest? How do you cope with a bully? How do you get your own way from time to time?

People tell me it would be a very brave person who claimed to have solutions to such a disparate range of social issues. In the main, though, I believe most work relationship problems fall into a few neat categories, all of which can be aided with a few simple skills.

Look for these calm solutions:
The 100 Percent Effort .... page 159
Managing Difficult People .... page 228
The Art of Negotiation .... page 241
Calm Self-Defence .... page 247

Assertiveness

As industry, commerce and the public service are forced to become more competitive, there is a corresponding pressure for employees of these organisations to develop their assertiveness.

Although assertiveness would be equally at home under the earlier headings of Control or Self, it is at its most necessary in the area of interaction with others.

You will have noticed how much frustration and feelings of impotence in workplaces can be attributed to lack of assertiveness on the part of the individual – particularly if you work with large or changing groups of people. While some will try to dismiss this as a failure of management in its responsibility to protect 'weaker' employees, this will be no comfort to you if you happen to be in this position.

For you, the only solution is to learn to be more assertive.

Look for these calm solutions:
How Susceptible Are You .... page 12
How to Get What You Want......page 232
Speaking Your Mind..............page 233

External social pressures

A major cause of stress in the workplace is one that can only loosely be defined as 'Personal'. Mostly this relates to non-workplace relationships – family, friends, lovers, potential lovers – or issues that involve them.

Often, the divided responsibilities that arise when you combine work and family life may seem insurmountable. But, in the main, they can be kept in perspective if you follow a few simple steps:

(i) Know what you want from your work.

(ii) Have strategies for how to achieve this.

(iii) Share those strategies with your partner, family or any other stakeholder in your career.

Look for these calm solutions:
Undividing Responsibilities ....page 166
Life Priorities Calculator .... page 91
Hit the Tub........................page 316
Diffusing Anger ....page 230
The Get Stuffed Fund.............page 224
Plan a Variation..................page 221

5. Change

I once worked with a woman – a leader in her field – who, upon taking over the general management of a company, immediately had all the senior executives change offices. 'Change upsets all their comfort zones,' she confessed. 'By the time they've readjusted, I'll be in control.' It worked. She was a very powerful woman.

Manipulative, yes; certainly not good management by today's standards; but extremely effective in upsetting the status quo.

Today, change is the only thing in our jobs that we can be absolutely certain of. Not only is change inevitable, but it is happening exponentially. And it will continue this way.

If you dislike the idea of change – and most people do – the prospect of having to confront an increasingly more dynamic, fluid and possibly even disrupted world can be terrifying. Because when the status quo is upset, it is natural to become insecure and tense. You become blinded by the prospect of loss or failure, rather than inspired by the possible advantages.

But change has brought countless benefits. Enhanced methods of production and organisation continue to push up our living standards. We have better medical services, safer transport systems, better disease control, cheap communications, accountable government ...

As long as you can appreciate that more good comes from change than bad – which statistical evidence confirms – you can strive to ensure that change works for *your* benefit. For the improvement of *your* life. *Your* work. *Your* well-being.

In addition, because of our increased expected lifespans, and our seemingly insatiable desire for improved leisure and entertainment, change can work in our favour from a job satisfaction point of view. Maybe now is the time to be thinking about a change in career direction for the next stage of your life ...

Embrace change for the good it can bring you. Accept it because of its inevitability. And not only will you feel more relaxed about your world now, but the potential for future success will be loaded in your favour.

Look for these calm solutions:
The Change List..................page 267
Never Too Old to Become Calm..page 269
A Change for the Better..........page 271

6. Physical

Five thousand years ago, most stress suffered by human beings was physical – you either caught your prey, or it caught you; you escaped the bushfire, or got sizzled; you found a cave to sleep in, or froze. Then, when people started to work for a living, stress got more complicated.

One hundred years ago, the most common source of workplace stress would have been the physical conditions you had to work in: environmental factors such as heat, cold, humidity, darkness, glare, dryness, wetness, combined with occupational factors such as unsafe work conditions, poor lighting and bad ventilation.

Today's workplace may be equally as stressful, but it is usually much less physically threatening. This has been one of the great advances of the industrial age: the physical causes of stress are nowhere near as pronounced as they were a century ago.

Nevertheless, they do exist. Extreme environmental discomforts apply to industries like diving, mining and firefighting, while others are affected by noise, vibration and various forms of pollution such as odours, gases, dust and poisons.

The common causes of physical stress, however, are more mundane. For example, many people find standing all day behind a serving counter to be as stressful as it is uncomfortable. Many who spend their days in front of computer monitors have similar complaints. So do those on the production line, in hospital casualty departments, and in the market garden. Shift workers endure physiological pressures that most of us have never contemplated.

While you may think that none of the above occupations seem all that physically stressful in themselves, they can have debilitating effects on those who work in them.

Generally, though, physical causes of stress require physical solutions – some of which are obvious (and possibly beyond the scope of this book) and some of which are covered later in the book.

7. Lifestyle habits

I have never been able to understand the omission of this category in the popular lists of workplace stress.

Surely the life you lead *outside* the workplace is potentially one of the major causes of stress inside it. If you smoke, have a heavy coffee habit, stay out late every night, don't exercise, drink too much, don't get enough sleep, fight with your spouse, or have any one of a hundred different habits, chances are you're going to be more susceptible to the emotional and physical stresses of work.

To overcome this, you don't necessarily have to change your lifestyle habits in any way. All you have to do is acknowledge that these are contributory factors, and learn to compensate for them.

Look for these calm solutions:

YOUR PORTFOLIO
OF CALM
SOLUTIONS

FIRST,
MAKE A DECISION

THE MOST IMPORTANT step in making the most of your work is deciding what you want to get out of your work.

> Make the decision today to concentrate your energy on the things that are important to you, such as becoming calm.

The only way to do this is to challenge what you believe in and what you think you want from your work, then to plan accordingly. If you can work towards goals that *you* define and that *you* believe in, you will be calm and contented in what you do.

Here is a simple technique to help you to order what is important in your life.

THE LIFE PRIORITIES CALCULATOR

The purpose of the Life Priorities Calculator is to help you determine your life's priorities. Is your top priority work? Position? Money? Success? Family? Happiness? Are your relationships more important? Do you just want to meet people? What will be at the top of your list?

The Life Priorities Calculator will help you to decide.

If, after completing this test, you decide (for example) that success in your industry is your priority, you can then focus on achieving that success. Once you've embarked on that mission, many of the unrelated stresses and frustrations of everyday work will either disappear or be reduced in significance.

To use the calculator, you need to sit somewhere quiet.

Before you begin, spend a couple of minutes doing nothing but listening to your breathing.

When you feel comfortable with this, imagine yourself at sixty-five years of age. Imagine what you'll look like, and what you'll be doing.

Next, think back over the life you have led ...

Your Life Priorities Calculator

Think back over the life you've just led up until sixty-five years of age. Now, having done that, rate the following in order of importance to you.

- I was a success in my job
- I earned a lot of money from my work
- I rose to the top of my profession
- I helped others and shared my good fortune with them
- I became managing director
- I owned a fabulous house and car
- I worked at my relationships with friends
- I spent my best moments with my family
- I took the time to develop my relationship with my partner
- I had some fantastic holidays
- I learned many life-enriching skills not related to my work
- I found every day to be an adventure
- I wrote a book/built a house/learned the violin/sailed around the world/did a PhD
- I took good care of my health
- I spent every moment I could with my children when they were young

While this is by no means a definitive list of goals, it will help you to order your priorities. You may discover that work priorities – money, position, 'success' – are at the top of your list. If so, you can make the choice that you are going to succeed in your work at all costs, confident that having made such a decision only failure will cause you stress.

On the other hand, you may decide that relationships or life-enriching aspects of life are at the top of your list. If this is the case, then it is pointless allowing concerns about your work to keep you from following these activities.

Either way, you will have made a decision. If your decision is the latter (the relationship or life-enriching course), you can approach your work with diligence and sincerity, but without losing sleep over career manoeuvres or prospects for advancement. It may offend your work ethic, but it will enhance your life satisfaction.

Each of us has only a certain amount of psychic (that is, non-physical) energy to devote to our life activities. To concentrate it on the things that are important to you is a sure way to succeed; to squander it on things that are unimportant would be a shame.

Make the decision today.

> **Look for these calm solutions:**
> Breathing Calm ....page 103
> Basic Visualisation
> Template ....page 118

SECOND, TAKE A CALM BREATH

THERE IS ONE character-
istic common to stressed
and nervous people. It is
the way they breathe.

> Master your breathing and you'll be
> able to find a calm sanctuary in even
> the most stressful work environments.

Invariably, tense people breathe in short, shallow
breaths. The pattern of their breathing is tense and skittish.
Because the breaths are short, you need more of them to
fill your lungs each minute; and because these breaths
come and go so rapidly, you never really expel all the stale
air in your lungs – it just sits there, more or less
permanently.

Breathing in this way sets off a stressful physiological
chain-reaction: it limits the amount of oxygen in the
bloodstream (while failing to reduce the level of carbon
dioxide), which causes a constriction of the blood vessels
throughout the body, which reduces oxygen to the brain,
which, in turn, promotes feelings of tension and
nervousness.

A calm, relaxed person, on the other hand, breathes
differently: their breathing is slow, measured and deep.
The pattern is tranquil and relaxed. This means more
oxygen is forced into the bloodstream, more carbon
dioxide is removed, and more oxygen gets to the brain,
which, in turn, encourages the release of endorphins (the

The effects of emotional state on breathing

	Extremely nervous	Nervous	Normal	Calm
Breaths per minute	35–40	20–28	12–18	6–8
Volume of air inhaled each breath (mL)	170–150	300–215	500–330	1000–750
Stale air expelled per minute (mL approx)	100	2400	4200	5100
Retained stale air per minute (mL approx)	5900	3600	1800	900

tranquillising hormone), which helps you to feel calm and relaxed.

The conclusion: if you want to become calm and relaxed, all you have to do is ensure your breathing is slow, measured and deep.

Could it really be as easy as that?

At the risk of sounding glib or overly simplistic, if you want to know how to become calm and relaxed – quickly, surely and effectively – learn how to breathe properly.

Master your breathing and you'll be able to find a calm sanctuary in even the most stressful work environments. *Remember* to master your breathing and you'll be able to cope with practically any pressure, as and when it arises.

Slow, measured, deep breaths. That's all it takes.

BREATHING CALM

Breathing is unique among human functions in that it's the only involuntary physical activity you have conscious control over. When you can control the way you breathe, you can influence your health, well-being, the way you think and your overall state of mind. More importantly, you can influence all those states – physical as well as emotional – through the few steps that follow.

I have to confess that I was not the first to discover this piece of magic about breathing – the Chinese and Indians have been aware of it for almost 5000 years, and have spent this time integrating it into their martial arts and meditative rituals – but I can show you how to learn the best part of this knowledge in seconds!

This is called Breathing Calm.

It is the basis of *all* calming techniques. (It is also the basis of most athletic and performance techniques, and could easily be the basis of all your outstanding work performances – but that's another story.)

Breathing Calm is the most important physical exercise you will take from this book. Unless you have already mastered this skill, no other single exercise – whether from yoga, tai chi, meditation, autogenic exercises or biofeedback – will serve as well in helping you to become and remain calm whenever and wherever you need to.

The beauty of Breathing Calm is that it can become the springboard for all other calm disciplines, including yoga, tai chi, meditation and so on. Its other beauty is that it involves only three steps, so you can teach yourself how to do it in minutes.

The three steps are:

(i)   Breathe deeply.
(ii) Breathe slowly.
(iii) Listen.

1. Breathe deeply

Ask most people what breathing means to them and you'll get a strange look; surely breathing is something that just happens and warrants neither study nor analysis.

Even if it did warrant some degree of study, surely you would already be considered expert at it; after all, you've been breathing successfully since the moment you were born.

As for deep breathing, you're an expert on that, too. Remember all those things you learned in front of the physical education class, or in the gymnasium, or in the army?

Let's put your skills to the test. Try doing this while standing directly in front of a mirror.

Take a deep breath. A giant one. The biggest, fullest deepest breath you are humanly capable of. The way you know to get the maximum volume of air into your lungs.

Try it now.

Note what you did with your shoulders and chest.

Your shoulders would have risen, the upper part of your chest would have lifted dramatically, and your stomach would have sucked in (see A in the figure below).

You would have been concentrating on the upper part

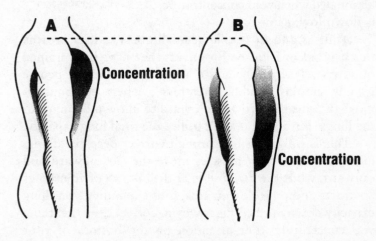

A deep breath

of the chest. 'Chest out, stomach in'; just like you were taught as a kid, right?

Unfortunately, you were taught incorrectly. (Although singers, dancers, actors and some athletes may have been taught differently.)

The correct way to take a deep breath, to really fill your lungs with air, does not involve lifting the shoulders or puffing out the upper chest at all. Quite the contrary. It involves concentrating on the *bottom* of your lungs, sucking the air in right down low. Near your navel. So that you can feel your stomach swell as the air sucks in (see B in the figure above).

Take a look at the figure opposite, at the way your lungs expand in each circumstance, and you will see how little comparison there really is. The quantity of air inhaled when you're concentrating on your upper chest (see A) is significantly less than the quantity of air inhaled when your concentration is down low, as in B.

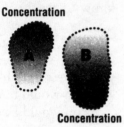

Concentration

Concentration

Lung expansion

Athletes and fit people generally believe they breathe this way unconsciously. But unless they have been trained otherwise, I seriously doubt it. Athletes and fit people usually employ 'middle breathing', where the muscles move the ribs upward and outward to allow more air into the lungs. But it still doesn't utilise the total lung capacity.

This is only possible through correct deep breathing. Here, the *intercostal* muscles move the ribs upward and outward, while the *diaphragm* at the bottom of your lungs contracts and pulls downwards, thus expanding your lung capacity downwards. This is why in correct deep breathing you concentrate your attention on the bottom of your lungs.

Imagine this

Imagine your lungs as a long, rigid cylinder, as in A in the figure below. At the bottom of this imagined cylinder is a soft, flexible material like balloon rubber. This is your diaphragm. When you inhale, forcing the air into the rigid cylinder of your lungs, the only way to accommodate all this extra air is for the soft elastic material at the bottom to expand, as in B. Then, when you stop inhaling, and the

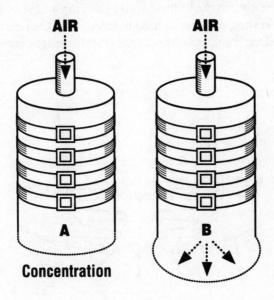

Visualising a deep breath

downward pressure of air ceases, what happens? The soft elastic material contracts back to its normal shape, and the air is forced out.

So, all you have to do is concentrate your breath at the bottom part of your lungs, rather than at the top. When you do this, and feel your diaphragm expand, everything else takes care of itself.

How's it feel?

Of course, reading this, and perhaps even imagining this, may not be sufficient for you to really get a feel for how deep breathing is meant to work. Here's a simple exercise to help you feel how your diaphragm expands when you are breathing correctly.

Place your hands on your hips (see below) with your forefingers just about touching your navel. Your thumbs will be resting in the hollow above each hip and your fingers will be resting on your stomach, stretching just below your navel. (Don't get too obsessive about the exact placement.)

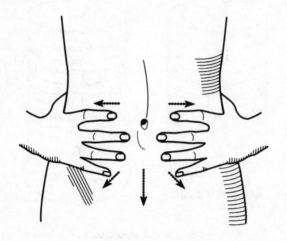

Feel your abdomen expand

Now, making sure your shoulders do not rise, take a breath until you can feel your abdomen swell beneath your fingers and thumbs. Concentrate on the *bottom* of your lungs as you inhale. Ensure your shoulders do not move. As your diaphragm expands to accommodate your breath, you will feel your abdomen press out beneath your fingers.

Now exhale slowly and evenly until you feel your abdomen fall.

That's deep breathing, the first step in Breathing Calm.

2. Breathe slowly

Remember how those tense or nervous people breathe? In short, shallow breaths. Rapid. Skittish. The tempo of the breaths adds to their feelings of tension, while the frequency prevents them from expelling a satisfactory volume of stale air.

You might find an extremely nervous person will breathe 35 to 40 times a minute, expel very little stale air at all, and hover on the brink of hyperventilation.

A person not so nervous might breathe 20 to 28 times a minute – not hyperventilative, but still rapid and tension-building, and still expelling an inadequate proportion of the stale gases.

Now we get more relaxed. A 'normal' emotional state

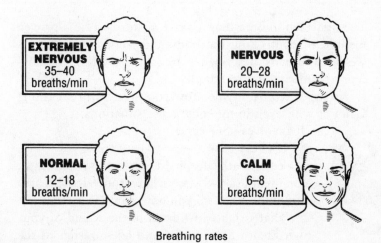

Breathing rates

would see the breathing rate drop to 12 to 18 breaths a minute. If you breathe at this rate under normal conditions, you will generally be feeling reasonably relaxed.

However, the ideal breathing rate for becoming calm – that is, the ideal rate for Breathing Calm – is only 6 to 8 breaths a minute. When you're relaxed, you'll find it easy to lower your rate to 10 to 12 breaths a minute; 6 breaths a minute may take a little more concentration but is quite achievable and comfortable. (Experienced meditators will do 4 breaths a minute at times.)

Breathing deeply at this rate will provide the maximum volume of oxygen to your bloodstream, and allow you to expel the maximum volume of stale gases. That means you will not only start feeling much more relaxed, but you will also be able to influence the way you feel.

Breathe deeply, breathe slowly, and you will be calm.

Now, what does it take to be able to relax – almost immediately – and to be able to do it at will?

3. Listen

The final step in Breathing Calm transforms a time-proven method of controlling the body and emotions – such as we have already described – into a fast-acting, readily-reproduced calming technique.

In other words, it will allow you to perform Breathing Calm at will, even in the most tense situations.

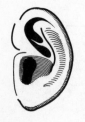
It involves your ears.

It's very easy.

You breathe deeply (down low in your lungs). You breathe slowly (anywhere from 6 to 8 breaths a minute). Then all you have to do is listen.

That's right. Just listen to the sound of your own breath as it comes and goes. Listen to the inflow of cool air through your nostrils. Listen to the sound of your warm breath as you breathe out through your mouth.

Just listen. That's all you have to do. Breathe deeply. Breathe slowly. And listen.

You will find this technique works in the most unlikely environments. By concentrating this way you will easily hear the sound of your breathing 'inside' your head, even in the noisiest conditions. As long as you listen for it, you will hear it. Clearly. Just as you would if you were floating or swimming under water.

Try it for yourself. Wherever you are now, whatever you're doing, take a deep breath, and listen to the sound of your breath as it comes and goes.

How easy was that!

Breathing Calm

1 Breathe deeply (use the bottom part of your lungs).
2 Breathe slowly (6 to 8 breaths a minute).
3 Listen to the sound of your breath as you
   inhale – the air coming in through your nostrils.
4 Listen to the sound of your breath as you exhale – the air
   coming out of your mouth.
5 Repeat for 60 seconds, or indefinitely.

Working towards long-term calm

If you want to stay calm all the time, concentrate on breathing correctly all the time. While learning is easy, remembering takes effort. Years of poor breathing habits are not instantly overcome; all that shallow breathing has probably weakened the diaphragm and abdominal muscles, which take practice to get back into shape.

Practise during moments of calm, and Breathing Calm will come naturally when stressful moments arise. The more you practise, the more intuitive it becomes. And the more you practise during calm moments, the more you associate feeling calm with this activity.

Calm posture

In addition to habit and technique, there is another attribute that will influence the way you breathe. Your posture. Even the slightest slump of the shoulders can have a limiting effect: it reduces the volume of your chest cavity which, in turn, causes you to breathe with your upper chest (shallow breathing) rather than your ribs and diaphragm.

Yet, with a simple adjustment to your posture, amazing things become possible. Open up your chest cavity and air floods into your lower lungs. This, in turn, flushes more waste materials from them and eases muscular tensions around your stomach and rib areas. And as these tensions release, correct breathing starts to become automatic.

Look for these calm solutions:
Straight to Calm ....page 292
The Sound of Calm...............page 280
Grin and Bear It ....page 289

THIRD, SEND YOUR SUBCONSCIOUS TO WORK

EARLIER, I WROTE that if you trust your intuition to guide you to the best solutions, you will have access

> Most stress results from what happens in your thoughts, rather than what happens to your body.

to some of the most powerful techniques in this book.

Many of these techniques require a degree of trust in your intuition or your subconscious to function at their optimum. This is not unusual. *All* significant improvements in life require this trust in greater or lesser degrees.

To many people in the workplace, however, this is an anathema. They have built their careers on being logical and unemotional, and on striving to be in control at all times. To stray from the practical, rational path is not encouraged. As a result, they begin to develop a bias towards a certain way of thinking – 'left-brain' thinking. If you examine the figure on the next page, you will begin to see why left-brain thinking dominates business, industry and most workplaces.

The human brain is divided into two hemispheres. Essentially, the left hemisphere is used for structured, reasoned, analytical thought processes – the type of thinking that is common, expected and highly regarded in most workplaces.

The right side of the brain is associated with more creative, imaginative, abstract, or emotive processes. As a result, it is usually used *less* in day-to-day work activities.

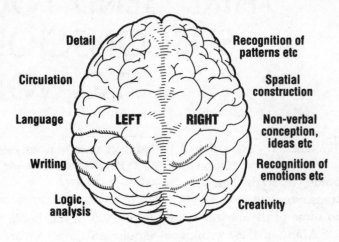

Activities of the brain

In spite of the fact that many occupations would profit from more right-brain thinking (creative, imaginative), the left-brain approach (structured, reasoned, analytical) tends to dominate. Even in industries that you would imagine were more creative and imaginative, such as advertising and television, this continues to be the case. Considering this left-brain domination, you can see how difficult it might be to convince some people to utilise their subconscious or intuition. After all, utilising such resources hardly seems reasoned or logical.

Or does it?

The logic of the subconscious

The activity of your subconscious is a simple part of your normal brain function. It relates to things that are not the focus of your attention, but are still being recorded (or observed) elsewhere in your consciousness, that is, in your subconscious.

If I were to convince you that putting your trust in your subconscious was essential to most, if not all, great achievements in life, you'd say it would also have to be a benefit in your occupation.

This is true.

In terms of controlling the emotions, your subconscious is significantly more powerful than your conscious mind, and immeasurably more powerful than the total weight of your willpower. Performers of great feats know the subconscious can help achieve things they would never be able to achieve if they relied solely on reason and willpower.

This is why most great achievements in life – be they work, creative, athletic or calming – are only achieved with the full and active support of the subconscious.

When you watch the karate master preparing to smash five bricks with his forehead, you will see a faraway, unfocused look come into his eyes. He may tell you that this is the process of focusing or harnessing his *chi* (life force), but in effect he is recruiting his subconscious – because it will be his subconscious that allows him to believe he can achieve things we all 'know' can't be done (such as smashing five bricks with your forehead).

You will see that same unfocused look in the eyes of great musicians before they hit the high points of performance. And in the eyes of boxers, sprinters and swimmers before the competition begins.

I've seen it in the eyes of business people before they pull off the big deal. *And you will often see it in the eyes of people who are becoming calm in stressful situations.*

Call it what you will, this is a simple process of inviting your subconscious to participate. If you know how to use your subconscious and learn to trust it, you can achieve almost anything – including becoming calm in situations that you would normally find stressful.

But first you have to learn how to trust it.

A familiar truth

I'll give you an example of the subconscious's effectiveness that you're probably familiar with.

Have you ever said to yourself, when going to bed at night, 'Tomorrow I will wake at 7.00 a.m.'? Sure enough, after you've done this, you wake next morning just as the clock moves past 6.59 a.m. How can this be? How can it be so accurate?

While it is true that scientists have recently discovered a part of the brain that is not only responsible for time-keeping but is extraordinarily accurate, you have no way of accessing this with your conscious mind. You can practise all you like, use all the willpower you are capable of, but you will fail, because you cannot access this part of the brain with your conscious mind – only your subconscious.

The wonder and the beauty of your subconscious is that it works best when you *believe* it will work best. Trust your subconscious to wake you at 7.00 a.m., and you will wake at 7.00 a.m. Every time, on the dot, without fail. (If you tell me you've tried this mental alarm clock method and it didn't work, I will say that you didn't trust your subconscious. Trust it and it will work for you, nothing is surer.)

I am not exaggerating. It will happen every time.

Your subconscious achieves other 'impossible' things in life with monotonous regularity. One of the most graphic demonstrations is the way you will hear your name mentioned on the other side of the room at a noisy party – from a distance you would consider impossible to hear any word of conversation. Similarly, it is your subconscious that warns you the person you were just introduced to is untrustworthy, or the stretch of path ahead conceals a pitfall.

Your subconscious will also help you to become calm.

Are you too smart for this?

Deep down, many intellectually-oriented people are sceptical about the power of the subconscious. They have so much faith and vested interest in the cognitive power of their brains, that they refuse to accept there could be something else at play which is equally as powerful in shaping their life – or, horror of horrors, even more powerful. These people love to say, 'prove it' (which, of course, there is no obligation for anyone to do). Secretly, they believe that if they can't see or hear it, it can't possibly exist.

If you have faith only in what you can see – or *believe* you can see – you might like to consider this: a great proportion of the 'visible' information that passes from your eyes to your brain is far from visible. It does not go to your visual cortex (in the thinking/reasoning part of your brain) at all, but scatters to limbic ('non-conscious'/emotional/motivational) parts or, even more bizarre, to the auditory cortex part of your brain that allows you to hear. So while you may be consciously aware of *some* of the visual information you are taking in, much of it is headed to parts of your brain that relate to 'non-conscious' functions such as feeling and intuition.

Other senses work this way as well. Much of the information you hear, for example, does not go to the cognitive parts of your brain, so you cannot be consciously aware of all you are supposedly hearing.

In addition to this, there is a well-documented psychological state where you actually *see* sounds, and *hear* colours. This state, known as *synaesthesia*, is where you perceive a stimulus detected by one sensory system in another sensory system. Artists and musicians know it well, but some scientists believe we are all capable of it at some time or another – if we pay attention.

How does it make you feel to realise you aren't seeing or hearing all the things you are looking at or listening to?

The good news is that your *sub*conscious has immediate access to all this information – both conscious and unconscious. Thus armed, it assists you to perform seemingly impossible feats. It makes you aware of an approaching car, even though you are looking in the opposite direction. It draws your eye to your own name on a newspaper page, even though it is buried in thousands of tiny words in tight columns. It warns you of someone's hostile intent even though their words may be friendly.

It can also help you to achieve greatness, to overcome problems and to become calm.

Some of the techniques that follow require the support of your subconscious. If these techniques feel right to you, and if you subsequently trust your subconscious to make the most of them, they will work for you.

Managing your subconscious

Knowing that your subconscious can be a powerful ally is only one part of this story; getting it to work for you, in your quest to stay calm at all times, is more important.

While discussion of the subconscious may seem technical or academic, it requires no special training or study to make it work for you.

The first step is to abandon your willpower. Once you

have done this, choose any of the following routes:

(i) Imagination
(ii) Repetition
(iii) Seduction

Imagination

The more disciplined among us have been trained to believe that by applying sufficient willpower we can achieve whatever we set our minds to, that the sheer weight of will and personality overcomes all subconscious urges or compulsions.

I'm sorry to have to tell you that this is not so.

As far as your subconscious is concerned, your imagination is infinitely more powerful. I'll give you an example: you know your chances of being attacked by a hooded monster in a darkened cemetery are about one in a billion. You also know you stand a much greater chance of being run over by a bus or dying of food poisoning. Why, then, does your pulse rate soar as you walk through a cemetery at night, yet it hardly alters as you cross a busy road eating a hamburger?

It's because of your imagination.

The power of your imagination escalates in direct proportion to the amount of willpower you exert trying to control it. To continue the cemetery analogy: the more you try to use your willpower *not* to think about hooded monsters, the more you'll think of them as you tiptoe through the tombstones.

If you want to influence the way you think and feel, therefore, you must appeal to your *imagination* rather than your intellect.

Later you'll read about visualisation techniques that help utilise the power of imagination to overcome stressful feelings and situations.

Repetition

You've seen enough hypnosis on television to recognise the hypnotist's favourite device: repetition. He makes the same suggestion over and over again. Perhaps he phrases it in different ways, but he repeats and repeats.

Any form of repetition has a non-discriminating effect on the subconscious. If you talk of your work being a pain in the neck enough times, chances are you'll develop tense neck muscles whenever you're there. Repeated negative suggestions (or thoughts) will induce failure, accidents and illness. Conversely, repeated positive suggestions can make someone a success, and can overcome problems and adversity.

Why? For one reason: repetition tends to dominate conscious thought, thus allowing more space for the subconscious to be influenced. This enables you to concentrate in ways sheer willpower would never permit. When you can concentrate like this – not through willpower, but through the *absence* of conscious thought – your subconscious is at its most receptive. And that's the best time to effect positive change.

If you want to influence your subconscious, repeat, repeat, repeat – with positive words (affirmation), actions or thoughts.

Seduction

The subconscious cannot be bullied into behaving rationally. Not by logic, willpower, commonsense or any other mechanism. That is not the way it works.

For it to accept one of your logical, hard-edged, black-and-white, practical demands – that is, a command from your will – it has to be *seduced* into responding the way you want it to. It has to be charmed, cajoled, tricked into performing what you ask of it.

This is achieved through suggestion.

Unlike the conscious mind, the subconscious has no ability to discriminate: under the right conditions, any suggestion you present to it will be taken on board and acted upon (as long as it is not too contrary to your general beliefs or desires).

Understanding this power of suggestion permits a great salesperson to exert their influence over a customer, causes healthy people to ail, causes ill people to recover, allows martial artists to perform great feats, and enables sportspeople to win. This understanding is also the basis of hypnosis, self-hypnosis and many self-help programs.

This is why a conversation about itching will cause you to want to scratch. It is why pretending to be tired will make you yawn. It is also why people who talk about success are often successful, and why failures talk about failure. This phenomenon is known as 'applied suggestion'. It can emanate from someone else (such as a complainer, a salesperson, or a hypnotist) or from yourself, but once the suggestion is accepted by the subconscious, the subconscious sets about transforming it into reality.

Thus, if you keep telling yourself *positive, calming* things, then you will achieve them. If you are persistent, this will work; there is nothing surer. More powerful still is *visual* suggestion. If you can mentally 'see' these positive things, these calming things, and especially if you can 'see' yourself participating in them, then you are well on the way to achieving them.

FOUR
TOOLS OF THE
SUBCONSCIOUS

IT COULD BE argued that there are hundreds of tools that you can use to influence the subconscious and so achieve the things you want to achieve in the workplace.

> The subconscious often behaves like a small child; it loves to be entertained and to play games, and thrives on dreams, emotions, abstract ideas, concepts, pictures, ideals and rich visuals.

I have simplified this process by dividing these useful tools into four categories – mainly because each of the tools works brilliantly, but also because I have done quite a lot of research into their effectiveness.

Each of the categories is presented as a template – a base technique or formula that you can add to or modify, according to your need or likes. They are:

(i) Visualisation
(ii) Affirmation
(iii) Self-hypnosis (and meditation)
(iv) Assumption

Get to know these basic techniques, then you can refine or augment them, in order to tailor your own solutions to specific workplace problems. Initially, though, they are techniques to be used at home – to prepare you for things that may happen at work; they are not necessarily designed to be used in the workplace itself, except perhaps during quiet times.

1. Visualisation

The cliché that 'a picture is worth a thousand words' was never more true than when used to describe a picture's (even a mental picture's) influence over the subconscious.

You know this from your own experience: the street fight you witness is much more offensive than the one described to you over the telephone; the glimpse of Tom Cruise in the flesh is infinitely more memorable than a lurid description of him in a magazine article.

So, if you feed your subconscious with powerful visual images – *positive* visual images – your subconscious is much more inclined to take those images on board.

Thus, visualisation is the most powerful technique you can employ for bringing about mood or behavioural change – because it appeals to the imagination, the picture-forming faculty of the mind.

Visualisations require only the most basic level of imaginative skill. If you doubt your ability to visualise, carry on as if you can do it easily. It will work just as effectively.

Following is the master technique for visualisation. It is designed to be varied as the need arises, but in any form it is singularly powerful.

The silver screen

This has been designed for our electronic, multimedia age. The technique employs an item of (imaginary) technology that is familiar to all of us: a big, silver movie screen (see next page). Instead of trying to imagine or visualise in some poorly defined area of your mind, you simply imagine the visualisation taking place up there on the big screen.

You perform all of what follows with eyes closed.

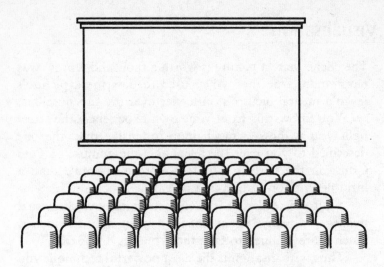

The silver screen used in visualisation

First, choose an image that best sums up the way you would like to feel. If you're feeling overworked and highly stressed, the image you choose might be one of yourself at work feeling calm, relaxed and completely in control. Alternatively, the picture may be pure escapism. In a luxuriant, peaceful rainforest. Or on the beach of an idyllic South Pacific island.

Once you have decided on the image that most appeals, you project this image onto your big silver screen; that is, you imagine it appearing there.

Still with your eyes closed, absorb all the visual details of the image on that screen: the carpet of leaves on the rainforest floor, the long stretches of white, sandy beach on the island.

When you can see this image clearly, imagine yourself climbing up into that screen, so you become part of the image.

Observe yourself in that rainforest. Or on the sun-bleached sands of that tropical island. Note what you're wearing, the relaxed way you're standing, the way the breeze blows your hair, the calm smile on your face.

Now imagine what you'd be seeing if you really were up there on the screen. 'See' the surrounding scenery through your own eyes.

At the same time, you begin to 'hear' the sounds of that location as if you were really there. The waves lapping at the shore. Or the songbirds in the rainforest.

Then 'feel' what it's like to be standing in that scene. The warmth of the sun on your body. The cool breeze on your face. The bed of leaves or the soft sand beneath your feet.

When you feel that you are really experiencing being in that particular place, take a snapshot of the scene. Or freeze the frame. Complete with all the images, sounds and feelings.

Then just pause and luxuriate in that feeling.

Within seconds, you'll be feeling calm and relaxed – as if you really were on that wonderful island, or that quiet rainforest, of your imagination.

Look for these calm solutions:	
Breathing Calm	page 103
Straight to Calm	page 292
The Sound of Calm	page 280
The Positive Picture	page 188

Basic Visualisation Template

1 Enjoy 5 minutes of Breathing Calm. Listen to the sound of your breath coming and going.
2 When you are relaxed, close your eyes and imagine a huge silver screen before you.
3 When you can 'see' that silver screen, picture the most relaxed environment you can imagine. Examine this place in detail.
4 Now imagine yourself climbing up into that image. See yourself up there – exactly as you would like to be – always acting, speaking and thinking *positively*.
5 Now that you are part of the scene, 'see' everything about you.
6 'Hear' all the sounds around you.
7 'Feel' the breeze, textures and temperature.
8 When all of that is firmly implanted in your mind, take a 'snapshot' (or freeze-frame) of yourself, complete with all those images, sounds and feelings.
9 Relax, and let the positive feelings work their way through your consciousness (no effort is required).
10 If necessary, repeat the exercise.

2. Affirmation

Affirmation is a technique well known to hypnotherapists, psychotherapists, promoters of self-improvement courses and, most of all, producers of self-help audio tapes. The process is known as self-instruction or auto-suggestion, and it is one of the easiest techniques to apply.

Affirmations are simply a set of words that depend on repetition for their power. As these words are repeated over and over, they begin to influence the subconscious and become self-fulfilling, with the words or sentiments you choose determining the results you achieve.

It sounds simple, and it is simple. But affirmation is

an enormously powerful tool for change – especially in the areas of adding calm and order to your life.

Choosing the right words

The words you choose for your affirmation should be in the present tense, and must be simple, active and positive. There is no room for sub-clauses and qualifications, just simple, straightforward, positive suggestions. Example: 'I am enjoying my work more and more. Every moment of it becomes more and more fulfilling.'

As well, because you want to appeal to the imagination more than the intellect, the use of emotive words ('enjoy', 'love', 'admire', 'confident', 'happy') work even more powerfully.

And, most powerful of all, are picture-forming words that appeal to your imagination. Words like 'I look', 'people see me', 'I keep my head held high'. These are not always easy to integrate into an affirmation, but if you can think of ways of doing so, all the better.

Say, for example, your greatest concern at work is an intimidating boss who has a habit of denigrating your efforts and qualities. To counter this, you choose words for your affirmation that are directed solely at the *solution* you desire – not words that address the negative characteristics of your boss or your relationship with your boss.

The focus of your words should be on yourself and the way you feel – after all, you are all that counts in this equation. It serves no purpose to add phrases like, 'my boss thinks I'm wonderful' if you don't believe it. Work on your own attitudes and abilities, and let the other issues take care of themselves.

The words you might choose in this particular instance may be something like:

I feel complete confidence in my skills and abilities in

my job. I know that I can achieve anything I set my mind to. I radiate calm and confidence to all around me.

Try saying those words a few times to yourself – authoritatively – and notice the difference they make to the way you feel. If you repeat them several times a day, you'll change the way you feel about yourself in a very short time.

If you don't feel these words are achieving what you want to achieve, choose another set of words. Once again, choose simple, active, positive words in the present tense.

Keep repeating them to yourself – as loudly as you can get away with – until your consciousness is filled with them. Do it for at least five minutes each time. When your mind wanders, think nothing of it and simply come back to those words.

Look for these calm solutions:

Breathing Calm ....page 103

Turn Off the Noise................page 277

Say You're Secure.................page 223

A Positive Word ....page 184

Talk Yourself into It ....page 214

Basic Affirmation Template

1 Enjoy 5 minutes of Breathing Calm. Listen to the sound of your breath coming and going.

2 Choose positive words/phrases that:
- reflect how you would ideally like to be;
- are simple, active, positive and to the point;
- are in the present tense; and
- appeal to the imagination or emotions, rather than the intellect.

3 Keep repeating these words to yourself. Repeat, repeat, repeat.

4 Do this several times a day.

3. Self-hypnosis

There's something exotic-sounding about the expression 'self-hypnosis'. It conjures up images of stage magicians, and silly subjects getting sleepier, and sleepier, and sleepier . . .

The reality, of course, is not so exotic. Self-hypnosis is a simple, highly accessible skill that almost everyone can use and feel comfortable with. And, in most respects, it is far removed from the stage hypnosis you are aware of.

The main difference between third party hypnosis (stage or clinical hypnosis) and self-hypnosis is who calls the tune. In one instance, you open your subconscious to the guidance of another person – the hypnotist – while in the second instance, you conduct the entire business yourself. In both instances, though, *you* exercise ultimate control over all that takes place.

The techniques of affirmation and visualisation that we have just covered are, in many ways, similar to self-hypnosis. All three techniques involve *applied suggestion* – where you provide certain input to your subconscious – and all three have similar outcomes, in that your subconscious then begins to direct your conscious mind. (This is how you overcome seemingly irrational fears, stresses and feelings.)

So, how do you perform self-hypnosis?

One way is to visit a hypnotist and get them to give you a post-hypnotic suggestion that allows you to enter a hypnotic state whenever you choose. Most people, however, will choose to use the simple technique that follows.

The technique of self-hypnosis

Hypnosis of any kind consists of two steps:

(i)   inducing a trance; and

(ii) presenting a suggestion that your subconscious will turn into a realisation.

Even though the word 'trance' by itself is usually enough to conjure up all sorts of dark and mysterious images, it is a completely natural, everyday event that each and every one of us has experienced. Yes, even you.

Have you ever been on train ride, with nothing to do but look out the window and listen to the clickety-clack of the wheels? Do you recall on that occasion how you 'stared into space', 'daydreaming', 'not conscious of thinking about anything in particular'? Have you even been given a massage, a facial, or even a haircut and found yourself 'daydreaming', possibly even nodding off?

That was a trance. Very likely, it was every bit as deep and meaningful – for however brief a period – as any hypnotic trance. It may have been for only a few minutes, it may have been only a few seconds, but it was a trance. Exactly the same sort of trance that they use on stage. Exactly the same sort of trance you can use in calming self-hypnosis.

This hypnotic state differs from your normal waking state in a number of significant ways. Paramount among these is your focus. In your normal waking state, you can be aware of hundreds of different stimuli all at the same time; in the trance state, you focus all your attention on one thing. In the waking state, your awareness is broad and all-encompassing; in the trance state, your awareness is focused, heightened and more intense. This intensified awareness is what causes your subconscious to be so receptive to the suggestions you will give it.

And, just as you did not fall into a deep, deep sleep, or lose control on those everyday occasions when you experienced a trance state (on the train, in the bath, having a facial), nor will you when you perform the following.

1. Inducing a trance There are thousands of ways to bring about a trance state, but here's a simple one I came across that has a proof stage built into it (for the novelty more than anything else).

In essence, it's nothing more than a process of filling up your senses with the sights, sounds and feelings around you, then narrowing these down, one by one, while your attention becomes more and more focused.

What could be simpler than that?

To start with, find yourself a quiet place in a dimly lit room. Kick off your shoes, loosen your clothes, sit down and make yourself comfortable.

Sit there a couple of minutes using Breathing Calm.

Before you do another thing, tell yourself – with conviction! – that the moment you reach the trance state, your chin will lift; slowly, surely, and of its own accord. This will be a signal from your subconscious that you have reached the desired trance state – the state where your subconscious is most receptive to any suggestion you might give it. (There is nothing magical about this: it's just like the mental alarm clock we covered at the beginning of this section, page 108.)

Let your hands rest comfortably on your lap, not touching one another.

Focus on one bright spot in the room. Maybe it's a reflection on a brass door knob, or a patch of sunlight on the floor.

Fix your attention on that bright spot.

Now, *using only your peripheral vision*, note six different things you can *see* in that room. Next, without allowing your eyes to stray from the highlight you are staring at, note six different sounds you can *hear*. Once again, without allowing your eyes to stray from the highlight you are staring at, note six different things you can *feel*.

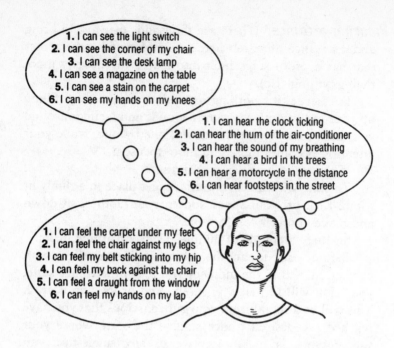

1. I can see the light switch
2. I can see the corner of my chair
3. I can see the desk lamp
4. I can see a magazine on the table
5. I can see a stain on the carpet
6. I can see my hands on my knees

1. I can hear the clock ticking
2. I can hear the hum of the air-conditioner
3. I can hear the sound of my breathing
4. I can hear a bird in the trees
5. I can hear a motorcycle in the distance
6. I can hear footsteps in the street

1. I can feel the carpet under my feet
2. I can feel the chair against my legs
3. I can feel my belt sticking into my hip
4. I can feel my back against the chair
5. I can feel a draught from the window
6. I can feel my hands on my lap

Next time around, note only five of those things you can see. And hear. And feel. (All the while focusing on that highlight.)

Then note only four things.

And three.

And two.

And one.

Then you will probably notice that your chin has tilted upwards of its own accord. You will probably get such a surprise that you will jolt yourself out of your lovely, peaceful trance state at that instant. (This last part of the process, the automatically tilting chin, is nothing more than a once-only trick to demonstrate how your subconscious can communicate with you. As it has no other role, you can discard it in the future.)

2. *Presenting the suggestion*   The words that you used in the section on affirmations (page 119) are known as auto-suggestions. If you want to, you can use the same words in self-hypnosis.

If, for example, all you want from self-hypnosis is to feel calm and relaxed, you may choose words such as these:

More and more, I am relaxing into a state of great peace and calm. I am feeling content, tranquil and at ease with the world. I radiate peace and calm to all I come in contact with.

(Notice how all the words are positive, emotional and in the present tense?)

The object of calming self-hypnosis is to feed those words to your subconscious *after* you have reached the trance state. There are two easy ways of doing this.

The first is to know the words by heart. Then, at the outset of your self-hypnosis session, instead of telling yourself your chin is going to lift, instruct yourself to recite those words when you reach the trance state. Your subconscious will take care of the rest.

The alternative is to record the words on a tape recorder, and instruct yourself to turn on your message once you have reached the trance state. (Make sure it's at low volume.)

Look for these calm solutions:
Breathing Calm ....page 102
The Sound of Calm...............page 280
Straight to Calm ....page 292

Basic Self-hypnosis Template

1 Sit in a comfortable chair. Remove your shoes. Rest your hands apart, comfortably on your lap.

2 Enjoy 5 minutes of Breathing Calm. Listen to the sound of your breath coming and going.

3 Tell yourself that you're going to recite your auto-suggestions once you enter the trance state. (Or prepare a pre-recorded tape.)

4 Concentrate on one visual bright spot in the room, and continue to focus on that throughout.

5 Using only your peripheral vision, note six different things you can see in that room.

6 Note six different things you can hear.

7 Note six different things you can feel.

8 Then note five different things you can see. And hear. And feel.

9 Repeat this process noting four. And three. And two. And one.

10 Recite the auto-suggestions to yourself. Alternatively, play the pre-recorded tape.

Meditation

No doubt there will be many diehards who will be aghast at my suggestion that meditation is a tool. They will argue, I expect, that meditation is a state of being, maybe even a sacred gift, and certainly not something to be considered a mere tool of the subconscious.

You can believe that if you wish.

Or, you can take the pragmatic approach (which I do) and use the *exercise* of meditation – as opposed to the philosophy – as a tool of the subconscious. This is a tool that helps you to become calm, to become positive, to solve problems and to improve health.

In short, meditation is a state of altered consciousness

where you feel deeply relaxed and removed from the outside world, yet at the same time wide awake and as one with a much larger world (the more you study the various meditation techniques, the more you get to appreciate the paradoxes).

The practice of meditation is both pleasant and beneficial to those who use it. And the more you use it, the more pleasant and beneficial it becomes.

This topic is covered in more detail later in this book (see page 325). Alternatively, you will find a specially designed animated section on the Calm Centre's Internet site (http://www.calmcentre.com) that will take you visually through the steps.

4. Assumption

Sometimes you can feel very inadequate being a human being. All that intellect and willpower at your disposal, and you still can't control how you respond to the most uncomplicated situations. You're feeling tense and apprehensive about something, and you know it's silly to feel this way, yet even with all the intellectual and personality resources you possess, you can't do a thing about it.

Now you know the reason for this – your willpower has no influence over your subconscious.

In many ways, the subconscious behaves like a small child; it loves to be entertained and to play games, and thrives on dreams, emotions, abstract ideas, concepts, pictures, ideals and rich visuals.

One of the most effective means available for influencing your subconscious was one you perfected yourself at a very tender age. This technique allowed you to escape the drudgery of normal life, and could transport you into fairy castles or the Batmobile in the blink of an eye. It allowed you to be as tiny as a thimble or as tall as a tree. It is your ability to pretend. To play imaginary roles.

Because it is creative and playful, and filled with unreal imagery, pretending – or *assuming* a role – is a powerful way to appeal to the subconscious. Some of the most skilled psychotherapists, particularly those who work with hypnosis, utilise this device to overcome the barriers and intrusions of the conscious mind. By having subjects pretend to be something or to feel a particular way, instead of actually trying to achieve it, they side-step conscious inhibitions, and recruit the subject's subconscious in their efforts.

This means success comes a hundred, even a thousand, times faster than if the conscious mind were trying to do it alone.

The technique of assuming

The following will show you how to use the Assumption technique to become calm and relaxed. (With slight modification, it could help you overcome shyness, become a non-smoker, improve your sporting prowess, or perform well in an unfamiliar situation.)

In the first instance, you conjure up in your mind all the characteristics you would exhibit if you were a totally calm person: what you'd be wearing; how you'd be taking it easy; the relaxed gestures you would use; the slow speech. Got the picture?

Now for the technique.

You simply *assume* that you're feeling this way. Act out all those calm actions; speak with that slow calm voice; move like a calm person would move. In other words, you assume that you're calm and relaxed. You assume that you're in complete control of the situation, and every other situation like it. *Assume* you're familiar with this feeling of peace.

If you do all that, guess how you'll be feeling after five minutes? Exactly, you'll feel calm.

And if you want to make this experience even more profound, you apply this one, subtle twist: you assume that everybody else sees you as the calm and relaxed person you're assuming you are.

Do this sincerely and diligently, and you'll believe it yourself in no time.

Basic Assumption Template

1 Enjoy 5 minutes of Breathing Calm. Listen to the sound of your breath coming and going.

2 When you are relaxed, close your eyes and imagine a huge silver screen before you.

3 Imagine an image of yourself on this screen as calm, relaxed and at peace with the world (or whatever characteristics you choose). Note how you're breathing, speaking, moving.

4 When you have a clear image of how you look, turn off the silver screen and open your eyes.

5 *Now,* do the following as you go about your normal business:

- Assume that you are exactly like the person you imagined. (This is only make-believe, so be as extreme as you like in these pretensions.) Assume you are calm. Move like a calm person, speak like a calm person, act like a calm person.

- Then assume that others see you the way you're imagining you feel.

Now you can become calm ...

WHEN THE
CAUSE IS TIME

Ask most hardworking people what is the one thing that causes them concern in

> Most time pressures are caused by heads, not clocks.

the workplace, and chances are their answer will relate to time.

Or lack thereof.

Perhaps you can understand this. After all, the world gets busier and busier by the day, and the one thing in life you have no control over is time. Or do you?

Why is it that some hardworking people manage to accomplish more in one day than others accomplish in a week? Are they superhuman? Do they enjoy some exclusive skill which others do not? Do they have some magical means of controlling time?

Probably not. While they may possess certain time-management skills or techniques, their real advantage is almost certainly one of attitude or perception – how they *perceive* time, not the amount of time they have at their disposal. Because, as we have already discussed, most time pressures are caused by heads, not clocks.

Here are a few techniques that will assist you in controlling that head of yours and, as a result, your perceptions of time.

Controlling time

Let's make this short: no-one can control time. Not you, not me, no-one. All you will ever be able to control is events, and perhaps the amount of time they consume. So the notion of 'controlling' time consists of:

(i) controlling the events that take up your time; and

(ii) controlling the way you look at time.

The Number 1 time offender

It's time to identify one of the worst 'time' offenders in the workplace. It's not a person, it's not a work practice, and it's not an attitudinal problem.

It's a wristwatch.

If you tend to be Driven in your behaviour (see page 25), chances are you'll glance at your wristwatch about a hundred times a day. Every time you glance at it, you create a pressure for yourself: 'I must get this finished by . . .'; 'Look how little time I've got left . . .'; 'How will I ever finish this . . .'; 'I just don't have the time'.

You will still do these things whether you're wearing a wristwatch or not. But something even more important happens when you're not wearing one: you begin to behave a little like an Easygoing personality – someone who is more casual about time, deadlines and so-called time pressures.

WATCHLESS PRETENCE

Think about these facts for a moment:

(i) 'Easygoing' people do not worry unduly about time, deadlines or other time pressures.

(ii) 'Easygoing' people do not get withdrawal symptoms if they forget to wear their wristwatches on any occasion.

(iii) 'Easygoing' people are so casual about time that, sometimes, they elect not to wear a wristwatch at all.

Now that you and your subconscious are aware of these statistics, the simple act of removing your wristwatch could be made to remind you to act like an Easygoing personality, and to be more relaxed about time. This could be your first step towards becoming calm.

If you think this is trivial, do yourself a favour and try it once. You'll find your subconscious loves playing the game, and will respond handsomely.

To make it more powerful still ...

To take this little game into another dimension, you can use the Basic Assumption Template from page 129. Once you have done that, it is a simple matter of applying this technique wherever and whenever you desire.

Every time you want to become less concerned about time, all you have to do is remove your wristwatch, recall the Easygoing characteristics that you witnessed on your imaginary silver screen (in Visualisation), and leave the rest to your subconscious.

Breathing Calm .... page 103
Modelling Calm .... page 260
Pretend to B .... page 206

Watchless Pretence

- Enjoy 5 minutes of Breathing Calm. Listen to the sound of your breath coming and going.
- When you are relaxed, close your eyes and imagine yourself on a huge silver screen, calm, relaxed and at peace with the world. Note how much more Easygoing you feel not wearing a wristwatch. Notice how deadlines seem not to loom so threateningly, how you have plenty of time to complete your work, how you do one thing at a time and enjoy it.
- When you have a clear image of how you look, open your eyes.
- Now, remove your watch and go about your normal business.
- Assume that you are exactly like the person you imagined. Assume you are Easygoing. Move like an Easygoing person, speak like an Easygoing person, act like an Easygoing person unconcerned about time.
- Then assume that others see you the way you're imagining you feel.

While we're on the subject of wrists ...

There are a couple of other little techniques I've collected over the years that relate to the wrist, though not necessarily to time. Both of these utilise simple acupressure techniques to induce a state of calm.

The techniques themselves require minimal effort. Once you know where the relevant pressure points are, all you have to do is apply a firm downwards pressure on each of them with a straight forefinger.

(i)   Apply the pressure as you breathe out. Release it as you breathe in.

(ii) Repeat this process several times: press as you breathe out, release as you breathe in.

Easy, isn't it?

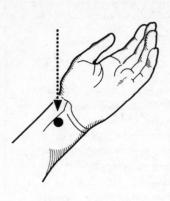

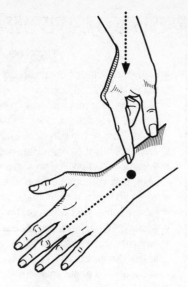

This acupressure point is known for the treatment of anxiety. It's located in the centre of your wrist, in a line directly up from your middle finger, about two thumb widths from the bottom of your palm, There is a natural groove, just behind your wrist bone.

This second point – an alternative to the first – is on the upper side of your wrist, directly up from your middle finger, about two thumb widths above the crease of your wrist. You will feel an indentation.

THE THREE LAWS OF TIME AND EFFORT MANAGEMENT

Anyone who faces time problems will agree that the greatest time wasters (that is, the greatest stressors) are not the major projects, but the minor ones, the ones that maybe you shouldn't even be bothering with in the first place.

While we must be wary of oversimplifying complex problems, there is a simple set of 'natural' laws that relate to time and effort management. Somewhat unimaginatively, these are called The Three Laws of Time and Effort Management. I have seen ample proof of their potency over the years, and I commend them to you as a simple prescription for planning and keeping your work efforts in perspective.

(1) Things you really want to do generally take twice as long to accomplish, cost twice as much, and bring only half the rewards you (or your boss, board, shareholders, spouse and bank manager) anticipate.

(2) Difficult work tasks invariably appear greater when you're approaching them rather than when you're performing them. So, things you don't want to do only take half as long, cost half as much and often bring twice the rewards you anticipate.

(3) Eighty percent of your time and effort will usually be spent on projects that account for 20 percent of your rewards.

1. The law for planning your time

When it comes to planning a desirable task or event – and this also means planning your expectations for it – remember the first law: things generally take twice as long, cost twice as much and bring half the rewards that you anticipate. If more business ventures were planned this way, there'd be a dramatic drop in the number of failures. If more people planned their work days and work lives this way, there'd be much less frustration when they fail to accomplish what they planned to do within a certain time frame.

Plan with these benchmarks in mind, *then strive to improve on them in the execution!*

2. The law for applying your effort

The greatest sufferers from time pressure tend to be procrastinators.

Whether pressure causes procrastination, or vice versa, I have no idea. What I do know is application is a more efficient way of dealing with time-related pressure than procrastination. Once you start working on a task, the time you need to devote to it seems to diminish. The sooner you start work on something, the less time you have to allow for it to be completed.

The trick is simply to start working.

3. The law for investing your talent

You can waste a lot of time and energy pursuing unprofitable, frustrating, time-consuming courses of action. The old 80:20 formula applies as much to time as it does to effort: 80 percent of your efforts produce only 20 percent of your results, and vice versa.

Be brutal about deciding which tasks are worth investing your time and effort in. Concentrate on these tasks first of all.

Life Priorities Calculator .... page 91
The Power of No ....page 143
The Nice Way to No..............page 145
Creative Long-Range Planner.....page 171
The Unconscious Planner ....page 177

**Applying the Three Laws of
Time and Effort Management**

- When planning desirable tasks or events, allow for them to take twice as long, cost twice as much and return half as much as the stakeholders anticipate – then improve on it.
- The sooner you start a task, the less time you will need to complete it. Procrastination makes projects longer.
- Concentrate your effort on the 20 percent of works that will produce the best results.

Depressurising deadlines

For many, if a deadline has been set, a problem has been created. This is particularly so of certain personality types (see pages 20–21) and of certain industries. Check out any deadline-intensive occupation, or any deadline-oriented person, and you will find a hotbed of stress-related problems.

Setting deadlines may be an effective time-management tool, in the sense that it overcomes procrastination and gets things done, but it also adds stress to the working day. As the deadline nears, and the task demands completion, tensions build.

True, there are those who work better, and feel more secure, only when deadlines are set. However, deadlines are an additional work pressure and do create problems.

Why?

Most people will tell you something about 'running out of time'. I don't accept this.

In my observations, an impending deadline bothers people, not so much because of their perception of time, but because they see it as a looming, threatening, end point – in other words, an irrational threat created by their subconscious.

This is understandable. The meaning of the word is steeped in brinkmanship. Even the sound of it is threatening. DEADLINE!

Yet, with a minor redefinition of your task, you can remove this threat altogether – yes, by using your subconscious.

ALLOCATING TIME FOR CALM

Redefining a task to remove the deadline pressure is simple. Instead of thinking of it in terms of deadlines, you simply change the terms of reference to 'time allocations'. So, if the task has to be completed by the same time next week, instead of setting a deadline, you allocate a certain amount of time for the task.

← TIME ALLOCATION →

In this instance, it would be seven days. Or, if you like big numbers, 168 hours. But what's more important than the number of hours is the fact that you can modify this allocation at your whim – allow yourself 144 hours, or 99 hours, or 12 hours.

See what you've done? While it is usually somebody else who sets deadlines, it is *you* who makes time allocations. So you're in charge of your own destiny. And people who feel in control of their own destinies suffer less from work-related stress. (Of course, if you squander the hours you allocate to a task, be prepared for the resultant pressure when you only have limited hours left.)

If you ever feel that a deadline someone sets doesn't allow room for effective time allocation, the time to negotiate this is at the outset of the project – not towards the end.

Look for these calm solutions:

Life Priorities Calculator .... page 91
The Power of No .... page 144
The Nice Way to No .... page 145
The Art of Negotiation .... page 241

Allocating Time for Calm

- Negotiate deadlines at the outset of, or as early as possible in, the project.
- If a deadline is set by someone else, *immediately* translate it into a time allocation.
- Vary the time allocation a little so that you know you are in control.
- For larger projects, write that time allocation down. Then keep a record of the hours you spend.
- For larger projects, continually relate the hours you have spent to your time allocation.
- Relax in the knowledge that you alone are in control of your own time.

Procrastination

Time management experts know the most debilitating time-related practice in the workplace is procrastination. They also know it is the most difficult to remedy.

On the surface, you would think procrastination should lead to feeling more relaxed about life. Postponing all the difficult, less pleasant tasks to the last moment should – one would imagine – allow hours of lazy pleasure followed by a brief flurry of hard work. Unfortunately, it doesn't work that way.

Postponing what you know has to be done only adds to the pressure in your work life. Because the tasks you postpone are invariably the ones you enjoy doing least, you have all these unpleasantries banking up, banking up, banking up. Thus, procrastination has a negative effect on your productivity. Worse, it has a damaging effect on your self-esteem and your stress levels because it allows events to control you, rather than the other way around.

This is why I believe procrastination is one of the dominant, though least visible, stress-builders in the workplace.

While procrastination builds tension, action leads to calm. Deal with each problem as it arises, and you will have cleared the way to peace of mind. But how do you overcome the tendency to procrastinate?

Most time-management experts advise you to set deadlines and thus create a sense of urgency for each task. But we know deadlines to be yet another stress-builder, so a more complete solution is required.

THE PROCRASTINATION ELIMINATOR

Procrastination arises from the fallacy that we will have more time in the future than we do right now to perform today's tasks.

As well as being inefficient and unproductive, this belief also contributes to stressful feelings at work. The way to overcome it involves seven steps.

1. Divide large tasks into smaller tasks

You've read this before, haven't you? No more excuses, now's the time to put it into practice.

If you have a large task, sometimes its sheer size or complexity gives you an excuse to keep putting it off. However, almost all large tasks can be broken down into a series of smaller ones.

Once you have isolated these smaller tasks, the overall task no longer seems so daunting.

2. Write them down

Dividing your large tasks into a series of smaller ones in itself leads to more efficient treatment of the detail – and that has to be good for your work. To add a little discipline to your program, write down each of the tasks in a place you can continually refer back to.

3. Allocate time for each task

Once you have written down your list of tasks, allocate time to perform each of them. You'll feel more in control if you do this rather than setting deadlines.

4. Rush headlong into the part you like *least*

As procrastinators leave the less pleasant tasks to last, their procrastinations invariably lead to feelings of dissatisfaction.

This is easily overcome simply by reversing the order of your inclinations: do the less pleasant tasks first, then keep the easier ones as a reward at the end.

The instant you have defined your different tasks, throw yourself into the one you'd like to do least of all. The momentum you establish in doing this will carry you through the rest of the project.

5. Turn your work into a game

You don't expect grown-ups to have fun with their work, do you? Well they can. And they should. If you can turn your chores into a game – racing yourself against the clock; pretending to be a rocket scientist rather than a typist; perfecting your telephone voice – you'll not only be recruiting your subconscious to the task, but time will positively fly.

6. Document your rewards

If you want to make a practice of overcoming procrastination, then you have to train yourself to see the benefits. A shortcut to this is to build a reward into your program. This may be something tangible, like a treat of some kind, or something more work related, like you'll take an hour off work to walk in the park.

To make this reward even sweeter, and to give it additional importance, write it down – alongside your list of tasks and time allocations.

7. Apply 100 percent effort

Finally, when the time comes to commence the task – especially the less pleasant parts of it – approach it with total concentration and effort. Then, not only will the task pass quickly, but you will derive an unexpected level of satisfaction from it. (You will also perform it more efficiently, but that's another story.)

> **Look for these calm solutions:**
> Allocating Time for Calm ....page 138
> Play with Yourself ....page 316
> The Three Laws of Time and
> Effort Management ....page 134
> The 100 Percent Effort ....page 159

The Procrastination Eliminator

- Divide large tasks into smaller tasks.
- Write them down.
- Allocate time for each task.
- Rush headlong into the part you like *least*.
- Turn your work into a game.
- Document your rewards.
- Apply 100 percent effort.

Overwork

When you survey people in the workforce today, and ask what causes them most distress, you will find one cause mentioned over and above all others.

Overwork.

Increased productivity demands over the last decade means that people really are working longer, with less support, than at any other time in recent history. But have workloads really increased that much? Are we really overworked?

Even if the answer were no, the *perception* that we are overworked exists, and that is just as problematical as the reality.

Overwork seldom means overworked. It simply means that there are too many work demands being made on your available time. If you had an extra 12 working hours in the day, and the same amount of work to do, chances are you would not be overworked.

So, now that you've narrowed the problem down – that of too many demands being made on your available time – it becomes a simple matter to solve it.

THE POWER OF NO

Have you ever wondered why you allow so many demands to be made of your available time? Chances are it will not be a failure of planning, or an overestimation of your capacities, but the simple inability to say 'no'.

For the sake of your own health and efficiency, this is a skill you would do well to acquire. But how? Where do you draw the line, when do you say 'no'?

Here are three simple steps that will make it easier:
(i)   Set goals and outcomes for every aspect of your work.
(ii) Take on only what will help you achieve those goals and outcomes. Say 'no' to everything else.
(iii) Ignore all arguments to the contrary.

The starting point is your outcome: at the end of the process, what will you have achieved? How will you have benefited? How will you feel? Once you have worked out your outcome, write it down at the top of a blank sheet of paper – use positive language, in the present tense – and list your goals beneath it. (Goals are the steps to achieve on the way to your outcome.)

Then, when somebody asks you to take on a task you hadn't allowed for, you have three clear choices:

(i) Say 'yes' if it will help you achieve your outcome or your goals.

(ii) Say 'yes' if it will assist someone in a serious matter, without impacting negatively on your outcome or goals.

(iii) Say 'no'.

Learn to say 'no' when necessary, and not only will you feel better in yourself, you will work more efficiently for having said so.

Look for these calm solutions:

The Art of Negotiation .... page 241

Speaking your Mind .... page 233

How to Get What You Want ...... page 232

The Power of No

- Set goals and outcomes.
- Start at the outcome: at the end of the process, what will you have achieved, how will you have benefited, how will you feel? Then define your goals (the steps to achieve along the way).
- Write your outcome at the top of a page, set out your goals beneath it.
- Evaluate all requests according to what you've written on your page. Say 'yes' to those tasks that will help you achieve your goals and outcomes. *Quickly* say 'no' to everything else.
- Resist all arguments to the contrary.

THE NICE WAY TO NO

If you're one of those people who cannot refuse extra work demands, invitations or requests for assistance, and if you have been suffering the consequences of taking on too much, you would profit from developing one powerful skill: the ability to say 'no' (nicely) when you have to.

There are sound, businesslike arguments why you should acquire this ability: when you overextend yourself, stress levels rise, efficiency decreases, productivity goes out the window and all functions are stretched and at risk. You've probably seen the statistic that most business failures are the result of many small problems rather than one large one.

Saying 'no' when you have to, therefore, should not present you as lazy, anti-social, negative or uncooperative. If anything it should paint you as someone who is efficient and in control of their work day – especially if you explain why you're saying 'no'.

There are two steps that will make this easier for you:
(i)   establishing your priorities; and
(ii) rationalising your refusal.

Establishing your priorities

How do you know which tasks to accept and which ones to reject? In the first instance, you have to determine what is important to you.

For big picture or macro decisions, use the Life Priorities Calculator on page 91, or the Creative Long-Range Planner on page 171. These will help you determine the priorities of your life – work, position, money, success, family, happiness and so on.

However, for the day-to-day decisions about your capacity, there is no substitute for detailed planning. The

essence of work planning is determining the following:
(a) the tasks you have to do;
(b) the time you have allocated for them; and
(c) their order of priority.

Once these have been taken into account, you'll be in the position to calculate your capacity to take on additional tasks.

Rationalising your refusal

Many people who realise they're not in the position to take on additional requests still feel uncomfortable about turning them down – this is why they take on so much in the first place.

If you suffer from this 'niceness', you will need to rationalise your refusals, and the most successful way to do that is to have a work plan, even if this is only for your own benefit.

This is not a formal document, nor is it one you will necessarily show anyone else. It is simply a list of the tasks you have to do, in order of importance, accompanied by the time you allocate for each.

When your day or week has been planned this way, you will find it easy to say how your time allocations will not permit additional tasks or favours.

> **Look for these calm solutions:**
> Life Priorities Calculator .... page 91
> A Positive Word .... page 184
> Creative Long-Range Planner.....page 171
> The Unconscious Planner ....page 177

The Nice Way to No

- Establish your priorities: the tasks you have to do, in their order of importance, and the time you have allocated for each.
- Write them down in a work plan (for your own use).
- When additional requests come that cannot be accommodated in your work plan, politely decline them – citing your work plan.
- Have faith in your work plan if negotiations are attempted.

KNOW YOUR LIMITS

Probably the most valuable piece of information you can possess when you're under threat from overwork is knowing what your limits are – as they apply to your time, resources and capabilities.

Once you know these limits, it becomes easier for you to determine what you are capable of handling or achieving.

This applies as much to the positions and responsibilities you assume as it does to tasks and deadlines.

Information overload

Information overload. Too much information, too many new developments, too much change. Today this is one of the most common causes of workplace stress – particularly among executives, the media, those in information technology, health and virtually any area of technology.

The world's knowledge seems almost infinite. Much of that information is now available to you – through e-mail, the Internet, libraries, universities. How are you going to keep up? How are you meant to protect the expertise you've built up over the years? What is the value of that expertise when knowledge is expanding so rapidly? And how are you ever going to absorb all the information that crosses your desk on the average day?

The above concerns are real. The problem of information overload is not.

In the great majority of cases, the problem simply does not exist. Few people in the workforce are ever *overloaded* with information. No-one forces them to consume all the available data. They are simply given many, many options to choose from.

Are options something to fear? Is choice something worth getting stressed about? If it is, there is no justice, because an even greater proportion of people in the workforce cite *lack* of choice as the main cause of workplace stress.

The moment you replace that word 'overload' with 'choice', the problem diminishes. And that is the sheer wonder, the beauty, of living in this age: you have so many choices when it comes to the information that can help you in your work.

If you believe you have to consume *all* this information to succeed, you have reason to be stressed. But you don't.

We pause for a grandmother story

As I was writing this, I remembered a story about my grandmother. In the early part of the century, she and her husband joined a gang of railway fettlers who were hired to build a rail link to a remote part of the Australian outback.

One of the young men in their crew was an unfortunate soul who was unskilled in almost all the basic refinements of life. If it weren't for the food parcels his sister sent on the weekly supply train, he would have starved. He almost starved, anyway. Having no concept of menu planning, he'd consume every morsel of the week's food she sent the instant it arrived. Then he would go without until the arrival of the next food parcel.

Being aware of this, my grandmother began to invite him to their place to share their modest meals. Imagine the table: a platter of potatoes, another of corned meat, yet another containing a loaf of bread. But whichever platter was directly in front of the young man, he would devour all that was on it. Nothing she could tell him about sharing, or waiting, would dissuade him – if it was in front of him, he had to eat it all. Choice was never an issue; he was compelled to consume.

In many ways, the information-'overloaded' executives of today are like that young railway fettler of 1921. They have this obsessive belief that whatever is put in front of them – not food this time, but information and research – has to be consumed.

But it doesn't. It is nothing more than an array of options for you to choose from.

INFORMATION EMANCIPATION

We live in an enlightened age. Whatever your interest, whatever your occupation, you have a wealth of research and information to choose from in order to perform your duties to your fullest.

This is not information overload. This is choice.

All you need to take advantage of it is some forethought, a few filters and a little discipline.

Forethought

This all boils down to planning. Using the Life Priorities Calculator, determine what is important to you, your career and your life. When you have isolated what is important, write it down.

To achieve this objective, you will probably require a degree of information and data.

A few filters

Now that you have determined what is important in your life, it is time to apply a few filters. Use any of the planning techniques listed below to determine the filters you will need. Write down your information filters. You should only have to do this once or, at most, every year or so.

(i)   The first filter is deciding whether you intend to be a generalist (with a broad overview, but less detailed knowledge of your topic) or a specialist with a narrow focus of knowledge.

(ii) The second filter is occupation-based. What field are you working in *now*, what field might you be working in *later*, and what field would you *like* to be working in (assuming that it is neither of the others)?

(iii) The third filter is geographic, or market-based. Where do you intend to compete or perform your work? Where is your market today? Where will it be tomorrow?

(iv) And you progressively add more filters according to your needs, interests, goals or ambitions.

(v)   The role of the final filter is to filter all of your filters: can any one expert or source of information substitute for any of them? (For example, if you said your future market was Asian-based, would it be better to hire an Asian expert occasionally rather than trying to broaden your expertise to encompass Asia?)

A little discipline

This is the easy part. All you need now is a little discipline. When information is presented to you, you apply the above filters (which you keep on a list in your drawer). Or, if you have an assistant or secretary, you have your assistant apply those filters.

Information that does not meet the criteria of your filters is ignored. Don't try to think who it would be useful to, as this can be stressful and time-wasting in itself. If information does not pass your filters, it is ignored or rejected.

It can't be as easy as that, you're thinking. What if you're the chief executive of a large organisation and *all* of the information passing your desk is relevant to your organisation and, as a result, relevant to you? How effective are your filters then?

Once again, you choose your own filters. Chief executives of large organisations must be generalists rather than specialists, so their very first filter eliminates most of the information generated by the organisations they head.

So, if you have a task to do, you follow the same two steps people have done throughout history: you gather the *information you need*, then you act on that information.

The question is: what information do you need?

Information Emancipation

1 Use the Life Priorities Calculator to determine what is important to you.

2 Write down what is important to you.

3 Use planning techniques to determine the filters you will use on information.

4 Are you a generalist or a specialist? What field are you (will you be) working in? What geographic/ market filter should you apply? What other filters?

5 Write down your information filters.

6 Is there any one expert or source of information that could remove the need for any of the above filters?

7 Now assess all information presented to you according to those filters.

8 Reject all information that fails your criteria. (Don't lose sleep trying to think who else could use it.)

One more consideration on this topic of information overload is, for many, the intrusive nature of e-mail. Some people I know receive up to 500 unwanted messages a week.

While you can ignore the unwanted letters that arrive in the post each day, it is more difficult to ignore your e-mail. Unless you have the right software. Most dedicated electronic mail programs now allow you to filter e-mail according to sender or topic. If you find your e-mail intrusive, you need this software: a small price to pay to remain calm.

Look for these calm solutions
Life Priorities Calculator .... page 91
A 30-Second Course in Marketing ....page 237
Creative Long-Range Planner.....page 171
The Unconscious Planner ....page 177

Your time

Now we come to the part that can save your life, your health and your sanity. It also relates to time.

Those of us in the workplace who are slaves to time – and, let's face it, most of us are – invariably overlook a vital element in our personal development. This is recharging time. Development time. Survival time.

It's the time you get purely for yourself, for your own indulgence. And guess what you have to do – absolutely nothing!

As much as the worker in you will protest otherwise, it can be a powerful use of time to do absolutely nothing occasionally. You're probably thinking you already do this. Maybe you think you do it regularly. If so, great.

But very few working people do!

Not procrastinators. Nor those we categorise as loners (which many hardworking people are), with minimal social life and, you would assume, plenty of time on their hands. Not even those we would categorise as lonely (which, once again, many dedicated working people are).

Because of the combination of an overstimulated society, and a misplaced work ethic, very few people *ever* permit themselves any significant 'self time', where they loll about by themselves and do absolutely nothing.

Before you scoff, let's look at what it takes to do 'nothing'.

SELF TIME

Self Time is simply a period of time you set aside *each day* for being. For seeking release from the pressures of everyday life. For enjoying your own self.

Self Time will take 15 to 30 minutes, even longer if

you choose. It can be first thing in the morning, last thing at night, or any time in between. Self Time allows no company, no stimuli, no entertainment, no trying to solve problems, and certainly no thinking about work. When you try it, it may seem more difficult than it sounds. That's because you have been conditioned to think this is indolence, a waste of time.

Nothing could be further from the truth.

After spending this Self Time a few times, you will become addicted to these moments. You will think nothing of rising 30 minutes earlier in the morning to be able to indulge yourself this way. You will think nothing of stealing these precious moments from your lover or your children – because it will mean the time you *do* spend with them will be enriched.

Fifteen to 30 minutes a day. Every day. Just to enjoy yourself.

Whether you use the time to meditate, to practise Breathing Calm, or to sit and stare at the wall is unimportant. What is important is that you make the commitment to spending the time, doing nothing, each day.

If you're a busy person, with no free time (so you believe), you'll probably think this 15 to 30 minutes could be used more profitably by catching up on your reading, watching the news on television, chatting to your spouse or children. This is not so.

Your Self Time does not have to encroach on the important times of your day. It is meant to encroach on the *un*important times of your day: it's up to you to decide what is unimportant. (Incidentally, how many highly stressed people do you know who swear by the so-called relaxation method of 'veging out' in front of the television? No matter how unchallenging the program, viewing television is stimulation, not relaxation.)

And while we're discussing what is important,

consider this: if you use Self Time regularly, you will worry less, be less prone to stress-related problems, your health will be improved, and your life will be enriched and extended. In other words, taking time off for Self Time is an extremely productive activity for every busy person.

Look for these calm solutions:

Breathing Calm ....page 103
The Calm Technique..............page 325
The Calm Space ....page 287
Grin and Bear It ....page 289
Idling..............................page 216

Self Time

- Choose at least one 15- to 30-minute period, *every* day, that you designate as Self Time.
- During this time you do nothing. You entertain no company, receive no stimuli, conduct no problem-solving, and there's certainly no thinking about work. You don't listen to music or talk to your dog.
- Use this time to meditate, to practise Breathing Calm, or to sit and stare at the wall. Do it regularly and you will worry less, you will be less prone to stress-related problems, your health will be improved, and your life will be enriched and extended.

MEETING TIME

Equally as important as scheduling Self Time during your day is to allow yourself a little time throughout your working day. If your daily routine involves many meetings or appointments, adopt this simple scheduling practice and you'll add years to your life expectancy.

The principles are simple:

(i) Depart 10 minutes early for all outside appointments. Not only will you avoid the stress of hurrying, but if all goes well you'll have 10 minutes to relax before your next engagement.

(ii) Schedule a 15-minute buffer between engagements. Ideally, this will give you a little stress-free space between them, but at worst, it means your meetings will not overlap.

> **Look for these calm solutions:**
> The Calm Agenda.................page 180
> Idling..............................page 216
> Allocating Time for Calm.........page 138

WORK ONE DAY AT A TIME

The best piece of advice I can give to anyone who believes they are overworked or lacking in time, but who knows the value of planning, is this: know when to call it a day.

Have a 'turn off' moment – when your foot touches the pavement outside the office, or when you enter your front gate – that you activate religiously every day. Whenever that moment arrives, purge all work-related thoughts from your mind. Indulge yourself. Entertain yourself.

Work to your maximum during the hours you allocate, then leave it all behind when you go home. (If work must be done at home, then set aside a designated period of time to complete it, and ignore it until that time.)

Remember that you can easily pick up tomorrow where you left off today.

> **Look for these calm solutions:**
> Allocating Time for Calm.........page 138
> Decision Time.....................page 175
> The 3-Point Execution............page 176
> The Unconscious Planner.........page 177
> Self Time.........................page 153

Now you can become calm ...

WHEN THE CAUSE IS CONTROL

Do you ever feel that you're not in control of the events that make up your working life or, worse, that the events control you? Do you feel that you'll never get on top of your work, or that

> **How can I control my . . . ?**
> You cannot control a difficult boss/employee/doorman/airconditioner.
> You would feel much better if you concentrated on trying to control, not the events that cause negative stress, but how you *respond* to them.

you're trapped on a circuit that's taking you nowhere? Do you feel that it's always someone else who is calling the shots?

You're not alone. Many people, even managers and chief executives, feel like that.

But how much control can you really exercise?

Just as you cannot control time, you cannot really control the things that go on in your world. Even chief executives exert very little control over their world. The only thing in life you can ever count on controlling is yourself: your actions, your attitudes, your perceptions. Bring *them* into line, and you'll be surprised at just how much in control of your work it is possible for you to feel.

Take control of your life

Think about the people you know who seem in control of their destinies and, at the same time, are calm and at peace with the world. In other words, those who seem most in control of their lives.

Are they rich and powerful? Are they famous or highly accomplished? Are they business owners, politicians or the directors of large organisations?

They may be. But the people I think of are very different. I think of the itinerant surfer who chases waves from one fantastic beach to another. The small baby playing endlessly with a rag doll. The artist on the side of the hill who sees nothing but the canvas before her and the landscape beyond. The man on the production line who whistles constantly, and seems fascinated by the passing parade of canned fruits.

What do these people have in common? What do they have that you don't? It's not necessarily their job, their wealth or their lack of sophistication. Nor can it be the level of control they've been awarded or had legislated for them.

What they have in common is a total involvement in what they're doing. This involvement allows them to feel they're in control of what they do, and this is what gives them their worry-free attitude.

You will see evidence of this when you watch a master cabinet-maker at work, spending hour after hour chiselling morticed joints on a drawer (when it could have been nailed in seconds), seemingly deriving peace and pleasure from this tedious activity. Don't you wonder how satisfaction can be derived from something that would quickly drive you round the bend?

When you see a highly-efficient checkout operator at work, treating every customer like a long-lost relative, interested in every little bit of their small talk, scanning every grocery item as if it were of great significance, don't you wonder how they can do this all day yet never seem frustrated?

The answer to these questions lies in an individual's capacity to be wholly occupied by the present. Or, to put it in Zen terms, to live wholly in the moment. (You will recall that the most effective suggestions for the subconscious to take on board are those that are phrased in the present.)

People who choose to live life this way – wholly occupied by the present, as opposed to worrying about the future or having regrets about the past – have tapped into the secret to feeling calm and in control of what they do.

What follows is a technique that will help transform any work – even the most mundane, repetitive tasks – into a calming and intensely satisfying exercise.

Because when you employ the 100 Percent Effort, you are 100 percent in control.

THE 100 PERCENT EFFORT

Say, for example, you have a 200-page document to type. Not a document of interesting information, but a tome of fairly turgid technical stuff. There are two ways you could approach such a task.

You could do what most people do: remind yourself every 30 seconds what a boring task you have in front of you, how long it is until lunch, how unfortunate you are in having to re-type the most uninspiring document in creation, how you'd rather be watching the tennis on television, and how you're not going to receive a single note of praise for your efforts because you're not even sure who you're doing it for.

Or you could look at it another way.

You could start by accepting what is. The task is a given, and unless you can change or reject it, it should be made the most of. That being so, your challenge is simply to turn it into a creative and fulfilling exercise.

You do that by dedicating yourself to doing the best typing job you are humanly capable of. You immerse yourself in the detail so that not a word is misspelt; and the layout is perfect. In other words, you are 100 percent immersed in the effort, 100 percent in control.

Guess what happens? Within minutes, you're engrossed in your task. You might not notice it, but you're more calm and relaxed than you thought you were meant to be at work – even with all the concentration you've been applying. Better still, you find that time has flown and the chore has passed in an instant. And, best of all, you have derived an unusually high level of satisfaction and fulfilment in having completed the task to the best of your abilities – because you were in total command of what you were doing.

As meditators well know, dividing your attention creates tension, while concentrating your attention on only one thing is both calming and efficient.

Indeed, it is the most efficient way you can work!

Look for these calm solutions:
An End to Boredom .... page 164
Work One Day at a Time .... page 156
The Calm Agenda .... page 180

THE JOY OF REPETITION

My mother's aunt felt she had the best job in the world. For many years she worked in the sweaty basement laundry of a city hospital. She found the hot, repetitive, labour-intensive work to be both stimulating and immensely fulfilling.

Here's how she made it stimulating.

At work, you can't always avoid the mundane. Some jobs are repetitive by nature, as are some tasks. Most people find these tasks to be frustrating in the extreme.

Data-entry operators who key in numbers all day long are susceptible to stress-related disorders. Workers on assembly lines often report getting little satisfaction from the repetitive nature of their work. Indeed, any worker who is asked to do the same thing, day in, day out, views this repetition with unease.

Yet, there can be a positive side to repetition. Repetition is the key to many subconscious-influencing techniques such as self-hypnosis and affirmation. It plays

161

a major role in most meditation styles. You've already read about a meditation aid known as the 'mantra', a word or sound that is repeated over and over to ease people into the peaceful meditative state.

What makes one form of repetition calming, while another can be its most frustrating opposite? It all relates to the amount of control you have, or don't have. Or *believe* you don't have!

In meditation, you are in complete control: you can stop when you want to, you can go and get a cup of tea when you choose, and you can abandon it altogether should you so decide. However, on the assembly line, at the sorting table, or the data-entry keyboard you are denied control; someone else is usually in charge, enforcing the repetition.

There is a simple work technique that will take the repetitive or mundane nature of any task and turn it into a calming, fulfilling exercise. It is the 100 Percent Effort technique I have just outlined.

Apply 100 percent concentration and effort to your task, and the repetition will begin to work to your benefit. Immerse yourself totally in the task, so that you achieve the very best result you are capable of, and you will find the task becomes almost like meditation, calming and satisfying in its own right. (This is the 'Little Way' made famous by St Thérèse of Lisieux a couple of centuries ago – a way my mother's aunt understood well.)

 ## ASSUMING CONTROL

Early in my career I had a relatively junior position in a large advertising agency. Having little idea of what was possible or impossible at that age, I mentioned that I might be the person for a senior management position they were considering. My boss said politics were such that someone my age wouldn't normally be considered for such a position. 'But why don't you just *assume* you have it. Act like you're already in the job, and chances are everyone will just assume you have the capabilities.'

Not knowing any better, I took his advice. And guess what – it worked.

Now I know that one of the greatest limitations to getting ahead in life is your own perception. If you perceive yourself as a junior, you'll always be a junior; if you perceive yourself as a pawn, with no control of your own, you'll always be a pawn with no control of your own.

On the other hand, if you perceive yourself as an employee of significance, someone who exercises control over what you do, then you're half way to actually achieving it.

And the best way to help you perceive yourself in this light is to actually assume the role that you assign for yourself.

Look for these calm solutions:
Basic Assumption Template ......page 129
Breathing Calm ....page 103
Modelling Calm ....page 260
Assume You're Secure ....page 222
Pretend to B ....page 206

CONTROL ONLY WHAT YOU CAN CONTROL

Life is full of things you can't control. You can't control time, you can't control other people to any major degree, and you can't control the world about you. All you can really control is your actions, your attitudes, your perceptions.

Accepting this can be a great source of comfort in your work life – especially if you have a tendency to want to control things.

If you want to be calm and satisfied, and feel like you

have some control over what you do, adopt this simple formula: attempt to control only what's possible for you to control.

Use the Plus and Minus Method from page 198 to define your goals and outcome. Using the same technique, differentiate between the things you can influence the results of, and the things that are beyond your control.

Then, devote all your energies to those tasks you can influence.

> **Look for these calm solutions:**
> Plus and Minus Method..........page 198
> Creative Long-Range
> Planner............................page 171

 ## AN END TO BOREDOM

Do you think you've got a boring, repetitive job?

Boredom is one of work's most common stressors. Indeed, as much stress is caused by boredom as is caused by overwork. When you're frustrated by the absence of something satisfying to do, your tension levels escalate. So, too, when you have repetitive tasks to perform.

The secret to eradicating boredom from those mundane tasks is to get pleasure and satisfaction from the mundane.

Use the 100 Percent Effort technique on page 159 to squeeze every last drop from the moment. Total preoccupation with what you're doing will overcome your boredom, and it is a sure way to become calm and relaxed at the same time.

Here are a few more ways to put an end to boredom.

Find the value in your work

Even the most mundane task has its value – if you're prepared to search for it. Once you have found this, you'll know how to find satisfaction in your work. Then, feeling calm will not be far behind.

Search for that value.

Work harder

The difference between total drudgery and noble, uplifting work is often a simple matter of application. It doesn't matter what you do, if you throw yourself into your work, you'll forget about your tensions and worries before you know it.

Concentrate your attention. If you're typing, make every word a masterpiece. If you're cleaning, make every surface brilliant. If you're driving a cab, make every fare the best your passenger has ever had.

Make it a challenge

Many of the stresses you encounter each day eventuate for no other reason than that you seem to do the same old thing, the same old way.

So, turn the work you do into a challenge. Vary the way you do things from time to time. Purposely take a different route (even if it is longer or more difficult). Add your own variation to your routine.

It's a small change, but it can make a big difference.

Look for these calm solutions:
The 100 Percent Effort .... page 159
Search for the Upside .... page 190
Make Fun of Work .... page 207

UNDIVIDING RESPONSIBILITIES

For many, this will be the most important topic raised in this book: how to balance work with young children.

One of the most challenging life issues many face today is that of being a working sole-parent, or a working parent who is saddled with all the child-raising responsibilities (or possibly the responsibility of dependent adults). Even in the most well-organised households, this creates conflicts of responsibility, which inevitably cause stress.

So, how can you manage these twin isues: work and family? How can you get satisfaction from both, without sacrificing interest or reward from either?

I appreciate the complexity of the issue as well as the fact that, for some, there will be no simple solutions. But there are procedures that can lessen your stresses if you find yourself in these circumstances. They are:

(i)   Prioritise your responsibilities.
(ii) Be open with all parties.
(iii) Have reliable help.
(iv) Keep your own time.

Prioritise your responsibilities

In the interviews I conducted in researching this segment, I was surprised to discover there were three sets of forces at play in many work/child-rearing circumstances.

In each case the parent believed there were only two forces at play – child-raising and work – yet a third kept raising its head, time after time. Indeed, often it was this third force that (in my opinion) was the most confusing of all.

If the first two forces are child-raising and work, the

third is social: what do you do with the rest of your time. The common responses to what I have just written are 'What social life?' and 'What time?', but social pressures can be every bit as stressful, and as divisive, as the other two. Especially for sole-parents.

Earlier we covered a process for determining the most important elements in your life, the Life Priorities Calculator. There will never be a more important use of this one-off exercise than here. What is *your* top priority? Is it work? Is it your child or children? Is it finding someone to share your life (and responsibilities) with? Is it saving your marriage?

Once you have decided this priority, other interests in life can be viewed with lesser significance. Getting your life into balance then becomes a matter of rearranging your other interests to accommodate your main priority.

Say, for example, your priority is the welfare of your children. While your job security may be central to that issue, your career advancement may not be so vital. As a result, you may decide to make a few sacrifices on the career front *and* the social front for the sake of your main priority and your peace of mind. You would do this in the understanding that most priorities change every few years.

There will be occasions when you believe circumstances don't allow the luxury of this prioritisation. Even if you believe that, I urge you to go through the process involved in the Life Priorities Calculator. You may be surprised by what you discover.

Be open with all parties

It's a small point, but one often overlooked. If you have a young child or children, it is usually to your advantage if your employer or manager is aware of your situation. You may fear such knowledge could be an impediment to your advancement and, as unprincipled and anachronistic as this attitude may appear, this will sometimes be the case. But if you want to avoid some of the stresses of dual-responsibilities, you will need to be open with everyone from the beginning.

Part of this openness can be ensuring that your child or children are aware of your circumstances (assuming they are of the age to understand). Sharing decisions and responsibilities may then be empowering for all parties.

Have reliable help

Even though it may prove to be your greatest obstacle, the next requirement is an essential – to have reliable child care. Someone you can rely on for child-minding or child-collection while you're at work, and someone you can call on in an emergency.

Not surprisingly, the first is harder to come by. I wish I could offer a simple solution.

Emergency help should be easier. You may choose a relative, or it could be another working parent that you have reciprocal arrangements with so that, in an emergency, you can call on them and they can call on you. Another alternative is to find a surrogate grandparent (I advertised for one once and was amazed at the number of unattached grandmothers who claimed to be grateful for an occasional 'family' responsibility).

Keep your own time

It's vital that you devote at least 20 minutes a day purely to your own needs, for your own indulgence. This is Self Time – where, by doing absolutely nothing, you retreat from the pressures of everyday life and rediscover the meaning of calm.

Do this regularly and all aspects of your life will seem better.

Now you can become calm ...

WHEN THE
CAUSE IS YOU

Now you know. By far
the greatest cause of stress
in the workplace is not
time, lack of control or

> The greatest cause of stress in the workplace is *you*. What's inside your head.

other people. It's you. What's inside your head.

The good news is that the solution is waiting in the
same, easily accessible, place – your head.

By adjusting your perceptions, your attitudes and the
way you respond to work situations, you can eliminate the
majority of workplace problems. In many cases, without
leaving the comfort and security of your own chair.

The solutions that follow address the more common
areas of workplace stress. These include the *inwardly-
focused* attributes such as fear, anxiety, ambition, guilt,
ego, insecurity and lack of focus, as well as the *externally-focused* areas such competitiveness, envy, lust and
anger.

In relation to all these stressors, the most important
skills for you to take from this book are an ability to plan,
combined with a leaning towards the positive.

Plan to be calm

The ability to exercise a degree of influence over what you do overcomes one of the most prevalent stressors in the workplace: lack of control.

As you now know, you cannot control time – you can only control events, and perhaps the amount of time they consume. The most effective tool for giving you control over events in the workplace is planning. Planning your work, planning your day, planning what you want to achieve from your work.

Poor planning causes frustration, procrastination, restlessness and many other problems. Good planning helps you to stay calm. Following, therefore, are a number of planning techniques for you to choose from.

CREATIVE LONG-RANGE PLANNER

I spent many years working as a strategic planner for large businesses. While much of this work had a marketing intent, on many occasions it had a corporate focus as well.

Probably the most fascinating insight to come out of all those years of dabbling in the future was this: most individuals and corporations do not know how to plan.

They try hard. They believe they're planning. But the approach they usually take is more suited to accountancy than shaping the future. This is the approach used by 99 percent of large organisations around the world. And it is seriously flawed.

The way it is meant to work is straightforward and predictable.

Your starting point is today. Reality. You say, 'Here we are today, $2 million in debt, low staff morale, tariffs about to be dropped in several countries, all our

THE FUTURE

**How will
we get there?**

NOW

technology is on order – where do we want to be in three, five, ten years from now?' Then you start planning. One logical step after the other – away from the reality of today and all the things you know to be true – headed towards some glorious success out there in the haze somewhere.

There's just one problem: in the overwhelming majority of cases, it doesn't work. (It's also a particularly masculine way of planning, but that's another story.)

It doesn't work because it takes a structured, analytical, logical (or left-brain) approach to an issue that defies lineal thinking: predicting the future.

'No problem,' they say when this is pointed out. 'We'll hire professional forecasters to make the predictions. Then we can use our linear approach to do the job.'

But it still doesn't work. You simply can't have a vision of the future using a left-brain approach. That's not how the mind works.

A more effective approach is the reverse of this. Some call it 'deconstruction' or 'reverse engineering'. It involves the creative, picture-forming, *right* side of the brain, and it's a far more holistic way to plan.

To activate it, you start with a situation that is pure fantasy: 'Here we are in 2005, our business dominates the widget market, etc.'

Then, using your creativity, imagination and whatever other resource your subconscious can muster, you retrace your steps.

'Now it's 2001. What did we do to get here?'

And you work back. All the way back to today.

It works. And it works because it uses the only part of your brain that can come to grips with an abstract concept like 'the future' – your right brain.

Think ahead, then work back. It is the most powerful long-range planning technique in existence, and more and more of the leading organisations are discovering it.

Some argue that this approach is too technical or theoretical. (The professional strategic planners won't; as soon as they read this they'll be busy revising their approaches.) However, it is only the *explanation* that is theoretical. The practice – especially when there is a group of people involved – is simple, engrossing and enjoyable.

If your occupation is such that you need to do large-scale planning, you'll find this approach produces better results than any other. If your needs are personal, for those times of your life when you have to think through your own needs in relation to job, career or personal life, the Creative Long-Range Planner will prove invaluable.

THE FUTURE

What did we do to get here?

And here?

And here?

NOW

How to do it

The process takes 10 to 30 minutes – a small amount of time to devote to making the major decisions of your life. You may choose to repeat it often, to formulate details of the various steps along the way.

Begin by sitting somewhere quiet. Spend a couple of

minutes doing nothing but listening to your breathing. When you feel comfortable with this, imagine yourself or your business at some defined time in the future. Imagine what you'll look like, who you'll be working with, what you'll be doing.

Once you have a complete picture in your mind – how it looks, what it sounds like, what it feels like – it's time to start retracing your steps.

First, think back a year before then (or two years, or a month, or whatever interval you think appropriate). Formulate a picture. Without thinking about it, write down the details you are aware of on a sheet of paper. Try not to be critical about what you've written.

Next, think back further still, getting closer to today. Once again, quickly write down the details on another sheet of paper.

Continue doing this – step by step – until you arrive back at today.

Now you will have several sheets of paper in front of you. These contain the big picture of your vision. With your eyes open and fully alert, review these notes. These are not designed to be insights, but a road map for your planning.

Simply take each of those pages and use them as the stimulus, or brief, for the detailed planning of the particular phase it refers to.

Look for these calm solutions:
Life Priorities Calculator .... page 91
Basic Visualisation
Template .... page 118
Basic Assumption
Template .... page 129

Creative Long-Range Planner

1 Enjoy 5 minutes of Breathing Calm. Listen to the sound of your breath coming and going.

2 When you are relaxed, close your eyes and imagine a huge silver screen before you.

3 When you can see that silver screen, picture yourself – or your business – at some defined stage in the future. Examine all the surroundings and physical attributes in detail.

4 Now see yourself climbing up into that image.

5 Note what you can see around you. Hear all the sounds. Feel the textures, temperature, wealth, praise and so on.

6 Now, think back a year before then (or whatever interval you choose). Formulate a picture. See, hear, feel what it's like to be there.

7 Write down the details on a single sheet of paper.

8 Think back yet another year (or whatever period you choose), getting closer to today.

9 Quickly write down the details on another sheet of paper.

10 Continue this process until you arrive back at today.

11 Review the sheets of paper and use them as a road map for your detailed planning.

DECISION TIME

Here's a simple piece of advice that transforms stressed, chaotic people into models of calm and organisation (comparatively speaking, of course).

Simply put aside 20 minutes a day for decision-making and organisation. Use the time to plan your day, to tidy your desk, to arrange your tools, to set your objectives.

Allow yourself no other thoughts or interruptions during that time.

It might seem like a big chunk out of your day, but you'll save that 20 minutes many times over just by being organised. If your position does not allow you 20 minutes to spend this way, start work 20 minutes earlier – consider it a small investment in feeling better and calmer about your work.

THE 3-POINT EXECUTION

In the workplace, it's useful to have a simple working procedure for those numerous occasions when you need a strategy to help you achieve something specific, or simply to help you through the day.

(We assume you've already applied the Life Priorities Calculator to determine what's important to you in your work life.)

The 3-Point Execution is almost obvious. It involves three stages.

The first stage is determining what you want to achieve. To do this, spend an hour by yourself, away from all distraction or interruption, and decide exactly what positive outcome you want. Alternatively, use a technique such as the Creative Long-Range Planner. (Be sure to make the outcome positive.)

The second stage is a planning exercise where you work out the blueprint for achieving what you want to achieve. This may have a number of different steps in it. The outcome, plus each step, must be written down. Spend as long as you need writing this down.

The third stage is the implementation procedure. The 100 Percent Effort is the most powerful technique I have encountered. Most workplace frustrations can be overcome, and interpersonal tensions and aggravations reduced, when you

Look for these calm solutions:

Life Priorities Calculator .... page 91
Creative Long-Range Planner.....page 171
The 100 Percent Effort ....page 159

totally immerse yourself in the process of your work. That is what the 100 Percent Effort is about.

The 3-Point Execution

1 Determine what you want to achieve.
Take an hour to decide what you want to achieve. You will then have one positive outcome in mind.

2 Determine how you're going to achieve it.
What is your blueprint for achieving this outcome? This is clearly an easier question to ask than to resolve. Businesses, governments and individuals spend inordinate amounts of time and effort wrestling with this one issue. *This step must be written down on paper.*

3 Immerse yourself in the process.
Use the 100 Percent Effort to achieve what you want to achieve, and to increase your efficiency and your job satisfaction in the process.

THE UNCONSCIOUS PLANNER

Let's say it again: people who plan their work days suffer less from stress-related problems than those who don't plan. Not a bad reason to plan, is it?

I know, I know: you don't have enough time for traditional planning methods, you're too busy doing your job, and traditional planning is so 'left-brain' and boring anyway. You'd be surprised how many people use those excuses.

What if I told you there was a way to do your day's planning that *wasn't* boring, that didn't take up *any* of your precious work time?

It works like this: choose a repetitive activity that you do on a daily basis, preferably in the mornings. This should be something you do almost on remote control, that requires little brainpower. It could be your workout in the gym. Or the 30-minute walk you take after waking. It could be the housekeeping routine you follow every day before going to work. Or your 30 minutes of meditation. It might even be the tedious bus ride to the office.

The object is to use this time to do your day's planning – in detail. The secret is to do it without giving it another thought.

The way you do this is simply to put your subconscious in charge of the process. Give yourself a brief at the outset of your routine, tell yourself you will have a detailed plan in your mind at its completion, then forget about it.

This last step is important: forget about it. Get the whole planning process out of your conscious mind. Don't give it another thought.

Then, at the completion of your walk, or meditation, or bus trip, the answer – your day's plan – will be just sitting there at the fore-front of your mind waiting for you to write it down.

It works every time. Flawlessly.

Look for these calm solutions:
Life Priorities Calculator .... page 91
The Calm Space .... page 287
The Calm Technique .... page 324

The Unconscious Planner

1 Choose a routine activity that you do every morning, more or less on remote control.
2 Give yourself a brief at the outset of the activity, telling yourself that you will have a detailed solution at the completion, *then forget about it.*
3 At the completion of your routine, your detailed plan will be at the forefront of your mind.
4 Write down your plan.

THE CALM WAY TO MAKE A DECISION

There are times, perhaps most of the time, when the most difficult action you can imagine is simply making a decision.

Not making decisions is easy. However, failing to make decisions leads to frustration. And frustration leads to feelings of tension and anxiety.

So, when you know there is a decision to be made, make a decision. Even a small one will do – a decision to make a decision. (There are many successful people who believe it is better to make a wrong decision than to make no decision at all. While I don't endorse that for everyone, there are occasions when it is sound advice.)

Here is the procedure that will allow you to make the best decision you are capable of at any particular time. Better still, it will allow you to do so calmly and quickly.

You take in all the available information. Then do whatever calculations or analysis is necessary. Now set yourself a brief (for example, 'Utilising all the information I have, my subconscious will tell me the best possible way to maximise returns on this particular investment').

Then do absolutely nothing for a few minutes while your subconscious sifts through the information and comes up with the best solution you are capable of at that moment.

This technique works handsomely. The only thing that will stand in the way is something I call 'left-brain arrogance' – when a person cannot accept that there is any physiological force that is the equal of their analytical ability. Such people should continue to slave over their analytical skills. The rest of us can take the easy way out: the calm way to make a decision.

Look for these calm solutions:
Life Priorities Calculator .... page 91
Creative Long-Range Planner..... page 171
The Unconscious Planner .... page 177

The Calm Way to Make a Decision

1 Do whatever research and analysis is required.

2 Set yourself a brief.

3 Put aside 5 minutes (longer if you prefer).

4 Move to another place.

5 Enjoy Breathing Calm for 60 seconds.

6 Instruct yourself that at the end of 4 minutes (or whatever time you choose), you will make a decision.

7 Let your intuition or subconscious guide you to make the best decision you are capable of.

8 At the end of 4 minutes, make your decision.

THE CALM AGENDA

There is nothing more frustrating or stressful than a long, unfocused meeting. Even short meetings can be trying since they interrupt whatever work pattern you establish for yourself.

There's no soft way to phrase this: meetings are the single greatest waste of time ever devised in the workplace. In many cases, they are a joke – a shelter for indecision and weak management. And the bigger they are, the more of a shelter they become.

If you're obliged to attend many meetings, you will profit greatly by adopting the principles of meeting management in the Calm Agenda. The results will improve and you will be calmer.

This presupposes that you can influence how these meetings are conducted. If you do not have this influence or authority, all I can suggest is that you photocopy this page and pass it on to those who do. You can always volunteer to write the agenda, of course, which gives you a degree of control – as long as you can persuade people to follow your agenda.

There are five principles to follow in the Calm Agenda, but we can summarise them as follows:

(i)   knowing why you're in the meeting; and

(ii) knowing you will get something out of it.

Unless every one of the following principles can be satisfied, I recommend that you don't attend the meeting. I guarantee it will be a waste of time for most people (except those who use meetings as a shelter for indecision and weak management).

> **Look for these calm solutions:**
> The Art of Being Heard...........page 255
> How to Get What You Want......page 232
> Under the Influence of Calm .....page 263

Calm Agenda

Here are the five essentials for a productive meeting:

- The outcome or outcomes of the meeting are clearly described at the top of your agenda (though not necessarily published this way if you don't want everyone to know).
- Only those who can make a real contribution may attend.
- There is a finite allocation of time to reach the defined outcome or outcomes.
- Any resolutions are documented.
- Someone in the meeting has the authority to act on the resolutions.

Unless every one of those principles can be satisfied, don't hold the meeting.

Some enlightened organisations have embellished these meeting principles with others. Here are a few of these for your consideration:

(i) Refreshments should only be served *after* a resolution has been reached (unless the meeting is with strangers).

(ii) Straight-backed chairs should be used in preference to lounging chairs.

(iii) All participants should stand rather than sit (eccentric, but effective for achieving things quickly).

(iv) Small talk is not permitted until after a resolution has been reached.

Follow those small steps and you'll be amazed at how much time and anxiety you save in your working days.

If you are in a position to put the Calm Agenda into practice, you will reap the productivity benefits that can come from a positive, well-run meeting.

A positive change

After the section on breathing, this is the most important section of the book. I would have given it the prominence of a chapter of its own, but it is so integral to how *you* feel, work and succeed, that there really is no other place for it than here – in the chapter devoted to you.

The key to achieving anything great in life is a positive attitude. Believe and you will achieve.

Big deal, you say, everyone knows that. Everyone knows that a positive attitude is all-important. However, while it may be true that they know this, not everyone follows the advice. Because it is difficult to be positive. Isn't it?

How can you be positive when the negative, adversarial nature of politics means the bulk of what you hear from your leaders is negative? When the bulk of what you read in the newspapers is negative? Or when the subject matter of movies, television, literature, even pop music, is more popular when it's negative than when it's positive?

The reason it is difficult is because you listen to *them*,

rather than to yourself. When you begin to hear *yourself* sounding positive, you're on the way to making a habit of it.

As discussed earlier, your subconscious responds most effectively when you feed it positive suggestions. Hypnosis, affirmation and visualisation work best when you use positive suggestions. So, too, when you issue instructions to subordinates, make requests of your superiors, and give recommendations to your peers.

Positive suggestions have the most positive effect. It sounds glib, I know, but it's interesting how many of the great truths in life also sound this way.

I've heard some so-called stress management authorities dismiss positive attitude as a way to combat stress: 'You can say, "I'm going to be calm at work today" all you like, and it won't make a gram of difference to your stress problems.'

If you'd used those words ('I'm going to be calm at work today'), chances are they *wouldn't* make any difference. Because those words do *not* represent positive thinking. They represent wishful thinking. Positive is, 'I am feeling calm and confident'. Wishful is, 'I *am going to* feel calm and confident'. See the difference?

It really is as basic as that. Almost every self-improvement or self-enlightenment technique that has ever been invented is based on this simple understanding: you have to do more than *want* something to work for you, you have to *know* it's going to work for you. When you are positive it will work for you, then it will work for you.

This is such an important understanding that I'll repeat it: when you are positive something will work for you, it will work for you.

A positive attitude helps you to achieve greatness, overcome adversity, transform weakness. It can help you to cure disease, win marathons and free yourself from the negative effects of stress. It can make you feel calm and happy. (Conversely, a negative attitude has been shown to make you feel lousy and have a damaging effect on your immune system.)

With a positive attitude and approach, you can be completely relaxed in conditions you never thought you'd be able to withstand. You can be calm within yourself, and a calm influence in the lives of those about you.

You may not have noticed yet, but you are already well down that path. At this very moment you are much closer to peace and calm than most of the population. Because you've taken the positive step of choosing to read a book such as this.

 ## A POSITIVE WORD

Whether you are conscious of it or not, the words you use have a profound effect on the way you think and feel. If you use positive, optimistic words, you will feel positive and optimistic. If you use negative words, you will feel negative.

It follows, then, that if you stack your vocabulary with positive words, you will develop positive feelings within yourself.

This is as easy to do as it sounds. All it requires you to do is pay attention to the words you use – the words you say aloud as well as the words you think to yourself – and to gradually replace the negative, or even neutral ones, with the positive. The more positive the words, the more pronounced the benefits.

Listen to your conversation and your thoughts. Strive to find the positive side of all you say and think about. When you do succumb to the negative, practise bombarding it with positive interpretations of the same thought.

Instead of 'I've got so much work to do', try, 'I'm fortunate to be fully occupied', or, 'It's rewarding to have useful work and challenges'.

Following is a list of words that illustrate what I mean. This list is by no means definitive, nor even an attempt to be partially complete, but it will give you an idea of what is possible.

Look for these calm solutions:
Basic Affirmation Template.......page 120
Talk Yourself into It ....page 213
The Joy of Repetition............page 161

Every time you get the urge to use a word like this . . .	. . . try to think of a way of using one like this, instead:
no	yes
can't	can
won't	will
maybe	certainly
tense	relaxed
chaos	order
problem	opportunity
okay	great
fail/failure	succeed/success
fear	confidence
ill	well
I hate	I love
bored	stimulated
panic	calm
miserable	happy
empty	fulfilled
lose	win
depressed	uplifted

POSITIVE CONTRIBUTIONS

We once had a very religious client who would not tolerate crude language of any kind. If you've ever been inside an advertising agency, especially one with a high proportion of gifted young artists and writers, you will appreciate how difficult it might be to keep those rebellious young tongues in check – not so much in the presence of that particular client, but when they were unaware of his presence in our offices, or when they were simply unaware of the effects of their everyday language.

To overcome this potential aggravation in the most positive way possible, we declined counselling and reward systems – neither of which had any great entertainment appeal – in favour of a more entertaining approach. A 'swear jar'. Every time someone let a profanity slip, they were urged by workmates to contribute a dollar to the jar. When the contents of the jar reached a certain level, someone was charged with the task of purchasing a cuddly toy for an underprivileged child, or someone in a children's hospital.

It was not meant to be a fine. Nor was it a 'negative reinforcement' (where pain or punishment is used to stimulate cooperative behaviour). It was a creative little game that appealed to the subconscious and reminded our writers and artists of something they really wanted to do: to keep on side with an important client. It made them *want* to find a positive outcome; it made them *want* to be aware of language they would normally take no notice of. Soon everyone was playing the game, and the corridors began to sound uncharacteristically wholesome for a young advertising agency.

I realised then that if such a technique could overcome negative language, it could also overcome negative attitudes.

The Positive Contributions jar

Here's a game you can play by yourself.

Take a small bottle or jar to work and keep it by where you work. Only you need to know its purpose. Every time you become conscious of a negative thought, comment or word, place a coin in the jar. Or a banknote (depends how badly you want to change).

If you're vigilant about this, you will have a jar full of money in no time. Now turn all those negative thoughts and comments into something positive.

Take the contents of the jar, and purchase something that will benefit someone less fortunate than yourself.

Then personally hand over the gift. (As this part of the exercise is done entirely for your own satisfaction, feel free to hand the money to charities, beggars, buskers – whoever you like.)

See what you've done? You've rewarded yourself (with satisfaction) for turning a negative word, thought or comment into something *positive*.

Once you have trained yourself to recognise subtle inclinations towards the negative, and are aware of these influences, you can set about substituting positive ones for them.

Positive Contributions

- Set up a small bottle or jar as your Positive Contributions jar.
- Every time you become aware of a negative thought, word or comment, place a coin in the jar.
- When the jar is full, purchase a small gift for someone less fortunate than yourself.
- Deliver the gift yourself (as long as you find this satisfying).
- Once you have trained yourself to be aware of your negative thoughts, words and comments, substitute positive ones for them.

THE POSITIVE PICTURE

Once you have got your positive/negative language in order, it's time to work on the *images* that formulate in your brain. (Remember mental pictures have the most powerful effect when it comes to influencing your subconscious.)

By choosing positive mental pictures, you can project onto your subconscious the positive outcomes you desire. And if you do it creatively, these images can transform your life.

The following technique should be as enjoyable as it is effective. Once again it uses the silver screen of the Visualisation Template to create a positive scene, then you imagine yourself as part of the scene. After that, developing a positive mental attitude becomes a simple matter of referring back to that mental picture, and you can do this in milliseconds.

A positive attitude

A positive attitude is more than a therapy; it's a pleasure in itself. Work at it and you will feel calmer and more in control. Every effort you make will repay itself over and over again.

Be aware of negative pressures and expressions. Substitute positive words wherever possible; pump up your vocabulary with them.

Use the silver screen to create an ideal image of yourself – always with a smile and boundless enthusiasm. Refer back to that mental picture time and time again throughout the day.

Look for every opportunity to laugh.

Finally, throw yourself into every activity you encounter. Even if the task is an unpleasant one, perform it as thoroughly and as conscientiously as you possibly can. This positive approach to work is one of the most well-established paths to peace and contentment.

> **Look for these calm solutions:**
> Breathing Calm ....page 103
> Basic Visualisation Template .....page 118

The Positive Picture

1 Enjoy 5 minutes of Breathing Calm. Listen to the sound of your breath coming and going.

2 When you are relaxed, close your eyes and imagine a huge silver screen before you.

3 When you can see that silver screen, picture the most positive (and probably relaxed) environment you can imagine. Examine this place in detail.

4 Now imagine yourself climbing up into that image. See yourself up there – exactly as you would like to be – always acting, speaking and thinking positively. Picture yourself with a smile and boundless enthusiasm.

5 Note what you can see around you.

6 Hear all the sounds around you.

7 Feel the breeze, textures, the temperature and so on.

8 When that image is firmly implanted in your mind, take a snapshot (or freeze-frame) of yourself, complete with all those images, sounds and feelings.

9 Relax, and let the positive feelings work their way through your consciousness (no effort is required). Luxuriate in that feeling.

10 To develop a positive attitude, refer back to that mental picture time and time again throughout the day.

SEARCH FOR THE UPSIDE

To round off this section on positive attitude – which I stress is the most important section in this book after Breathing Calm – I've contrived a little game for you to take through life. If you play it regularly, it will help you to feel calm and contented in your work, to a degree you would never have believed possible.

It is designed to be played many times a day. The more often you play it, the more enjoyable it gets and the more habitual it becomes.

It's called 'search for the upside'.

This is a simple mind-game of inverting perspectives. You apply it to all those events you would normally gripe about, or resent, or feel bad about. To play the game, all you have to do is find a positive side to things you would normally only see as negative.

This is not always easy to achieve. Often, you will find yourself having to turn negatives into humorous positives.

For example: it's pretty hard to find a positive side to being demoted. So you console yourself that it will now be someone else's responsibility to clean out all the junk in your filing cabinet that you've been planning to do for ages. It doesn't solve the problem, but it adds a touch of humour to something that is hardly humorous.

In cases like this, humour is positive. It will have a positive effect towards helping you feel good about yourself and your work.

Search for the upside, find the good in what you do and what happens to you, and you'll soon be able to transform even the most difficult moods and situations into something positive.

Then you can be calm.

Dealing with worries

Worry and anxiety have a lot in common. They are different conditions, but both are imagination-based and often lack substance. In layperson's terms: worries are usually about the specific, whereas anxiety is usually non-specific or general; worries relate to things and events, whereas anxiety is more of a 'feeling'. (Oversimplified, I know, but you get the point.)

Many of the remedies that follow, therefore, can be used for either condition.

The future of worry

The nature of worry is to be concerned about something that *might* happen. It is never about something that is taking place at that particular moment. Many worriers have difficulty coming to grips with the abstract nature of this, believing their problem is very real and present. But worry is, by definition, always future-oriented. For that matter, so is anxiety.

Knowing this is probably not going to make you feel better next time you start to worry. However, it will make it easier to come up with effective solutions – most of which are designed to make you forget the future and focus on the present.

THE WORRY ELIMINATOR

Irrational worries (which most of them are) should be able to be dispensed with as easily as a headache; if they're not erased altogether, then they should certainly be lessened in intensity.

The steps to achieving this are elementary:
(i)   Plan.
(ii) Reprogram your worries.
(iii) Look after the present.

Plan

Because worries are future-oriented – that is, about something that may or may not eventuate – they invariably relate to the unknown. The more you know about what's going to happen, the less you worry about it; even when it is something unpleasant.

When you're told you're going to be fired, you worry less than when you simply suspect it. When the X-ray tells you your wrist is broken, you worry less than when you were taken to hospital.

Knowledge helps alleviate worry. That is why we plan.

All well-run enterprises feature some degree of planning. It is a necessary art that not only allows for the correct allocation of resources, but also allows for the management of expectation (your expectation as well as other people's).

This management of expectations is the most crucial part of helping people to stay calm and contented in their work. You will see evidence of this in your own workplace: those who know what is expected of them, and have some idea of how their careers are mapped out, suffer fewer position-related anxieties.

This is why you should always insist on having a detailed job specification that not only defines tasks and responsibilities, but also measurement criteria.

I was raking through my memories trying to think of an appropriate demonstration of this from my corporate experience. Then I remembered a better one.

Take a lesson from my grandmother   My grandmother (yes, the same one) was one of those pioneering women who, during the Depression, accompanied her husband to the harsh, unforgiving Australian outback to make a life for their young family. Her two main concerns were employment (money) and food. To a struggling family with patchy work opportunities and extremely undependable food supplies at the best of times, this should have been good reason to worry. Three children under five with no understanding of or sympathy for the concept of food shortages should have been even more cause for worry.

Did she sit about worrying? No, she planned.

She planned to store two low-cost foodstuffs that they could survive on for extended periods: flour (for bread) and dripping (fat renderings from cooked meats). While this would have overcome one of her problems, it presented another: how could she keep three small children happy and contented on a sustenance diet of bread and dripping?

She planned this as well. From the time they arrived in the outback, her children knew of only one special-occasion meal. From time to time they had cakes, and roasts, and oranges, but these were never presented as special-occasion foods. For special occasions, only one dish was good enough – bread and dripping.

Then, when the harsh times came about, which they inevitably did, the children finally got to savour the treat they'd been denied all year: bread and dripping.

An elegant piece of planning, wouldn't you say? The perfect allocation of resources, accompanied by the creative management of expectations. If my grandmother were around today, I'd put her in charge of one of my businesses.

Reprogram your worries

Most worries are a product of your subconscious. They are, in the main, irrational – that is, you know they are groundless or unlikely to eventuate, but still you worry.

This is good news. You already know ways of getting your subconscious to perform the way you want it to perform. So to overcome or discard worries, you might use any of the four tools of the subconscious we have already covered: Visualisation – to see yourself without worries; Affirmation – to tell yourself you have no reason for worries; Self-hypnosis – to convince yourself you're worry free; and Assumption – to go through your days assuming you are worry free (which you will be if you assume a worry-free role).

Look after the present

Because all worries and all anxiety are based on the future, they're based on something that does not exist. In addition, most of these worries *never* eventuate. Never. When you look at it from that perspective, worriers generally don't have a lot to worry about at all, do they?

But most worriers worry out of compulsion rather than choice. So how can we change this compulsion, to allow them the choice?

Simple: use the 100 Percent Effort technique. It's the surest way to exist in the present and so derive all the calming and satisfying benefits associated with it.

> **Look for these calm solutions:**
>
> The 100 Percent Effort ....page 159
> The Joy of Repetition.............page 161
> Four Tools of the
> Subconscious.....................page 114

The Worry Eliminator

- Plan for the long term as well as for your short-term tasks. Knowing what to expect (because you've planned it) helps to alleviate worry.
- Write down your plan.
- Spend a few minutes enjoying Breathing Calm.
- When you are relaxed, use any of the four tools of the subconscious to reprogram your worries, so they no longer appear so threatening.
- Focus all your effort on the present, by using the 100 Percent Effort technique.

THE WORRY BREAK

This is a gem of time management. It horrifies some time-management experts because they believe it encourages procrastination. And, unlike the advice you get from these experts (almost always reasoned and left-brain oriented), this solution involves your subconscious.

One of the core beliefs of achievers, workaholics and time-management experts is you should never postpone things that are difficult or unpleasant. Generally, I agree with them, but worries and anxiety are in a category of their own. I want to show you how it makes great sense to postpone worries and anxieties wherever possible, perhaps even indefinitely.

So how can you postpone feelings that are the product of your subconscious, and more often than not, entirely irrational?

Use the postponing technique I call the Worry Break.

To be effective, it requires adding an element of formality – or, at least a degree of habit – to your worrying. You must set aside a specific amount of time at the same time every day for this activity. It could be 10 minutes, or it could be an hour. As long as it's the same every day. During this time you may be as bitter and as negative as you like because, at the end of the period, you will have dealt with your worries for the day.

Or until the same time tomorrow.

Every worrying issue that arises during your working day you officially postpone to the Worry Break. You note your worries, record the details required to make a decision (if one is required), then do your best to forget about everything until the time arrives.

Then, at the designated time, you let yourself go and have a really good worry. Even though this is technically just a postponing technique, nine times out of ten your worries will have vanished by the time you conclude the session.

As well, the beauty of this technique is that you have very little to do other than make the initial decision; after that, almost all of the effort is carried out by your subconscious.

The Worry Break

- Designate a certain time and place where you can conduct regular worry sessions. Same time, same place, every day.
- When worries, frustrations, irritations or anxieties arise during the day, postpone them until this time. Write them down, record the details required to make a decision (if one is required), then forget about them until the time arrives.
- At your Worry Break, devote all your attention to these concerns – for the designated period only.
- At the end of the period, move to another place and stop thinking about your problems entirely.
- Trust in your subconscious to have the solutions you require.

 AN APPOINTMENT WITH CALM

Here's a clever way of dealing with worries. It is not a technique you'd necessarily use to solve important work problems, but one for dealing with irrational worries that arise throughout the day or in the quiet hours at night.

This technique works on three levels: it appeals to the subconscious; it postpones the unpleasant; and it is actually a very efficient way of dealing with minor problems (because they often seem to vanish before you apply it).

All you have to do is make an appointment with yourself to sort out the worry later.

When the worries occur, don't pay them any special attention: just write them down and inform yourself you will deal with them at a specific time in the future, say the following day at noon. If the worries happen at night, write them down in a notebook you keep nearby, with the same objective in mind.

The idea is to turn this appointment with yourself into a ritual.

In doing this, not only do you postpone the worry to a time that *you* dictate – rather than wrestling with the worry all the time – but you are well advanced in finding a solution for it. If a solution is required, your subconscious will do all the work *before* the appointment time, and while it is searching for the solution you can go about life as usual.

Look for these calm solutions:
Four Tools of the
Subconscious......................page 114
The Calm Space ....page 287

An Appointment with Calm

- When worries or anxieties occur during the day or night, write them down, and make an appointment with yourself – nominating a specific time – to deal with them later.
- Forget about the issue until the appointment time arrives.
- When the time arrives, do all you can to resolve the issue – in the amount of time you have allowed.
- At the end of the period, move to another place and stop thinking about your problems entirely.
- Trust in your subconscious to have the solutions you require.

THE PLUS AND MINUS METHOD

You will notice that many of the techniques throughout this book require you to 'write it down'. You see this often in self-help techniques.

The power of this is that you use two senses (sight and

touch) to record one piece of information. As well, because you choose your own words, it forces you to pay strict attention to the composition of the information. The net effect of this is that the information is more firmly implanted in your consciousness. (There's also a side benefit, not to be underestimated, that you have a permanent record of the decision you have made.)

Here's another reason. When you toss a problem around in your mind, all sorts of unpredictable influences come to bear. This often results in the problem appearing more formidable, or more uncontrollable, than it really is.

When you write a problem down, however, you are forced to consider it more carefully. In the great majority of cases, it will appear less threatening than you thought.

The Plus and Minus Method is a worry diffuser. It works on the understanding that most worries are caused by the *expectation* that something will happen – not by something actually happening. Its purpose is to explore the possibility of your worry ever coming to fruition.

Here's how it works. Let's say your worry is that you might become unemployed and be unable to afford the payments on your new mortgage. At the bottom of your page, write down this worry.

Now, at the top of the page write the outcome you seek in relation to this worry. Make sure that it is worded positively and (according to your situation) realistic. Underline the words: 'I have a long-lasting and fulfilling job that allows me to afford my mortgage.'

On the next page, write this same outcome at the top, but not the worry.

Next, draw a line down the middle of the page. On the left write ' − ', and on the right write ' + '.

Now, on the left, list all impediments to achieving your outcome. And on the right, list all the opportunities or possibilities that exist (or what qualities or resources you possess) that will enable you to achieve the outcome at the top of your page.

Before you know it, the worry you wrote at the bottom of the first page will seem less important, perhaps even trivial.

Try it. You'll be surprised how effectively it works.

Look for these calm solutions:
The 100 Percent Effort ....page 159

The Plus and Minus Method

1 Use a notebook. At the bottom of the page, write down your worry.

2 At the top of the page write the outcome you seek when your worry is removed. Make sure it is worded positively. Underline the words.

3 On the next page, write your outcome at the top. Draw a line down the middle.

4 On the left, list all impediments to achieving your outcome.

5 On the right, list all the opportunities or possibilities (or the resources you possess) to help you achieve your outcome.

6 Then, using the 100 Percent Effort, set about achieving your outcome.

WORRY ABOUT THE BIG THINGS

I knew a man once whose philosophy advocated two neat ways of maintaining calm and perspective in his life:

(i)   Never lose sleep over small issues.

(ii) Treat *all* issues as small issues.

Such a philosophy can work for every one of us. And it works because it plays to a number of 'truths' that are already in place in our belief systems.

BIG worries warrant BIG hurt, that's just common-sense, isn't it? We'll never change that. Another one: little worries are mere trifles that don't really deserve the mental effort we allow them. Any sensible person would buy that argument, too.

Something that is probably not in your belief system at all is that BIG worries can be redefined as little worries. But you have to agree, if you *could* define them this way, you would be able to dismiss them with much greater ease.

Here's how you do it.

Sit somewhere quiet, and project yourself to some time in the future. Imagine yourself at sixty-five years of age (or later, if you like). What you'll look like, what your attitudes will be, and what you'll be doing.

When you really feel you have this sixty-five-year-old future perspective, review today's worry. Chances are it will quickly fade in significance.

> **Look for these calm solutions:**
>
> Four Tools of the
> Subconscious.....................page 114
> The 100 Percent Effort...........page 159

Worry About the Big Things

1 Enjoy Breathing Calm for 60 seconds.

2 On your big silver screen, try to imagine what you'll be like at sixty-five (if you're already about this age, pick any age in the future). Note your appearance, what you're wearing, where you'll be living. What sort of attitudes will you have?

3 'See' yourself climb up into that image.

4 When you feel like you are part of that future image, think back on the problem you're worrying about today. Imagine how important it would seem looking back. (Chances are it would hardly feature in your memory banks.)

5 Pause, with these impressions in mind, and allow today's worry to fade.

USING YOUR NOSE

Finally, we come to a delightful way to deal with anxiety – especially the non-specific variety that, usually with no foundation whatsoever, leaves you feeling something is about to go wrong.

This anxiety-reducing method uses essential oils.

Aromatherapy is no longer thought of as New Age. A form of Chinese herbal medicine, aromatherapy is being viewed more and more as a science: the science of aromacology, the study of the effects fragrances have on mood and behaviour. People in all walks of life now appreciate the benefits of aromatherapy, particularly in the way it can treat stress and encourage relaxation.

We now know that certain scents produce distinct physiological effects, particularly so in the area of relaxation. Research has shown that the scents of certain oils stimulate the production of serotonin in the brain. (Serotonin is the neurochemical that helps you to feel good, and is the focus for anti-depressant drugs such as Prozac.) We also know oils such as lemon and peppermint have a stimulating effect on the nervous system, and can actually increase productivity in the workplace. A mix of the two stimulating oils, rosemary and lemon, is said to improve concentration.

Floral scents, such as rose, lavender, orange blossom and chamomile, have a calming effect. Oils such as patchouli help eliminate anxiety and lift the mood, while sandalwood and nutmeg can help you shrug off the ill effects of stress.

Following is a list of oils that aromatherapists use in the treatment of anxiety. You will note that some of them have additional properties, in the sense that they invigorate (stimulate) at the same time as they relax. These are known as *adoptogens* and act as 'balancers' for the body. Others, such as patchouli, change in their effect – from uplifting to sedating – according to the quantity you use.

(Some say that pregnant women should avoid using basil, juniper, marjoram, melissa and clary sage.)

You don't have to be an aromatherapist to use essential oils. Experiment with combinations. For a start, experiment with bergamot, geranium, lavender, neroli and basil. For chronic anxiety, consider a combination of lavender, cedarwood and lemongrass. For intense, short-term anxiety, consider lavender, sandalwood and geranium. From the oils listed here, choose according to your

sense of smell – your nose will guide you to the ones that will be of most benefit. Three oils are an ideal number to combine.

Properties of calming oils

OILS	CALMING OILS	OILS FOR ANXIETY	UPLIFTING OILS	MOOD ELEVATING OILS	MENTAL CLARITY OILS
Basil	✓	✓	✓		✓
Bergamot	✓	✓	✓		
Cedarwood	✓				
Chamomile	✓	✓			
Cypress	✓	✓			
Clary sage	✓	✓		✓	✓
Geranium	✓	✓	✓		
Jasmine	✓	✓			
Juniper	✓	✓	✓		✓
Lavender	✓	✓	✓		
Lemon					✓
Marjoram	✓	✓			
Neroli	✓	✓		✓	
Orange			✓	✓	
Patchouli	✓	✓	✓ (in small amounts)		
Pine					✓
Rose		✓			
Rosemary					✓
Sage		✓			
Sandalwood	✓	✓			
Thyme		✓			
Ylang ylang	✓	✓	✓		

Now, use the pure oils in whichever way appeals to you.

Use a few drops in an oil burner: a discreet one near your workspace will be appreciated, not only by yourself, but by those around you as well.

You can also place a few drops on a handkerchief, to carry with you. Alternatively, when you go home tonight, add 10 drops to a warm bath or a few drops to a bland oil base (such as almond or jojoba) for massage.

One more note about my grandmother Lavender is probably the most widely used and acceptable oil – not only does it help you to relax, but it also eases aches and pains, such as headache.

My grandmother instinctively knew of its calming properties. Wherever she went she would carry a handkerchief perfumed with lavender water – a low cost luxury perfume item she would buy in volume from a pharmacy.

You can do the same. Add a few drops to your handkerchief and keep it handy for stressful moments.

Look for these calm solutions:
The Scent of Calm................page 282
The Calm Space ....page 287
The Sound of Calm..............page 280

B-type transformations

It may be politically incorrect to use psychological stereotypes, but we're now going to enjoy getting into a bit of serious Type A and B stereotyping.

In the main, people who exhibit Type A, or Driven, personality characteristics (serious, time-conscious, obsessive) are more susceptible to the problems of self-induced stress problems than their Type B, or Easygoing, counterparts who are relaxed, less obsessive, more outgoing. So, from a sheer feel-good point of view, it makes sense for you to want to be a little more Easygoing in your approach.

What about your work efficiency? Studies show that Easygoing people – even though they may lack some of the drive and ambition of their counterparts – are often better leaders, managers, communicators, and more efficient at the things they do. So, it makes good work sense to be a little more Easygoing in your approach.

Here are a few techniques that will trick your subconscious into believing you're more of an Easygoing personality – at least for some of the time.

PRETEND TO B

You can't get an easier technique than this. Check out the chart on pages 22–3 and study the characteristics of an Easygoing personality.

Then, using the Basic Assumption Template, imagine yourself with such a personality.

Once that image is set in your mind, it simply becomes a matter of assuming you are this personality type, and assuming those who come in contact with you recognise you as such.

> **Look for these calm solutions:**
> Breathing Calm ....page 103
> Basic Visualisation Template .....page 118
> Basic Assumption Template ......page 129
> Watchless Pretence...............page 133

TAKE AN EASYGOING BREAK

It's hard work having a Driven personality. You're the one who has to take work seriously, you're the one with all the ambition, having to work back each night, take work home with you, worry about it all night long. You're the one who has to carry all the responsibility ... or so you like to think.

Those Easygoings on the other hand really get it easy. They're more casual about working, maybe you could say more balanced in their approach. They have fun at nights and weekends, and never seem to worry about their work. They don't seem to have any time pressures at all. Yet, somehow, they always seem to get their work done.

It's not fair, is it.

That's why I've devised this simple technique especially for you. So that occasionally, just occasionally, you can share in all the benefits that your Easygoing counterparts enjoy.

It can only happen once a day. And it can only be for one hour. During that hour, you give yourself permission to enjoy all the relaxing benefits that come from being an Easygoing personality.

To begin with, you need to imagine what it's like to be this way – how it looks, sounds, acts and feels. You do this on your imaginary silver screen.

Somewhere in that image is an outward characteristic you can adopt and, later, use intuitively. Maybe it's a loosened tie, or casual shoes; maybe it's the way they stand or move; maybe it's just the absence of a wristwatch.

Now, using the technique that follows, use that characteristic to trigger those relaxed, time-oblivious feelings that Easygoing people enjoy.

At any time.

Look for these calm solutions:
Your Choice of Pressures ....page 210
How Susceptible Are You? ....page 12

Take an Easygoing Break

- Study the difference between Driven and Easygoing behaviour.
- Put aside one hour each working day for you to emulate an Easygoing personality. Mark the time in your diary.
- Choose at least one of the outward characteristics of an Easygoing personality (such as: moves slowly, doesn't wear a watch, is interested in things outside work, stops work at reasonable hours, doesn't rush from appointment to appointment).
- Assume that characteristic for one hour (your Easygoing Break). Notice how deadlines no longer seem so threatening. How it seems like you have plenty of time to complete your work. How you can do one thing at a time and *enjoy it*. How relaxed you feel.
- At the completion of your hour, pause for a couple of minutes to reflect on how comfortable you felt being an Easygoing personality.
- Every day, spend at least one hour being Easygoing. After a while, all you will have to do is adopt that outward characteristic (for example, taking off your watch) for your subconscious to recall those positive Easygoing characteristics, and to help you feel calm and relaxed.

MAKE FUN OF WORK

The classic Driven personality is rather serious. (You can understand this, considering the responsibilities they believe that they alone have to carry.) People who fall into this category are serious about their work and their ambitions, and they frown on the frivolous.

Conversely, people whose personalities tend to skew towards Easygoing are relaxed about the frivolous. Some of them even enjoy it. They know when to call it a day, and when to let their hair down and have a good time.

For their more uptight counterparts, therefore, adopting a few of those Easygoing traits can turn out to be very calming. The advice that follows relates to having fun. As you know, it's very hard to feel stressed while you're having fun. Better still, think how pleasant life would be if you could get fun out of your most time-consuming activity, your work. Think how calm you could be.

The game of work

The challenge here is to play a game with yourself as you work. The game is to find the humorous, entertaining or even ridiculous sides of everything that goes on at your workplace, and everything you do.

So next time the pompous executive from Personnel starts throwing his weight around, smile, because you see this image of him as a puffed-up baboon. Next time you're sent on yet another errand to the stationers, smile, because you can take a different route and pretend you're on an adventure. Next time you have an unpleasant or mindless task to finish, smile, because you have the opportunity to turn it into a mini-competition or a game. And the next time a demanding customer threatens to take her custom elsewhere . . .

Drive control

Take a look at the high-energy achiever types in your workplace. They will probably be intensely self-motivated, ambitious, time-conscious and have no time for 'frivolous' activities like play or relaxation.

Nine times out of ten, these people will be what we've been referring to as Driven.

If you fall into this category, you can overcome the

stresses that stem from overambition by using techniques that encourage more Easygoing behaviour. We covered several of these in the previous section.

An ambition to be calm

Ambition can be a good servant, but a tyrannical master. The pressures that come from uncontrolled ambition are not far removed from those that come from being deadline-obsessed: you set difficult benchmarks and time frames, then you pressure yourself until you either win through or give up in frustration.

Either way, the place you end up is a long way from calm.

Ambition is not a stressor in itself; many are enriched and invigorated by it, finding it gives their work direction and purpose. But when your ambition is coupled with unclear goals, you have a dangerous combination. Because you have all of the drive, with all its pressures, but none of the satisfaction that comes from having achieved your goals.

Therefore, the obvious way to derive peace and satisfaction through ambition is to have clear goals and objectives.

Look for these calm solutions:

Life Priorities Calculator	page 91
Creative Long-Range Planner	page 171
The 3-Point Execution	page 176
Control Only What You Can Control	page 163

YOUR CHOICE OF PRESSURES

The mental words you use when you're thinking things through is known as internal dialogue. While some people rely on this more than others, it is something we all do.

Some of us, however, go even further. Many times a

day we say things to ourselves that amount to more than just dialogue. Something inside you whispers that you ought to reply to that letter you received a few days ago, or give up smoking, or start exercising. Other times it will whisper that you have to see an investment adviser about your savings, or an optometrist about your eyes (computer screens are hell, aren't they). Sometimes you might even hear yourself muttering things aloud like, 'I must get that filing finished.'

Driven people do this most of all. They never give themselves a moment's peace. Their internal dialogue is loaded with expressions like 'must', 'have to', 'should', 'ought to' and so on. When you hear such people speak, even their *external* dialogue sounds the same. 'I *have* to finish this document by nine.' 'I *must* go to the bank before I stop for lunch.' 'I *should* speak to my boss about a rise.' 'I *have* to learn to get on with the new receptionist.'

Note the instructions they give themselves. These are known as pressure phrases or instructions: basically, it's constant, nagging little reminders that you're not doing all you should be doing, and that you *must* and *should* achieve more and more. The mental words themselves create pressure. They produce stress. Not only do they set an endless agenda, but they perpetuate the feeling that there's always more to be done. They never give you the time to reflect and be satisfied with what you have achieved, because there is always something else that *has* to be done.

I know it's unkind to write this, but Driven people thrive on pressure phrases; it's fuel for their restlessness, it excuses their tension and anxiety.

Yet, simply by choosing a few different words for this internal (and external) dialogue, you can eliminate much of the pressure that accompanies it.

Once you have achieved that, you can substitute words

that actually encourage you to feel the way you'd like to feel. Use any suite of words you like – about having choices, about being happy, about being calm – and you'll soon begin to feel that way.

But the first step is substitution. Substitute 'choose to' every time you get the urge to say 'have to' and you will feel an immediate change in your attitude. Tell yourself: 'I choose to finish this typing by nine' . . . 'I *choose to* mark these essays before I go to lunch' . . . 'I *choose to* be more tolerant of the new director of nursing' . . . and you will feel the change almost immediately.

And, if you believe you'd profit from being let off the 'have to' hook altogether, you can choose even softer options: substitute 'can' for 'have to'. Now, you would tell yourself: 'I *can* finish this typing by nine (if I choose)' . . . 'I *can* do the mail before I go to lunch (if I choose)' . . . 'I *can* be more tolerant of the new receptionist'.

Whichever choice you make, the new freedom these internal dialogue phrases allow will help you feel more relaxed and comfortable about your work and duties.

Look for these calm solutions:
Basic Affirmation Template . . . . page 120
Pretend to B . . . . page 206

Your Choice of Pressures

- Listen to the language you use in your external and internal dialogue.
- Replace the pressure phrases like 'have to' with more moderate words, such as 'choose to'.
- If you want to be under even less pressure, substitute 'I can' or 'I may' instead of 'I must'.
- Use this language, not only for internal dialogue, but for your conversation as well.

SET YOUR OWN BENCHMARKS

One of the less attractive infatuations of the nineties is with a process called 'benchmarking'. This begins with a measure of performance and productivity – often flamboyantly described as 'world's best practice' – against which your performance and productivity is ultimately compared.

Not surprisingly, very few processes ever measure up to 'world's best practice'. And, even for those that do, the pressure continues. Because the instant you make it and become the world's best, you become the object of everyone else's benchmarking. So it is endlessly competitive.

Every person who gets embroiled in this evaluative process becomes a victim of the process. You either measure up, or you're a failure. This is no way to maintain calm and nurture self-esteem.

My recommendation is to ignore all this 'world's best practice' benchmarking nonsense. (I'll give you a tip from the inside: much of it *is* pretentious nonsense.) Then, set your own performance standard. Set your own benchmarks to meet or surpass. Move at your own pace.

This is not an excuse to do less work. The second part of my suggestion is that you employ the 100 Percent Effort technique, so that when you work, you are wholly involved in the process of meeting or surpassing the standards you have set.

This total involvement means you can achieve great things, and become calm in the process.

Look for these calm solutions:

The 100 Percent Effort ....page 159
Life Priorities Calculator .... page 91
The Power of No ....page 143

TALK YOURSELF INTO IT

If you feel you're a slave to duty, or have this unfocused compulsion to perform better and better, you could profit from having a little chat to yourself from time to time.

Using positive, relaxing affirmations.

As you know, affirmations are a set of words that, through repetition, gradually influence the subconscious and become self-fulfilling. The words or sentiments you choose determine the results you achieve. Choose positive, easygoing words, and you will eventually become positive and easygoing.

It sounds simplistic, but it is a powerful tool for change. And it's so easy to do you've really got no excuse not to try it.

PERMISSION TO REJECT SUCCESS

If you promise not to tell any of my business associates I wrote this, I'll share a sanity-saving work secret with you.

From your first days at school, it's probably been drummed into you how important it is to succeed at everything you do. This adds a great amount of pressure to your life. It is no exaggeration to say that many, if not most, people measure their worth according to the success they have or have not had in their jobs. If they don't see themselves as successful in this role, their self-esteem suffers, which leads to them feeling miserable and stressed.

You don't have to feel this way.

There is absolutely no obligation for you to be

'successful' at all. Indeed, it's possible that you would be a far more relaxed person if you rejected this popular concept of success altogether. At the same time, however, you don't want to feel like a failure – which can be equally as demoralising and stressful.

So, how can you reject the need to succeed at work without feeling like a failure?

It's all a matter of how you define success. Chances are, your idea of success will have a lot to do with what others perceive as being successful – that is, the conventional measures of achievement. As well, chances are that you won't have given much thought at all to what it means to you (in a personal sense).

Yet, just by spending a few minutes using the Life Priorities Calculator, you would know exactly what success means to you – in all aspects of your life. It might have nothing to do with your job at all. It might relate to your efforts as a parent or a partner, or as a citizen. It might relate to your self-education, or your efforts to teach yourself Irish dancing. Only you can decide.

Once you have decided how you will measure your success, give yourself permission to reject everyone else's notion of what success should be, and then apply 100 percent effort to everything you choose to do.

Then you can be calm.

> **Look for these calm solutions:**
> Life Priorities Calculator .... page 91
> Creative Long-Range Planner ..... page 171
> Undividing Responsibilities .... page 166
> The Power of No .... page 143
> The 100 Percent Effort .... page 159

Take the time to be calm

Take a look around your workplace. Some of your colleagues will always be in a hurry: dashing to meetings, rushing in and out at the last moment, always up against deadlines.

As well as always being in a hurry, such people generally display certain 'hurried' physical characteristics. They speak quickly, breathe quickly, and gesture with short, sharp movements. They fidget, tap their fingers, move from one foot to another, and pat their pockets for cigarettes or gum.

These are the characteristics of a tense person.

The characteristics of a relaxed person are the opposite. They speak slowly, breathe slowly, and gesture with broad, languid movements. They loll about, look out the window, and generally appear to have all the time in the world. (And they probably do just as much work as their tense counterparts.)

Here are a number of ways designed to make you more like that relaxed person.

IDLING

You've heard the expression 'idling'? It mostly relates to car engines when the car is in neutral, and the revs are at the lowest. It is the most relaxed, energy-efficient way for a car engine to operate.

Humans can work that way, too.

Research into work habits has shown that the human body can only work a certain time without rest before performance begins to deteriorate. This time is known as the Rest–Activity Cycle. The average person's cycle is 90 to 120 minutes of activity, followed by 20 minutes of rest. While this ratio varies a little from person to person, and can vary to meet short-term demands, it is a cycle that must be respected. (There are health and performance implications in ignoring this.)

This 20 minutes of 'rest' can be your idling time.

The secret to successful idling time is not to rush to the coffee machine or the cookie barrel, but instead to set about becoming calm and relaxed. You do this by abandoning all your tense attributes of the past 90 to 120 minutes, and then adopting the *superficial* characteristics of a relaxed person. That's all you have to do. Just the superficial characteristics: the pace, the breathing rate, the slow movements, the relaxed speech.

That 20 minutes of physiological slowdown will help you remain calm and relaxed throughout the rest of your working day.

Look for these calm solutions:
Pretend to B .... page 206
Take an Easygoing Break......... page 206
The Sound of Calm .... page 280

Idling

- After 90 to 120 minutes of work, take a calm break.
- Make a conscious effort to slow down all your physical actions. Speak slower, even slower than you think sounds natural. When you move your feet and your hands, force them to move slower and more purposefully. Think about every movement you make. Slow and purposeful. Even slower than you think appears natural.
- Then slow *everything* down.
- Walk slower.
- Think slower.
- Speak slower.
- After 20 minutes of this, you'll be ready to face the rest of your working day.

LOOK FOR A LITTLE STRESS

It is a popular misconception that all stress is bad for you. Some of it is positively good for you. This positive stress – technically known as *eustress* – is the intense feelings that accompany the exciting things in life: a rollercoaster ride, a first date, a job promotion, a team win.

Not only can it make you feel good, but it is extremely beneficial in terms of life enrichment and helping you to relax afterwards.

If you work in an intense, high-pressure job, or if you are naturally inclined to be tense and overly-concerned about your work, you would profit from adding a regular dose of positive stress to your week.

Probably the most enjoyable positive stress happens by windfall. But there are elements you can generate of your own accord. Use the table below as a guide, and do what you can to add some to your life.

Positive stress	Negative stress
You're given an important promotion	You're threatened with retrenchment
You win an important piece of business	You lose an important piece of business
You meet the love of your life, by accident	You have an argument with your colleague
Your football team is just about to score	Your pay cheque bounces
You race your eight-year-old across the park	Your eight-year-old is in trouble at school
You ride the Big Dipper	You get a parking ticket
Your favourite singer appears on stage	You have unspecific worries

5 MINUTES TO LEAVE TOWN

What happens when you've followed all the advice in this book (up to now), you've thrown 100 percent of yourself into your work, you've convinced yourself that you have some degree of control over what you do, and still you feel trapped?

It's reasonable to expect this will happen from time to time. After all, nobody can perform at their peak week in, week out; even the most relaxed people feel under pressure at times.

These are the times to take a break.

You know what a circuit breaker it can be to take a small holiday at the times you need it most – a weekend away, a trip to the mountains, a day at the beach, a stroll in the park. There are times when such a break is essential.

But you can't afford a holiday right now? It's Friday and you haven't planned a thing?

Doesn't matter. You know what it *feels* like to get away on one of those escapades. If you closed your eyes, you'd probably be able to recall what it looked like, as well. Perhaps you could even recall what it sounded like.

With a modicum of effort, all these feelings, sights and sounds can come to your rescue when and as you need them. It only takes 5 minutes to bring them to life – whenever you feel the need.

> **Look for these calm solutions:**
> Breathing Calm ....page 103
> The Plus and Minus Method .....page 198

5 Minutes to Leave Town

1 Enjoy a few minutes of Breathing Calm.

2 When you are relaxed, close your eyes and imagine a huge silver screen before you.

3 Picture the most relaxed environment you can imagine. Probably somewhere you've visited in the past. Totally escapist. Examine it in detail.

4 Now see yourself climbing up into that image. See yourself up there – enjoying the moment, savouring the peace.

5 Note what you can see. Hear all the sounds. Feel the breeze, textures, temperature.

6 When that image is firmly implanted in your mind, take a snapshot (or freeze-frame) of yourself, complete with all those images, sounds and feelings.

7 Relax, and let the positive feelings work their way through your consciousness.

PARK IT

If someone told you that spending 30 minutes wandering through a leafy park or garden by yourself would reverse all the stresses and tensions that tear at you each work day, you'd shrug and say you already knew that.

Everyone knows that. But how many do it?

You have an excuse, of course; there's no such place near where you work. But are you sure? Don't you hate it when a visitor comes to town and, after a few days, points out all the wonderful little places in your suburb or area that you'd never noticed before? Aren't you amazed when you go to meet a friend only two blocks from where you work and suddenly discover a parade of new shops and restaurants?

This is one of the downsides of being such a

hardworking person. We become so engrossed in our insular little lives that we tend to overlook the beauty and comfort that's right beneath our noses.

The Park It technique involves a little search. It means finding a park or similar, somewhere near where you work. You'd be surprised how often such a place is within walking distance – yes, even in the cities.

Then comes the challenging part. You go there for a stroll. Not a work-out, not a fact-finding mission, just a stroll. Soaking up the atmosphere, letting go of your tensions, and just learning to be human again.

Walking in a visually pleasing, oxygen-rich environment like a park has an immediate and measurable effect on your stress levels. If you can manage it once a day you will be a much calmer person.

PLAN A VARIATION

Stress problems have a habit of becoming habitual.

You can break that habit by purposely stepping outside your routine, entering into some new activity – several times a day. It might be as simple as taking a brisk walk around the block instead of having a coffee. It might be a 5-minute meditation on the train, or in the bathroom. It might be 5 minutes of listening to relaxing music on your headphones.

Whatever you choose to do, it should be an unfamiliar activity, a break in your routine.

If you adopt the right approach, a break like this can be extremely beneficial in helping you to become calm.

Look for these calm solutions:
The Sound of Calm .... page 280
Diffusing Anger .... page 230
The Calm Space .... page 287

Secure is a state of mind

As the working world becomes more complex and less predictable, as the value of your expertise fades with time rather than builds (if it is not constantly nourished), it's understandable that insecurity should be on the rise.

It is difficult to feel calm and relaxed if you're feeling insecure.

There is nothing much this book can do to make your job more secure. The fast-changing nature of the world today means that no-one can be truly job-secure for any length of time.

However, you can be emotionally secure. Here, security is nothing more than a state of mind.

ASSUME YOU'RE SECURE

You can have your own custom-designed security-enhancer by using the Basic Assumption Template from page 129. Formulate a small routine to help you feel completely secure and at peace with yourself.

All you have to do is assume you're feeling how you'd like to be feeling. (Pretence is powerful because it *charms* the subconscious into reacting the way you want it to.) It doesn't matter how you are feeling in reality, you just assume you are feeling absolutely calm and secure. Assume you are absolutely confident about your ability to perform and do well in your position. Assume you are in complete control of the situation, and every other situation like it. Assume you're extremely familiar with this feeling of peace and security. Be bold in your pretence.

Then, assume that

Look for these calm solutions:
Basic Assumption Template ......page 129
Pretend to B ....page 206
Take an Easygoing Break.........page 206

others see you the way you are assuming to be. You'll be feeling secure in no time.

SAY YOU'RE SECURE

Remember in the film of *The King and I* how Deborah Kerr urged the children in her charge to 'whistle a happy tune whenever you feel afraid'? It was an effective little appeal to the subconscious to help them overcome fear and insecurity.

Positive affirmations work the same way: by repeating a particular set of words, over and over, you gradually influence your subconscious to take on the instructions in those words. Again, I emphasise that if you choose positive, easygoing words, you will eventually become positive and easygoing.

Here are a couple of word sets you can use to help you feel more secure. I'm sure you can think of others.

I feel complete confidence in my skills and abilities.

I know that I can achieve anything I set my mind to.

I radiate this confidence to all around me.

Or:

More and more, I am relaxing into a state of great peace and calm.

I am feeling content, secure and at ease with the world.

I radiate this peace and calm to all I come in contact with.

Then, use the Basic Affirmation Template to put these words into effect.

Look for these calm solutions:
Basic Affirmation Template ....page 120
A Positive Word ....page 184

DAYDREAM

All our lives we've been told that daydreaming is an indolent, time-wasting and self-indulgent activity. If teachers or disciplinarians can be believed, it is as undesirable as cheating or sloth.

They are completely wrong. Done properly, daydreaming is a positive, enriching exercise that should be actively encouraged in the workplace. All of us should indulge in it from time to time.

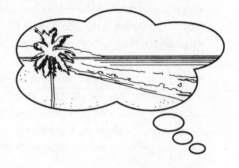

In every efficient person's work cycle there is a period designated for rest. Ideally, this rest will be 20 minutes in duration, and will involve a shift in emphasis from left-brain activity (analysis, logic, language) to right-brain activity (creativity, intuition, emotion).

And what's one of the most accessible right-brain activities? You got it. Daydreaming.

Follow 90 to 120 minutes of work with 20 minutes of daydreaming, and you're well on the way to becoming a calm and efficient worker. Better still, if you can daydream with a certain degree of forethought and intent, you can use it to achieve the things you want to achieve, such as feeling secure in what you do.

Daydream about being calm and secure, and you will feel calm and secure. But, best of all, you already know how to do it.

GET STUFFED FUND

'It's easier for you to be calm,' one of my employees once told me, 'you own the business. You can get by without me, but I can't get by without you.'

While many business owners would strongly disagree with that principle, you can understand her point of view: because she was dependent on her job, she felt she lacked choices. And, when someone lacks choices, they feel pressured.

You may be able to create your own choices.

One of the great tricks of choice creation was taught to me by my business partner prior to launching our first business. Admittedly, this ingenious stress-avoiding ploy is not within the reach of everybody, but, for those who can manage it, it can be very powerful.

He called it the Get Stuffed Fund.

Skimping and saving for the first few months, we put aside a small reserve with a single purpose: so that we always had a choice in who we worked for and what we did. With this fund in place, we believed we would always have choices.

By establishing such a fund for yourself, you can ensure you never feel trapped in your job, and will always be free to leave your employer if the situation warrants – in other words, the decision is yours. The size of the fund is calculated according to the size of the buffer you need between jobs, and by how much you can afford. Whether it's a four-week or a six-month buffer you need to feel secure, you plan accordingly.

Then you'll be the one who has choices.

Now you can become calm ...

WHEN THE CAUSE IS SOCIAL

DIFFICULT RELATIONSHIPS with other people in your workplace – workmates, supervisors, staff, other

> Managing relationships – with equals, superiors and subordinates – is an essential part of work practice.

department representatives – can be a source of great aggravation and distress.

Even if you're the most resourceful diplomat, it's not easy to deal with an authoritarian supervisor, an uncommunicative boss, an uncooperative employee or a spiteful colleague. And it's even harder to get your own way with them.

But there are ways to manage your dealings with other people. And most require a degree of assertiveness.

Assertiveness

It was once believed that the world neatly divided into three distinct personality types: 'assertives', 'aggressives' and 'submissives' (the latter type is generally described as 'passives', which I consider a poor description). While we must acknowledge that these are stereotypes if applied to individuals, they neatly summarise certain behavioural patterns. But these generalisations need not apply to you. Using any number of assertiveness-building techniques, you can train yourself to overcome aggressive or submissive tendencies. You can train yourself to become more assertive.

So what is assertiveness and what can it do for you?

Contrary to popular belief, assertiveness has little to do with having a loud voice, a pushy or domineering personality, or a reputation for outspokenness. In theory, it is nothing more than a determination to achieve certain things that you hold important, and to then stand by your determination. In practice, it is more to do with communication – being clear and forthright about your specific wants, needs or feelings.

You will note from the chart on page 20 how assertive behaviour appears significantly calmer than aggressive or submissive behaviour. Anecdotal evidence confirms this.

Ironically, I have discovered the people who suffer most from being unassertive in the workplace are *not* the submissive types at all (who are usually painfully too aware of their submissive tendencies), but the 'aggressives'. Aggressive types often believe they are being assertive when they are simply being aggressive. Believing they are assertive, yet accomplishing none of the things that assertiveness accomplishes, becomes doubly frustrating for them.

Second to these are the Driven (Type A) personalities

who are, in many cases, also unassertive. When this is pointed out to them, they passionately embrace assertive characteristics, but become frustrated when they do not immediately get their own way on matters. Assertiveness is no guarantee of getting your own way. (I stress once again that these personality groupings help us to understand behavioural tendencies, and should not be used to stereotype individuals, because no one person ever fits a stereotype exactly.)

If you are not naturally assertive, learning how to be more so in the workplace will help you to become calm.

As a result I have devoted quite a few pages to building your assertiveness skills. These won't immediately transform you from a mouse into a lion, but they will support you in times of conflicting opinions and wills, and they will help you to achieve what you believe it is important to achieve.

While you may not always get your own way, find the right words or even get your point across, you will know what it takes to be heard and noticed – and, for many, just knowing this is a step towards becoming calm.

MANAGING DIFFICULT PEOPLE

Trying to control other people in your workplace is a waste of time. And, to be frank, it's a bit impertinent to even attempt it.

Managing *relationships*, however, is an essential part of work practice. Whether your relationships are with equals, superiors or subordinates, the steps to follow are more or less the same.

A caveat is necessary here: even when you follow these steps to the letter, I can't guarantee you will exercise any more influence over others than you did before you read this book. What I can assure you, though, is that these steps will make your occupational relationships easier to endure. And if your objective is to feel calm about what you do, and to get satisfaction from your work, this is the way to achieve it.

The process for managing difficult people is relatively straightforward. But before you attempt it, you need to take three simple steps:

(i)   Decide exactly what you want from your work.
(ii) Make a plan for how you will achieve it.
(iii) Immerse yourself totally in the effort.

To begin with, you need to have determined why you are working in the first place, and what you hope to get out of your job. Depending on the decisions you arrive at, some of the difficult people you encounter will no longer seem important.

Next, use the Creative Long-Range Planner to formulate a plan for achieving your objective. This will take into account the difficult people who are impediments to your objectives.

Finally, immerse yourself in the task ahead.

When you follow these steps, you will suddenly realise that interpersonal relationships take on a new, and less personal, perspective. If, for example, you have decided that your reason for working is to cultivate relationships with people, then you will see a lazy workmate in a different light than if you have decided your purpose is accumulating wealth. Or if you decide your reason for working is to get to the top of the corporate ladder, you may see an ineffectual boss in a different light than if you have decided your purpose is that of being the most reliable employee.

You will quickly realise that the difficult people in your work life now fall into one of three categories:

(i) those who will assist you in what you intend to achieve;

(ii) those who stand in your way; or

(iii) those who don't really matter one way or another.

Those who will assist you should be nurtured. Those who will stand in your way should be circumvented. And those who don't really matter, don't really matter.

Managing Difficult People

- Use the Life Priorities Calculator to determine what you want from your work.
- Use the Creative Long-Range Planner to formulate a plan for achieving this. This plan will take into account the difficult people who may be impediments to your plan.
- Write down your plan.
- Immerse yourself 100 percent in everything you do.
- Reassess your difficult people into those who will assist you in your plan (to be nurtured); those who will always stand in your way (to be circumvented); and those who really don't matter.
- Relax and enjoy your relationships with the less difficult people you work with.

DIFFUSING ANGER

A common reaction to stressful situations is anger. Especially when frustration is involved.

Small children and animals have efficient ways of dealing with anger: they cry, or they physically attack the source of their frustration. Adult reactions, on the other hand, tend to be verbal – and things said in the heat of the moment can often lead to more complex stresses than the original aggravation warranted.

So what is the most expedient way to deal with anger?

You may not be able to avoid feeling angry, but you can lessen the damage it does to you. The way to do that is to head for the door. Walk. Walk quickly, for at least 15 minutes. While you're walking, observe every detail of the street about you.

For the first 10 minutes, your mind will be filled with all the cutting retorts and insults you should have said. The next 5 minutes, though, are where you avoid creating extra stresses for yourself on your return, because the chances are your responses will have moderated in those last 5 minutes. Then, when you return, you'll not say things you regret – at least, not without having weighed them up first.

Getting what you want

One of the most popular words in use by business and government these days is 'competition'. Competition between markets, job seekers, companies, departments and individuals. And as our world becomes more competitive, there is a corresponding pressure on each of us to be assertive in the workplace.

What does this have to do with a book on calm?

For a start, assertive behaviour is more relaxed and easygoing than either aggressive or submissive behaviour. More importantly, though, assertiveness helps overcome one of the dominant causes of frustration in the workplace – having no sense of control over what you do. This is why I devote so much effort to it.

HOW TO GET WHAT YOU WANT

Being assertive does not guarantee you will get what you want. Life would be pretty predictable if it did. However, what assertiveness *does* guarantee you is that others will know what you want – and that is an excellent starting point.

Know what you want

The first step to getting whatever you want in life is one that many people fail to take. It's simply identifying what you want. So much energy, emotion and creativity is wasted on the pursuit of vague, or non-existent, ideals. 'I want to be rich' is a vague ideal. 'I want to have $1,000,000 in liquid assets by the time I turn thirty' is a specific ideal.

Use the planning techniques from earlier in this book to identify the things you want from your work, and to determine how you will achieve them.

Write down your plan of action.

Once you have done this, you will be one step ahead of most of your work colleagues. So, when it comes to being assertive about what you want, knowing what you want is a great place to start.

Know what you can reasonably ask for

It's not easy to make a request if you have no idea of whether it's an acceptable request or not. Just as there is no point trying to stand up for your rights if you don't know what your rights are.

Because the rights that pertain to assertiveness always relate to one person in relationship with another, or to one request that evokes a corresponding answer, they always come in pairs. In no order of priority, some of these rights are:

(i) The right to ask for whatever you want.
(ii) The right to decline anything that is asked of you.
(i) The right to have firm beliefs.
(ii) The right to change your mind.
(i) The right to express your opinions and feelings.
(ii) The right to challenge anything you disagree with.
(i) The right to encourage a relationship.
(ii) The right to privacy.
(i) The right to succeed.
(ii) The right to fail.

To be assertive, you must be aware that each of these rights (along with your other basic human rights) is yours to exploit – and for you to respect in another's case. Know them, use them, encourage others to use them, and stand up for them whenever you feel they are under threat.

Look for these calm solutions:
The Power of No ....page 143
The Nice Way to No ....page 145
Control Only What You Can
Control ....page 163

SPEAKING YOUR MIND

The most fundamental of all rights in the workplace is your right to be assertive. Any manager who would claim otherwise, anyone who claimed to be affronted by someone expressing their opinion or asking for something they believed important, is out of place in today's workplace.

Being assertive, though, is more than just standing up for your rights. It's also about negotiating constructive change, having a constructive say, and initiating positive relationships.

The basic skill of assertiveness is to be able to articulate your request or opinion in a positive, understood way. To do so effectively, follow these three steps:

(i)   Know what you want to achieve.
(ii) Express yourself positively.
(iii) Know when to stop.

Know what you want to achieve

We have covered this in earlier chapters. Use the various planning techniques to decide what you want to get out of your work.

Write down what you want to achieve.

Express yourself positively

Several years ago, a large computer company you know perfected the art of communicating negatively, using the acronym FUD – fear, uncertainty, doubt – to describe its marketing methods. The intent of these tactics was to discourage computer purchasers from choosing any competitor product for fear that something calamitous would arise as a result of the decision. After several years of decline, the company realised negative communications do not pay in the long term.

Ask any advertising authority whether positive or negative communication techniques will achieve your result faster, and they'll tell you positive. (Positive communication is not always as much fun or as colourful for the copywriters, but it generally works faster and is more easily understood.) Any good salesperson will tell you the same. In areas where the deepest levels of persuasion are required – visualisation, affirmation, hypnosis, psychotherapy – positive language triumphs again. Indeed, many believe it is the *only* way to get through on these levels.

Positive language works the same way when you are being assertive. One simple, positive, constructive statement communicates many times faster than any negative one and, more importantly, has a much more positive effect.

So, instead of trying to couch what you say in soft, indirect words – whether to protect your sensibilities or those of your listener – choose a simple, positive statement or request. It works better every time.

Here are a few examples of how it works.

If your approach is negative or aggressive, the response is usually quick and cutting. As you can see in the top figure overleaf, after the response, the subject is closed. So, you either have to start again, or prove that you're not melodramatic – and that can seem melodramatic in itself.

If your approach is indirect and indecisive as in the middle figure, the response can be equally as indecisive.

But if you couch your comments in simple, positive words, asking for some sort of response as in the bottom figure, you're already well into the process of negotiation.

Positive, constructive, straightforward language, that clearly states what's on your mind, is impossible to ignore.

Know when to stop

I don't know whether this is a rule of assertiveness or of simple survival in a competitive world. It's knowing when to stop.

The most powerful weapon that police and auditors the world over have at their disposal is not forensic science or brilliant interrogative skills ... it's the mouth of the person under investigation. Most people don't

The power of positive language

know when to stop when trying to convince or persuade someone else.

Lawyers will tell you there are only four answers to be used when under investigation: 'Yes', 'No', 'I don't know', 'I can't answer that'. Any more will either get you into trouble, or prolong the investigation. (Note that this is a lawyer's perspective, not mine.)

The difference between a good salesperson and an also-ran is seldom how persuasive they are. Any persuasive person can talk you into *almost* buying something. Completing a sale, however, requires something more. It requires silence – with perhaps a little steering. The biggest mistake the also-rans make, is not knowing when to stop selling. Once the proposition has been offered, and responded to, it's time to shut up. Anything you say thereafter usually hinders the sale, rather than helps.

The same applies when you are being assertive. Know what you want to achieve, say what you have to in direct and positive language, then bite your tongue.

I'll give you an example.

Somebody in the office tells you you're fat, and you want them to know how hurtful and insensitive that comment was. (We're assuming here that you're going to use positive, straightforward language.)

Response A: 'I find that very hurtful.'

Response B: 'I find that very hurtful. If you were overweight and someone just blurted out that you were fat, how would you feel?'

Response C: 'I find that very hurtful. When I was thirteen, one of my parents was killed in a car accident, leaving me to fend for my three younger brothers. Naturally I didn't have time to look after my diet . . .'

You see? With Response A, the other person's imagination has to come into play – wondering how much you were really hurt, was it really such an awful thing to say, are they going to get into trouble and so on. Each of your words has an impact.

With Response B, where you made the same comment, but combined it with a reprimand, the other person is preparing their defence against the latter, so your first sentence is already forgotten.

With Response C, the other person is so unimpressed by the verbosity of your response, they're probably thinking up something even more cruel to hit you with when you've finished.

To be assertive, know what you want to achieve, then make your point in positive, straightforward language.

Look for these calm solutions:
Creative Long-Range Planner.....page 171
A Positive Word ....page 184
The Power of No ....page 143

Speaking Your Mind

- Know what you want to achieve. Use planning techniques to determine it. Write it down.
- When making your point, express yourself positively, constructively, concisely.
- Once you have made your point – clearly and positively – bite your tongue. Resist the urge to lecture, complain or soften your meaning.

A 30-SECOND COURSE IN MARKETING

You might well wonder why someone would want to include a course in marketing, even a 30-second course, in a book on being calm at work.

There's a simple reason: marketing, selling and

achieving what you want to at work all share three important principles.

They are:

(i) Base your actions on your 'buyer's' needs.

(ii) Find the positive in what you're proposing.

(iii) Get a response.

As well as helping you get what you want, these principles can also help you to become rich and successful (if that appeals).

In this instance, we are concerned only with the big picture principles, not issues of detail such as pricing, production, positioning (vis-à-vis competition) and so on, each of which have principles of their own.

Base your actions on your 'buyer's' needs

(I use the word 'buyer' here loosely. It could be your client, your customer, your boss – indeed any person that you want to accept your argument or point of view.)

You involve marketing actions when you want somebody else to accept your argument or offer.

To succeed, you must do your planning from this person's perspective. Whenever you have a request, complaint or point of view you want someone else to accept, instead of structuring your argument from your point of view – which almost everyone does – structure it from the other's point of view: 'what's in it for them'.

Say, for example, you want to transfer to another department.

You could come straight out and couch your argument solely in terms of your own needs: 'I'd like to work in sales.'

But such requests are easy to turn down. Much harder to decline is a request that's couched in the *other person's* needs: 'I'd like to prove to you that I could make a massive improvement in our total sales effort.'

Which is easier to agree to? The latter, of course.

The clearer and more compellingly you can present what's in it for them, the closer you will be to getting your own way in the transaction.

Find the positive in what you're proposing

We've dwelt on this a lot in *Calm at Work*. Positive suggestions and language are fundamental to almost every instance where you want to influence behaviour – such as in marketing.

You will find many advertising and marketing people who will argue with this, but they argue out of ignorance. You can't build a marketing success on a negative motivation; it goes against human nature.

'Use our sunscreen or you'll get cancer' will have little effect on the person you are trying to persuade. 'Avoid cancer by using our sunscreen' is much more powerful. Other than in politics, I am aware of very few marketing successes that have been built on a negative proposition. (Even though using reverse psychology or 'knocking' the competition may sometimes work, the marketing intent of these tactics is positive.) Sometimes a market leader will use a negative proposition to diminish the efforts of a competitor, as is often done in politics. Several insurance companies have also tried it – and failed; this is why today's successful insurance companies invariably focus on a positive benefit, such as peace of mind.

If you want to succeed, ensure you have a positive proposition, and make sure you present it in positive language.

Get a positive response

Marketing, like any other form of communication, is a two-way process. It cannot exist without a response from the recipient/receiver/listener.

You must ask for this. It is never sufficient to depend on the sensitivity or intelligence of the other party. You must clearly state the response you require – then wait for it to be delivered. 'Can I assume I have the position, then?'

> **Look for these calm solutions:**
> How to Get What You Want......page 232
> A Positive Word ....page 184

30-Second Course in Marketing

1 Plan your actions, and structure your arguments, according to your 'buyer's' needs and wants rather than your own.

2 Find the positive in what you're proposing. (Present it in positive language.)

3 Design your actions and arguments to elicit a positive response. Then clearly state the response you require.

Use the above three principles in all your workplace negotiations, and you'll stand a much better chance of achieving what you want at work.

THE ART OF NEGOTIATION

The nature of assertiveness is to strive for positive, constructive outcomes. This always involves another party. Unfortunately, this party may not share your vision, or your positiveness, or indeed care for your outcome in any way at all. This is why one of the core requirements of assertiveness is the ability to negotiate.

Now look what I've done: I've given you cause for

alarm. You know there are people who *try* to negotiate, and there are brilliant negotiators. There are even whole firms of specialist negotiators. What hope do you ever have against people like this?

None, of course.

But you won't have to. If your job did involve specialist negotiation responsibilities, you would hopefully have done a bit more preparation than reading a book on how to become calm at work.

In the context of this book, 'negotiation' may mean a combination of the different ways of resolving conflict and of achieving what you want. Such methods could include persuasion (selling), problem-solving ('how can we work together to resolve this issue?'), coercion (not a good idea) and instruction (depends on your position). Negotiation in this sense is not so much deal-making as picking your way through the subtleties of workplace relationships, terms of employment, task and deadline rearrangements, and things like that.

The following five steps are the keys to the personal, relationship-oriented negotiations you will encounter in most areas of the workplace.

The steps are:

(i) Determine your outcome.

(ii) Be positive.

(iii) Let the other person know you're listening.

(iv) Be prepared to offer an incentive.

(v) Be persistent.

Determine your outcome

Yes, it's the same one you've been seeing throughout this book. Use planning techniques to determine exactly the outcome you want from your work, and from every negotiation.

If you have a simple, clear outcome in mind you start with an advantage. Then, knowing what you want to achieve, you commence your negotiation with a proposal that will lead to you achieving this outcome.

Be positive

Simple, positive, constructive language is the most powerful weapon in your negotiating armoury. It communicates faster than any negative approach and it generates a more positive result.

Choose your language carefully – and resist all temptation to be clever, to match wits, or to score points at the other's expense.

Let the other person know you're listening

Professional negotiators will tell you that one of the most powerful skills they possess is the ability to listen.

You might think that if you know what you want to achieve, and are focused on this outcome, the thing you'd most want to avoid is being sidetracked by someone else's opinion or comments. Not so. Ignore your boss's comments, and you'll get nowhere fast. Ignore a colleague's comments, and you will sacrifice all ability to give and take.

Apart from its simple tactical wisdom, listening serves another purpose: it helps to reveal your counterpart's position. This happens particularly when *you* ask questions that cannot be answered with a simple 'yes' or 'no'.

These are the questions that begin with 'how', 'when', 'where', 'why' and 'who'. For example: 'How did you arrive at that conclusion?' 'Why do you think someone else would be as good in the position as I am?'

Asking questions also helps to diffuse the intensity of

the other party's arguments. If they know that each point they make is registering and being acknowledged, there is no incentive to add further emphasis to that point.

Taking it even further, by listening, by being aware of the other party's feelings – expressed or otherwise – you are in the position of being able to address possible obstacles before they even arise.

For example, if you know from someone's tone that they are too preoccupied to want to listen to your opinions, you can pre-empt their 'too busy right now' argument by saying, 'Thank you for taking the time to discuss this. I appreciate how busy you are at this time of the week.'

If you want to maintain the edge in your workplace negotiations, listen. And listen so that the other party knows you are listening!

Be prepared to offer an incentive

Negotiation is the process where you get what you want from someone who wants something from you. Your proposal, therefore, will contain a condition, and an offer.

Your offer will probably fall into one of two areas: a benefit for the other party or a compromise.

A benefit for the other party You've heard the expression, 'win win'. 'You win, I win.' *All* successful negotiations have an element of this in them. There are no exceptions. To be successful, *both* parties must feel they've come away with something and have succeeded to some extent.

Your challenge is to highlight the benefit to the other party if your outcome is realised.

The technique for doing this is known as 'If . . . then'. 'If you . . . then I . . .' For example: 'If you let me have that new computer, then I will be able to perform the work I do for you at a much higher standard.'

Do your homework on isolating these benefits to the other party, and your negotiations will be much more effective.

Compromise The second incentive that every negotiator must have in mind – preferably predetermined – is a compromise. What are you prepared to forgo in order to achieve your outcome?

Successful negotiators always work out what they're prepared to give way on *before* the negotiation begins.

Be persistent

Persistence is a vital part of negotiation. It works best when you've taken the time to figure out what you want to achieve from your work – and *only* after you've taken the time to work out what you want from your negotiation.

Before you begin negotiating, write down what you want to achieve from it. Make this objective as single-minded as you can. The more single-minded you are, the easier it will be to keep referring back to your point – no matter what arguments are raised, no matter what digressions are attempted, no matter how brilliant or skilled at negotiation your counterpart may be.

If your objective can be contained in a simple sentence, it will be difficult for you to be outwitted or outtalked, because all you have to do is return to that one simple sentence, restating what you want until your point is made. (Strictly speaking, this is not negotiation. But in most workplace situations, it can be a very useful tactic.)

The occasions when repetition is most useful are:

(i) When the discussion digresses into irrelevant (or unknown) territory.

(ii) When you are dealing with a skilled or manipulative negotiator.

(iii) When you are dealing with a fool.

(iv) When you lack confidence in your negotiating ability.

(v) When someone is trying to deny you your rights.

Repetition is a blunt tool. It does not lead to elegant conversation. But it will serve you in difficult times. As long as you have taken the time to identify exactly what you want out of the negotiation – before you begin.

Gender generalisations

It's worth making one more point here in relation to the different approaches of men and women to negotiation. While these are generalisations, it pays to be aware of them should they be pertinent in your case.

In conversation, men tend to pronounce and be adversarial; they interrupt, sidetrack, challenge and match input for input.

Women, on the other hand, are more inclined to seek agreement or consensus in conversation; they exchange information (as opposed to giving it), which means they are more skilled at listening.

In negotiation circumstances such as those outlined above, being a good listener can be a distinct disadvantage. If you want to listen, listen to yourself repeat that one simple sentence, returning to it over and over again until your point is made.

(This is simplistic, I know, but being aware of these potential differences can be beneficial if you work in an environment that is dominated by one particular sex.)

> **Look for these calm solutions:**
> Creative Long-Range Planner.....page 171
> A Positive Word ....page 184
> The Power of No ....page 143

The Art of Negotiation

- Determine your outcome. Use planning techniques to work through your strategies. Write down your objective in one simple sentence.
- Use positive, constructive language at all times.
- Let the other party know you're listening, and have some empathy with their point of view.
- Offer an incentive: What is the benefit to the other party if your outcome is realised? What compromise are you prepared to offer to conclude your negotiation? (Work these out beforehand.)
- Be persistent. Keep referring back to the one simple sentence that sums up your objective. Resist all efforts to digress.

CALM SELF-DEFENCE

The last, and perhaps most important, element of assertiveness is knowing how to stand up for your rights.

While the expression 'standing up for your rights' has a degree of combatancy about it, it doesn't necessarily mean being aggressive. It can be purely self-defence to be used against aggressors.

Calm Self-Defence is designed to protect you against such people, without losing your cool. It works just like in jujitsu: you use the other person's aggression or momentum to get your own way.

In a practical sense, the most common needs for Calm Self-Defence in the workplace occur when you are:

(i) defending your rights; and

(ii) dealing with criticism.

Defending your rights

There is a list of your basic workplace rights on page 233. There are many more than this, of course, and they vary from place to place, occupation to occupation.

When your rights are infringed, you have two choices: do nothing, and stew over it; or insist that they are respected. If you want to stay calm, it's best to do the latter and to address the matter before it makes you even more distressed.

The keys to this action are to:

(i) know what your rights are;

(ii) know what you want to achieve;

(iii) express how you *feel* about this infringement;

(iv) avoid criticising the other party; and

(v) bite your tongue.

You are already familiar with (i) and (ii).

The first words you utter should be to express how you *feel* about this infringement of your rights. While you may be dealing in facts, it is more disarming to express them in terms of how you feel. Now your communication is brought into a human focus, and does not become an abstract discussion on the rights and wrongs of certain behaviour.

Explain how you *feel* about this issue. Avoid lecturing, reprimanding or criticising the other party. Then, once you have made the point you want to make, bite your tongue.

No matter how much impact you think you have had, you must leave time for your grievance to register.

Dealing with criticism

Your work life will be much more relaxed and harmonious if you can find a way of dealing with criticism.

When criticism is presented in a negative, rather than a constructive, way we take it personally. When it is positive and constructive, it is easier to deal with. Provided your ego is under control, and you do not suffer too many aggressive tendencies, you may even be able to view constructive criticism as a way of learning and improving.

Dealing with negative criticism takes more effort. As we cannot easily change the carping habits of other people, we are obliged to acquire defensive skills especially for critics in the workplace. I have narrowed these to three basic techniques:

(i)   The Thrust
(ii) The Feint
(iii) The Parry

The Thrust   The Thrust is clearly the most aggressive of these 'defensive' techniques. It does not attack the other party, nor does it criticise or reprimand their behaviour. All it does is challenge their negative criticism, or, in a more subtle way, their right to criticise.

I must stress that the object here is to challenge the criticism – *not* to offer a defence. You want the other party to know you're aware of their tactic and that it is not appropriate, then to put a stop to it. Offering a defence simply justifies your critic's efforts.

The first step is to identify negative criticism. Although you will intuitively recognise it, you will find most negative criticism is shrouded in:

- Generalisation
- Instruction
- Comparison
- Subversion
- Condescension

Here are a few ways of handling negative criticisms. There are millions of other responses and turnarounds you could choose. Use your creativity to develop more.

Method	Criticism	Response
Generalisation	'You always . . .' 'That's typical of . . .'	*Ask for specifics.* 'When exactly did I . . .?' 'What exactly do you base that knowledge on?'
Instruction	'You should . . .' 'Why can't you . . .?'	*Point out your rights as an individual.* 'I may. Then again, I may not.' If you're speaking to someone like your boss: 'What should I do to . . . ?'
Comparison	'If I were you . . .' 'Other people seem to be able . . .'	*Point out your uniqueness.* 'It's important to be an individual.'
Subversion	'Are you capable of . . . ?' 'You may not appreciate . . .'	*Recognise the put-down.* 'I am very aware of my capabilities . . .' 'I always appreciate quality/ intelligence/whatever.'
Condescension	'Someone in your position wouldn't . . .'	*Make them prove their superiority.* 'What is it about my position that . . . ?'

If you recognise negative criticisms as such, and have the presence of mind to respond immediately, do so. But don't feel pressured, you can respond at your leisure – it is always your choice.

For your own peace of mind, though, either respond, or forget the issue altogether – there is nothing to be gained from living it over and over again in your mind.

The Feint This is a disarming technique to use on bosses or superiors as it immediately refers the responsibility back to them to justify their criticism. Be warned, though; it is not a conversation stopper. It invites further discussion, so be prepared for what it could reveal.

Unlike with the previous technique, the Thrust, this one is designed to arrive at a positive, constructive outcome – possibly resulting in you having to modify your performance or behaviour – not to challenge the behaviour of your critic.

Criticism	Response
'Your approach towards teamwork leaves a lot to be desired.'	'What should I do to improve it?'
'It's not the job for you because you're no good at office work.'	'In which way am I not good at office work?'

The Parry Often you will find that the criticism directed at you contains at least an element of truth. The Parry takes this element (or part of it), and reformulates it in a way that *you* find more truthful, or more acceptable.

In other words, you acknowledge part of the criticism, but you modify its scope.

Criticism	Response
'Your work is a disgrace. Your figures are sloppy; you mustn't pay any attention at all to what you do.'	'You're right, they were sloppy yesterday. But you'll find they look better . . .'
'I don't like your attitude to time. You're always late for meetings, and you never let anyone know where you are.'	'I have been late for a couple of meetings. I'm not happy about that so I intend to buy myself a watch.'

The secret to Calm Self-Defence is not to try to change the habits of others, but to shrug off the negativity that they spread. All you have to do is deliver your response, and banish it from your thoughts as soon as you possibly can.

Once you've got it off your chest, you can get on with being calm.

HANDLING HARASSMENT

The preceding segment is ideal for negotiating your way through the day-to-day antagonisms in the workplace. Sometimes, however, more serious strains can arise in the areas of harassment or unfair discrimination.

In the main, harassment is any behaviour that offends, intimidates or humiliates you. Discrimination is any unfair distinction made on the grounds of race, sex, age, disability, belief, marital status or any number of prejudices. Both can be extremely stressful.

Sometimes they are the result of a person or group using power inappropriately over others; at other times power is not an issue. The way in which harassment is manifested can vary from unkind jokes, to comments, to bullying, to outright physical abuse. *In all cases, such transgressions are an abuse of your rights and should not be tolerated in the workplace.*

In many countries, offences of this nature are illegal, and offenders can be prosecuted. In extreme cases, this may be your only course of action. Generally, though, such offences are the result of ignorance, insensitivity or rudeness, and may be resolved in less stressful (for you) ways.

So, what action should you take if you are harassed in your workplace?

In the first instance, you should recognise that it is

your right to expect this behaviour to cease. This is unquestionable. The next steps vary according to the confidence of the victim, the power of the offender, and the severity of the offence.

1. Ask the offender to stop

If you're a confident or assertive type, your very first action should be to ask the offender to stop. Before doing so, firmly state: 'I find [your behaviour] offensive' – so there can be no ambiguity over what you really mean. Then, ask them to stop.

Often the offender will be surprised to hear this. If no offence had been intended, they will appreciate this opportunity to correct their behaviour.

2. Take your complaint further

If, however, the behaviour continues, or if your position or confidence does not allow you to confront the transgressor, your next step is to take the complaint to your supervisor. In many countries, any person in this position is obliged to intercede on your behalf.

If the offender happens to be your supervisor, or in a more senior position than your supervisor, you might consider taking your complaint to one of the following:

- Your supervisor's superior
- The human resources manager
- The general manager
- The chief executive officer
- A member of the Board of Directors (who have very exacting legal obligations)
- A union representative
- Any of the anti-discrimination authorities in your country

These days, anyone in those positions would be likely to treat your complaint seriously.

Handling superiors

I'm going to share a few communication tips with you here that I've borrowed from some of the

> Read this section well. It could be the one that saves your sanity, makes your fortune and wins you your boss's job.

world's most successful corporate players. The people I've taken them from have *all* been major successes. Yet these techniques work equally as well for anyone in the workplace who wants to be heard: from courier to chief executive.

The techniques play no direct role in spreading calm other than helping you to get what you want out of work, and limiting situations that will ultimately cause you stress.

The focus of these techniques is one of your job's major sources of stress. Your boss.

Incommunicative, authoritarian supervisors, department heads and bosses have a lot to answer for in the spread of workplace stress – particularly when it comes to the level of control their subordinates believe they have, or do not have, in their work lives.

One way to overcome this is by having your own ideas and suggestions on how to enhance profits, productivity, efficiency or even your own role. But if your suggestions or requests are ignored, it only exacerbates your frustration and feelings of impotence.

How can you overcome this? How can you control your superiors?

The short answer is, you can't. At least, not with any

degree of success or consistency. All you can ever really depend on controlling is yourself. But if you can control how you relate to those you work for, you can be calm.

THE ART OF BEING HEARD

With a little preparation, you can make the people you work for clearly understand your needs or requirements, and perhaps even assent to your requests.

It's all to do with how you present your argument.

With a few simple skills, you can ensure everyone pays attention while you present your case. With a little forethought, you can ensure your case is presented in the best possible light.

Even if it is the smallest request or suggestion, you want it to be heard, understood and, ideally, acted upon. And unless you are a very powerful individual, this requires preparation.

The following formula applies whether you're making a major presentation or just asking for a pay rise. Get into the practice of using it – *even for the little things* – and you will be surprised at how much attention you can command in your workplace.

There are six important steps:
(i)   know;
(ii) plan;
(iii) rehearse;
(iv) assume;
(v)   ask;
(vi) bite your tongue.

Know what you want

As we have covered many times, the first step to success in any workplace endeavour is knowing exactly what you want to achieve.

Write it down. This will be your starting point.

Plan to be effective

You can spend days, weeks or even longer thinking about and working through some issues, only to have them ignored or dismissed in seconds – because you did not present them succinctly or authoritatively.

So, every important request or suggestion you make should be treated like a mission in its own right.

One of the biggest mistakes ever made in a work environment is to believe others are as interested in your ideas or efforts as you are. Even with your closest colleagues, this is seldom the case.

The second biggest mistake is believing that if you document these ideas or efforts, they will be read. Remember this is the age of 'information overload'; in the workplace, no-one reads anything they don't have to.

No matter what you do in relation to communicating with those above you, the very first step is being noticed. (Being heeded is well down the track.)

To be noticed, you need a strategy.

Present a powerful argument

Using the planning techniques we have already covered, formulate how to *present* your ideas or efforts. Maybe you should get a book on presentation skills from the library: it will be well worth the visit. And, please remember, this is not about the construction of your ideas or thoughts – you will have to use other techniques for that – it's solely about how you present your completed effort.

If you're too busy to go to the library, here's the basic formula for making successful presentations, or just getting yourself heard in any situation:

(i) Tell the 'presentee' at the outset what you expect to achieve from the presentation.

(ii) Present all your arguments with a beginning, a middle and an end.

(iii) If you're making a more formal presentation, use visual aids where possible. When using charts, use simple 6 to 10-word headlines (*never* whole pages of type on overheads or on computer screens).

(iv) Summarise.

(v) Ask for some kind of response.

Rehearse

Now you know why you're going through the process, what you're going to say, the visual aids you will use (if applicable), the summary you will make and, most importantly, the response you will request.

Even if you're a skilled presenter, the next step is vital. You rehearse every step of what you're going to do: every word, every request and, in the more formal presentations, every visual aid. Use whatever assertiveness skills you can.

This is not simply practice for the sake of practice. It's for conviction. Because if there's one thing more important than what you present, it's *how* you present it. If you know what you're talking about, and present it with conviction, everything else will take care of itself.

Assume

You know what you're going to say, you know how you're going to say it, and you've rehearsed the lot. Now you have one more thing to do: assume the character of an authoritative, achievement-oriented employee who is totally confident about their recommendations.

Use the Basic Assumption Template to achieve this. And remember the last part of it: to assume that others see you the way you are assuming to be (this is more for your benefit than theirs).

Now you are ready to convince or influence the authority figure in question.

Ask

Most presenters will go to all the trouble we have just outlined, then falter at the last moment. They do this firstly because they believed their argument or sales pitch was so compelling that no-one would be able to resist it; and, more importantly, because they did not tell the 'presentee' how they were meant to respond.

Even after having read that, I know the majority of presenters will still falter at this moment: they will not ask for the response they seek.

You must ask for some sort of response.

I will repeat that: YOU MUST ASK FOR SOME SORT OF RESPONSE. Your 'presentee' must be in no doubt what you are asking of them. They must have a clear, unambiguous picture of how you want them to respond following your presentation.

Bite your tongue

This is the one piece of advice that, in my experience, is overlooked by many of the great presenters. Good salespeople use it intuitively. I first became aware of it in the seventies in negotiations with senior Japanese businessmen (always men). Whether they meant it as a negotiating technique or it was just a confluence of circumstances, I have no idea. All I know is it worked. It worked for them and it will work for you.

It's silence.

After you have asked for whatever response you require, sit down, shut up and bite your tongue. No matter what temptation you feel to elaborate, to correct any possible misimpressions, to ingratiate yourself with your boss, bite your tongue and say nothing.

Even if the pause goes on for minutes (which some negotiators are good at), continue to bite your tongue. Because the onus now is on whoever speaks next.

You might believe that people in powerful positions are above this sort of manipulation. They're not. They're human beings. If someone makes a request of them that demands an answer, they will feel compelled to answer. (This is not to say they won't overcome the compulsion; but it will be there.) And, even if you don't get the response you ask for, their discomfort will still have the effect of making them take notice of your request.

> **Look for these calm solutions:**
> Creative Long-Range Planner.....page 171
> Basic Assumption Template......page 129
> How to Get What You Want......page 232

Slipstreaming

Until now, everything I've written about has required a degree of effort from you. For this section we'll take a little break and make life easier. Passive calm, if you like.

If you've watched much car or bike racing, you'll be aware of a technique known as 'slipstreaming'. It's when you manoeuvre your car or cycle into the slipstream (or forward air current) of the vehicle in front so that it expends all the energy, and you get a free tow in the slipstream of air following it.

Such a thing is also possible with calm.

MODELLING CALM

There's a psychological technique that's been in use for decades called 'modelling'. Generally, it's used for modifying behaviour and teaching new skills, as well as treating conditions such as fear and phobia.

In recent years, modelling has become popular in

sports psychology and various schools of psychotherapy. It is sometimes combined with hypnosis to intensify its power.

Modelling is as straightforward as its name suggests. You choose a role model, and you emulate how this role model performs under certain conditions. So, if you want to improve your golf swing, you might 'model' a successful golfer you see on videotape. Similarly, if you're a nervous, insecure clerk, you might 'model' a calm, confident, eloquent executive. (Method Acting, which rose to such prominence in the sixties, was a form of modelling.)

To do this successfully, you have to do more than copy the actual swing of the golf professional on television or the vocabulary of the executive in the corner office. You must copy *every aspect* of the person.

You note the way they breathe. You note the pace at which they speak. You note the way they fold their hands, and cross their legs. You note the way they move. And you concentrate on these seemingly unimportant details – not the golf swing or the vocabulary. Then, when it comes to making your golf swing, your subconscious puts together all the pieces so you execute the movement exactly as your role model would have done! It is your subconscious that does the work, not your conscious mind.

If you can find a calm role model, this is one of the fastest and most streamlined ways to become calm. Your role model spends a lifetime learning how to become calm and peaceful, and you come along and hijack all the benefits of their knowledge with only a few minutes' concentration.

Look for these calm solutions:	
Breathing Calm	page 103
Basic Visualisation Template	page 118
Basic Assumption Template	page 129
Pretend to B	page 206
Assume You're Secure	page 222
Watchless Pretence	page 133

Modelling Calm

1 Choose a role model who is the epitome of calm.

2 Closely observe every detail of this person.

3 Go somewhere quiet and enjoy 5 minutes of Breathing Calm.

4 When you are relaxed, close your eyes and imagine your role model on a huge silver screen.

5 Note how they breathe, the rhythm of their speech, the way they fold their hands, the way they walk and move.

6 When you have a clear image of how this role model looks and behaves, put yourself in their place, with exactly the same mannerisms and behaviour. (Your subconscious will fill in the details.)

7 Now, as you go about your normal business, assume that you are exactly like the person you imagined. Move like that calm person, speak like that calm person, act like that calm person.

8 Then assume that others see you the way you're assuming to feel.

CONSORT WITH THE CALM

I have to apologise for this. What I am going to advise is not particularly charitable, and not necessarily even fair. But it's an easy way to become calm and stay that way.

All you have to do is mix with calm people. Calm is catching, just as tension is. Mix with calm people, and you will be calm. Mix with Easygoing personality types, and you will pick up Easygoing traits. Conversely, keep your distance from the highly-stressed and, if you tend to have a Driven personality, stay away from these types as much as you can.

Look for these calm solutions:
How Susceptible Are You? .... page 12

Pretend to B .... page 206

Take an Easygoing Break .... page 206

Make Fun of Work .... page 208

Once you're calm and relaxed, you can go about spreading calm among your more tense colleagues.

UNDER THE INFLUENCE OF CALM

Here is a slipstreaming method where others use *your* slipstream; where they pick up on your sense of calm and adopt it for themselves.

What am I saying? Here you are reading a book on how to become calm at work, and I'm suggesting others follow your calm example. What is this man on?

This is a beautiful little technique that works in co-operative environments like meetings and team projects. It has the double effect of helping you to become calm, then, in turn, helping others to follow your example.

Have you ever noticed how easy it is for one anxious, hurried or angry person to quickly spread that feeling of unease throughout a group? All it takes is one uptight person to make a whole room tense. One angry person can inflame a room full of people.

There is justice in the world, however, because the converse of this is also true: a calm person can spread calm almost as easily as a tense one can spread tension. Just as you can soothe a distressed child by speaking softly, you can appease a tense or angry adult by breathing easily, speaking slowly and appearing totally calm. All it takes is one person exhibiting the characteristics of someone totally at ease and relaxed (use the Calm Assumption Template to do this), and you'll have the whole room following your example in no time.

This works even more dynamically if you slightly exaggerate your calm characteristics. Slow down your speech even more than you think sounds calm. Slow down your breathing and your movements, similarly. Only you will notice the exaggeration, and you'll be surprised how quickly this calm pace begins to take over.

(If there is a calm person and a very tense person in the same room, the results are less predictable. Probably, the tense person will be more aggravating, so is likely to have the greater influence. But, if you work at it, at least you can remain calm while the rest of the room goes to pieces.)

A calm postscript

Often when I speak about this technique to business groups, I get a strange response: 'We don't want a calm room, we want people active, firing on all cylinders, pumped up and ready to go.' Can't you just imagine some people saying that?

I can assure you that in every single case where that comment was made to me, it was delivered by a tense, troubled person – a spreader of tension.

You don't need adrenaline to be inspired. All you need is motivation. And motivation comes from calm just as effectively as it comes from pressure.

Look for these calm solutions:
Pretend to B .... page 206
The Sound of Calm .... page 280

Now you can become calm ...

WHEN THE CAUSE IS CHANGE

Today, the only thing you can be absolutely certain of in your job is change. Change is going to happen, although you don't know how it's going to happen, and when it happens it will shake up all your comfort zones.

> There was a huge outcry at the introduction of the electric refrigerator (some claimed it would cause things like cancer and infertility). Similar claims arose with the introduction of television, the microwave oven, the colour monitor and digital phone. The unknown invariably provokes fears.

And you can't do a thing to prevent it.

The variable in this equation is not whether you can influence change, but how you will react to it.

The normal reaction to an upset in the status quo is to feel insecure and tense – even when the status quo means maintaining something distasteful. The prospect of loss blinds most of us to the possibility of gain. Nothing new here: change has always aroused our fears. Many predicted the collapse of society as they knew it at the advent of the Industrial Revolution. There were similar fears when the locomotive made its debut. It happened again when electric power became widespread, and still later when cheap oil and the automobile changed the face of transport. And, contrary to the expectations of millions, civilisation did not come to a grinding halt when women won the right to vote.

In retrospect, each of those changes brought positive improvements to our world. And all but the most mean-spirited would have to agree they have changed our lives for the better.

We have better medical services, aeroplanes that are many times safer than the horse and buggy, better disease control in today's slums than in the high street of yesterday, cheap communications with friends and loved ones ... the benefits are endless. Even changes that are affecting our work lives – the new emphasis on competition and the dependence on information technology – have many benefits.

In addition to that, our living standards are rising faster, and our corporations are more open, accountable and employee-conscious than at any other time in history. Care for the environment is at an all-time high – yes, higher than at any other time in history. Our life expectancies have almost doubled in just a few centuries. In most countries, despots are not tolerated; racism is frowned upon; slavery is banished; we elect our politicians; and women have the same opportunities as men ... hey, there's a lot to be said for change.

And, every bit as evident, change has also been to our benefit in the workplace. Airconditioning instead of temperature extremes; carpeted floors instead of greasy wood or stone; jackhammers instead of picks, and forklifts instead of slipped discs; fast word processors instead of having to retype with every alteration; instant communication instead of ignorance; and enough regulation to ensure you never have to endure physical, emotional or moral discomfort again.

Why, then, are we so down on change? For a start, we've been too exposed to the militant change-haters. They've been praising the past and bleating about the evils of change since nine-year-olds were banned from the coal mines; and they are, in the main, forces of negativity. Whether they be journalists, politicians, ferals or clergy, they lack creativity and contribute little to society. They deserve to be ignored.

Take a positive view of change, and the benefits will ultimately apply to you. Recognise that you cannot have growth without change. Embrace change for the good it can bring. Strive to make it work for *your* benefit, for the improvement of your life, work and well-being. Strive to make change for the better.

Then you'll be calm about change.

THE CHANGE LIST

I'd love to tell you everything is wonderful in the world, but it doesn't mean much if you're not going to believe it. After all, if you don't feel everything is as rosy as it is made out to be, then as far as you're concerned, it ain't rosy.

This is why the following exercise is an essential for anyone who cannot overcome their apprehension about the rate of change going on in the world.

The purpose of this exercise is simply to determine whether change itself is, or is not, a benefit in your life. Having established this one way or the other, you can then work on your apprehensions knowing whether they are, or are not, without substance.

To perform it, all you need is a pencil and a sheet of paper.

Draw a line down the centre of the page then place a '+' in the left column, and a '−' on the right.

Under the '+' write down all the benefits you have derived as a result of change over the course of your life. (If you can't think of any, start with the list at the beginning of this chapter.)

Then, on the '−' side of the page, write down all the negatives that change has brought during the same time period. If you're like most people, you'll have roughly the same number on either side.

But that was only Step One.

Now, delete all the changes on the '−' of your page that are the result of normal human growth. Delete the reference to your daughter leaving home at eighteen. Delete the reference to a marriage problem resulting from ten years of *no* change. Delete any reference to your income tax rising, or the cost of living rising (in real terms, they are not rising to any degree). Delete the reference to your expanding waistline. Delete all references to things resulting from growing older. Delete references to all those generalised complaints (for example, decline in family values) that have always existed, but you didn't know they were so prevalent until the advent of the mass media.

And, if you're honest with yourself, guess what you'll be left with? Mostly '+', with very little '−'. (If, however, your imbalance is the other way around, go searching through the other techniques of this book, and you'll find the answer you're looking for.)

I can't guarantee that this understanding will immediately make you feel calm, but at least it can take some of the fear out of change.

Look for these calm solutions:
The Plus and Minus Method .....page 198
Pamper Yourself..................page 313

The Change List

1 Draw a line down the centre of a page. Place a '+' on the left column, and a '−' on the right.
2 On the left, under the '+', list all the changes that have taken place in your life that have made life better.
3 On the right, under the '−', list all the changes that have taken place in your life that have made life worse.
4 Now, delete all references in the '−' column to the things that are the result of normal human growth. Then delete all generalised complaints.
5 Review your list and assure yourself that change really can improve life, and is not to be feared. All you have to do is make change work for you.

NEVER TOO OLD TO BECOME CALM

You may think it's easy for someone of my years to write essays about the benefits of change. But what about the over-fifty-fives? Often the most vulnerable people in the workplace, how do they survive all this upheaval?

Many believe that one of the disadvantages of getting older today is the insecurity that begins to creep up on you between the age of fifty or so and retirement.

'I'm too old to learn something new.' 'I've spent years building my expertise; it's too late to develop new skills now.' 'If anything happens to my job, I'm stuffed; no-one hires fifty-five-year-olds.' 'What they want is the young and inexperienced; they're cheaper and easier to train.'

You've heard all these comments, probably even used a few yourself. And, as far as insecurities go, they have no more substance than those of any seventeen-year-old. Maybe even less.

In these times of ever-increasing lifespans, the old notion of 'work to sixty-five and retire' is fast becoming an anachronism. So much so, that many now refer to the Third Age of Employment – the new careers, the new opportunities that are being discovered, *after* the age of fifty-five, for the most fulfilling career phase of them all.

I know many such people. A close friend started writing at fifty-six and is today one of the world's largest-selling authors. Another friend is sixty-seven and is headed the same way. I know a woman who left a powerful executive position to study naturopathy; today she has a dedicated clientele and is doing famously. I know many who have gone back to university. I can tell you about a fascinating seventy-five-year-old, who was 'too old' to work in an office, yet is now booked solid by corporations with commissions for his 3-tonne marble sculptures. And, closer to home, I recently employed two potential retirees in their sixties to help train our youngsters; they've since become two of our most productive team members.

Age is no barrier to new challenges and successes.

If you're in this age group, and feel pressured by the circumstances I have just described, you can feel heartened by the number of new opportunities that are unfolding by the second. Forget what you hear about unemployment statistics: with longer lifespans, an aging population, and an insatiable desire for improved leisure and entertainment, the opportunities will continue to grow – if you are open to them.

These opportunities will mean much from personal growth and job satisfaction points of view. Maybe now is the time to brush off your ambition and start planning a glittering new career for the next stage of your life ...

Look for these calm solutions:
Life Priorities Calculator .... page 91
Creative Long-Range Planner ..... page 171
The 100 Percent Effort .... page 159
Permission to Reject Success .... page 214

A CHANGE FOR THE BETTER

So far in this section we've concentrated on the problems that arise, or are feared, from too much change. Now I want to draw your attention to an even greater problem: that of too *little* change.

You've heard the story of the tiger that paced its tiny cage, backwards and forwards, year after year. Finally, some kindly souls arranged for it to be moved to more humane surroundings with grass, trees, water and space. The only trouble was the animal could not relate to its larger, more natural world, and continued to pace backwards and forwards over the same cage-sized strip.

People get like this in the workplace. They become habit bound, locked into an ever-decreasing spiral of experience and outlook. This is as stultifying and unproductive as it is stressful.

A Change for the Better encourages you to broaden your perspective in a deceptively simple way. All you have to do is look for new ways of performing your everyday duties and work functions. By exploring these differences, you break stressful habit cycles, and you'll be surprised how effective these innocuous little routines can be in reducing tension. Here are a few ideas.

(i) Next time you're having a hard day, instead of going to the sandwich shop on the corner again, walk a couple of blocks and get your lunch from somewhere new. Observe the people and places you pass on the way: note how different life can be only a short distance from your work.

(ii) At the end of a tense work day, instead of taking the same monotonous trip home that you do every day, try a different route. Doesn't matter if it's longer. Pay attention to the streets you pass, the different character of the buildings. Note the activities of the street.

(iii) If you normally travel to work by car, take the bus one day. If you normally take the bus (and you're within range), use your feet. While you walk, observe the features of the houses and the looks on the faces of passing pedestrians – the sort of things you would never pay attention to under usual circumstances.

(iv) If you're a neat, orderly person, start work an hour early to set up a new filing system.

(v) If you tend to be an untidy person, start work two hours early to set up any sort of filing system.

(vi) If you always stop at 10.00 a.m. for coffee and crackers, switch to peppermint tea and fruit (this has a double benefit). Savour every bite.

The most important thing is that you purposefully break your routine, and then absorb all the details that accompany such a change. In doing this, you counter the effects of stress by broadening the perspective of your life, by taking the time to see and experience the bigger picture. By expanding your experiences, you expand your world. And by expanding your world, your everyday problems will seem smaller and less threatening.

Ideally, you will do this several times a day. Even if it's only for half an hour on the way home from work, it's a cheap and simple way of getting off the treadmill and escaping the stresses of everyday life.

Look for these calm solutions:
Plan a Variation...................page 221
Look for a Little Stress...........page 218

Now you can become calm ...

WHEN THE CAUSE
IS PHYSICAL

YOU HAVE READ that the most common cause of stress is what happens inside your head, rather than what happens to

> Some of the most pleasurable ways to become calm and relaxed are physical, and physical solutions are usually the answer to physical problems.

your body. This is why many of the techniques we have covered so far have been designed to influence the attitude, emotions and subconscious.

Yet some of the most pleasurable ways to become calm and relaxed are physical. In addition, physical solutions are usually the answer to physical problems.

So, what are these physical problems?

One hundred years ago, factors relating to the physical nature of the workplace would have been at the top of your list: noise, dangerous work conditions, uncomfortable accommodation, poor lighting and ventilation. These physical factors would have been supplemented by environmental factors such as heat, cold and damp.

For most of us today, pampered by our strict workplace regulations and our carpeted, airconditioned offices, these conditions seem remote and uncommon. Yet our workplaces can still be extremely stressful.

Today's physical causes of stress may seem benign by comparison, but they can be just as damaging. Those who work on today's production line, in hospital casualty, and in the foundry probably have physical stresses every bit as unwelcome as workers in the eighteenth century. Those who work in front of computer monitors all day probably have similar complaints to those who slaved over our forefathers' ledgers. And those who stand behind today's serving counter often suffer the same discomforts that shop assistants have always suffered.

One advantage you have today is that you can find a solution to your discomfort in a book like *Calm at Work*.

Calm the building

You've no doubt heard references to 'sick building syndrome', where the building itself is blamed for the malaise of the people who work there. Often, whether the building is sick or not, this is a real condition.

There has been quite a lot of research done on this phenomenon, some of which is worth reporting. In most cases, there was no evidence that the building itself was to blame. A few cases were really the result of chemical or fungal poisoning, while airconditioning systems – particularly older systems – were the culprit on other occasions; these were easily (albeit expensively) remedied.

Another suspected cause was the low frequency rumble of some airconditioning systems. In experiments we perform with music at the Calm Centre sound laboratory (cclab@netspace.net.au), low frequencies are used to entrain brainwave patterns so as to induce certain behaviours. By employing certain musical frequencies, we can arouse, stultify, induce lethargy, or even produce trancelike states in the listener. Most of these experiments take place in the 5 to 12Hz range, which is precisely the frequency range of some airconditioning systems. So a building's airconditioning system emitting the right low-frequency rumble could effectively induce any one of those states (arousal, drowsiness, lethargy, trance) in any person working there.

But the most widespread reported cause of discomfort was fluorescent lighting. You may not consciously see it, but fluorescent lights produce their brightness via a series of high-speed flashes or flickers. In countries with 50 cycle (Hz) electricity supplies (Europe, Australia, parts of Japan), these flickers occur at 100 flashes per second. In countries with 60Hz electricity supplies (USA and parts of Japan), they flash 120 times per second. At 100 flashes per second, some people's visual capabilities, and possibly even their equilibrium, are impaired. There's more than one reason why office fluoros are ugly things.

KILL THE FLUORO

Whether you believe you work in a sick building (unlikely) or not, you can improve your health and your tension levels by performing a small modification to your fluorescent lights.

Turn them off!

If you can't turn them off, get someone to remove the tiny starter cylinder which attaches near the end of the bulb. (For safety reasons, get an electrician to do this – even though it is a very simple procedure.) Removing the starter will stop the bulb from lighting. Instead, get yourself a regular, incandescent desk lamp.

In my experience, building maintenance people will replace this starter about three times before they realise you are having them removed. Then they'll probably take the easy way out and leave you in fluorescent-free peace.

Kill the fluoro and you'll be calmer for having done so.

THE IONS OF CALM

In the moments preceding and following electrical storms, the air becomes charged with wonderful little particles known as negative ions. On hot, windy days, when the breeze crosses large expanses of dry earth, the air is filled with positive ions – which some believe accounts for the increase in violence and madness on such days.

Negative ions freshen the air, assist your breathing and induce a feeling of calm and energy at the same time.

There are two reasons why they have a soothing, calming effect: the first is that they have a direct influence on mood because they stimulate the production of *serotonin*, which is the neurochemical that relaxes, overcomes depression and produces slow-wave sleep; the second is that they cleanse the air, as airborne dust particles become electrically charged and fall to the ground. (This is why recording studios and computer rooms install commercial ionisers to protect their sensitive equipment from dust.)

A simple, low-cost negative-ion generator, or ioniser, works wonders for countering the excess of *positive* ions generated by your computer monitor, fluorescent lighting and other electronic office equipment.

Simply plug one in and you'll soon find it easier to breathe – the air will seem cleaner, almost cool to the 'touch'. You will find these conditions to be refreshing, mood-enhancing, even uplifting.

Turn one on, and you'll thank me for this suggestion every day.

Calm the Building

- Have the tiny starter cylinder removed from your overhead fluorescent lights. Now you'll be in the dark.
- Install a regular, incandescent desk lamp (or lamps) to provide your lighting.
- Now enjoy being calmer and more healthy than you would otherwise.
- Consider installing an ioniser, or negative-ion generator.

TURN OFF THE NOISE

Silence is one of the great pathways to calm. If you've ever been to a place that is truly silent (under water, in the desert, in a sound-proof room) you will appreciate just how conducive it really is – after the initial discomfort of experiencing silence for the first time.

Once you begin to appreciate that silence is not so much an absence of sound as a presence of peace, you soon learn to revel in this wondrous state. This is why so many of the techniques mentioned in this book work better if you can perform them in silence. If you want to be peaceful, if you want to relax, go searching for silence. Absorb it, immerse yourself in it, hang on to it as long as possible.

But how can you find silence in a busy workplace?

Surprisingly, it is not at all difficult. You can find silence in the noisiest of places simply by performing the Breathing Calm routine, and by concentrating on the sound of your own breathing. Even in a rowdy office, even with a heavy rock band bending your eardrums, you can hear the sound of your own breathing – *if you concentrate on it.*

After you have done this a few times, once you can hear that sound, you will be well on the way to finding silence.

Look for these calm solutions:
Breathing Calm ....page 103
The Calm Space ....page 287
The Sound of Calm...............page 280

CREATE YOUR OWN SPACE

Confine a group of rats to too small a space and they'll gradually go mad and start killing each other. All animals and humans require a degree of space in which to thrive and remain peaceful. The less space, the more stress.

Since the eighties, the trend in office design has been to reduce the allocation of space for each employee. Hence, in the last decade or so, we've seen increasingly more people working in decreasingly less space. As office rents become more expensive, and as technology shrinks the size of machinery and tools, this trend will continue – a recipe for escalating workplace stress if ever you could design one!

Space is a conduit to calm. That's why it is easier to find calm from a position of spaciousness: in the centre of a room rather than the corner; away from the crowd rather than in the middle; in the open park rather than the crowded elevator.

So what can you do if you find the space that's been allocated to you is shrinking, and that your colleagues are moving closer by the day?

Obviously, there are physical things that can be done about it. The more compact your tools or work utilities, the greater the feeling of space you will enjoy. Space-creating qualities can be found in small footprint computers, typist chairs rather than executive thrones (choose the former), computer networks rather than stand-alones, electronic filing rather than cabinets, and wall shelves rather than desk real estate.

However, the real space-maker in your work area has nothing to do with any of these physical things: it's to do with what's in your mind. The more you can focus on the work you are doing, the less aware you will be of any intrusions on the surroundings in which you work. (Imagine how thrilled your boss would be to read this.)

To really focus on the tasks at hand, with an intensity that you've probably never managed before, you follow two steps.

The first is Breathing Calm. In doing this, you search for the silence within yourself. Focus on the sound of your own breath as it comes and goes, and the pressures and intrusions of the rest of the world will recede. After a few minutes of this, you will find yourself in your own world: calm, relaxed, and ready to transfer your focus to your work.

The next step is one you also know well. It's applying 100 Percent Effort to every task you do. Once again, this is a process of concentration, where you apply yourself to a single task at a time giving it your total effort, savouring every second and absorbing every minute detail of it. The net effect of this is that your world becomes the task at hand – which is calming, relaxing and a highly effective way to work. It also has the effect of de-emphasising all the other things around you.

By concentrating on these two techniques you could work in a shoe box, and still feel like you had all the space in the world.

> **Look for these calm solutions:**
> Breathing Calm .... page 103
> The 100 Percent Effort .... page 159
> The Sound of Calm .... page 280

Create Your Own Space

- Enjoy 5 minutes of Breathing Calm. Listen to the sound of your breath coming and going. Let this sound fill your consciousness until you feel calm and highly focused. After a few minutes, you will find yourself in your own relaxed world.
- When you are relaxed, apply the 100 Percent Effort to your work. Do only one thing at the one time. Commit to it as thoroughly, conscientiously and skilfully as you can.
- Try to exclude all external stimuli such as radio or conversation.
- Continue in this way until you are totally absorbed by what you are doing, until the task just 'does itself', and you feel calm, relaxed and at peace.

De-stressing the workplace

Some work environments seem to be perpetually tense places. Casualty departments of hospitals, tight-deadline newspaper offices, classrooms in difficult schools, crowded government departments – the list goes on.

The techniques for becoming calm should be the same from one place to another; however, the task is made more difficult by the surroundings.

If others will agree to it, a few simple de-stressing techniques can have a profound effect on your workplace. They are not designed to numb or placate, simply to ease the nerves and so enhance the working environment for each and every person who works there.

THE SOUND OF CALM

You know from experience that music can have a powerful effect on the emotions. Fashion-oriented workplaces where rock music plays all day, such as hairdressing salons and dress shops, set out to produce an ongoing state of excitement and arousal. Often, this causes major stress problems for their employees. (Some believe passive listening can be just as toxic as passive smoking.)

Music, however, can be as calming as it is stimulating. If used sensibly, it can have a calming effect on an entire workplace. When I recommend this, I often get disparaging grumbles about 'elevator music', and the bland intrusiveness it can have. But the type of music that I write about is about as far removed from 'elevator music' as the music of the Smashing Pumpkins is from Shostakovich.

Therapists have long known that music can cause a variety of physiological changes in a listener, not only in the obvious areas of heart beat and breathing rhythm, but in galvanic skin response, blood pressure, hormone levels, immune response and brainwave activity – it can even help in overcoming some learning disabilities. The fact that certain frequencies or cycles can draw you into a state of relaxation (alpha rhythms) or trance (delta) is common knowledge. But these frequencies or cycles cannot easily be produced, have no audible pitch, and are far from what you'd call music.

Theoretically, you could play these tones over an office PA system and send everyone to sleep. Or wake them up. But you wouldn't make them happy: that requires a level of musical talent which researchers seldom possess. (At the Calm Centre we have overcome this by teaming talented 'calm' composers, such as the *shakuhachi* grand master, Riley Lee, with technical experts – thus producing brilliant music that makes listeners feel calm, yet alert: a necessity in the workplace. If you're curious, you can hear some of this on our web site, http://www.calmcentre.com)

This is not to suggest that other forms of music would not succeed as well. Perhaps a Debussy *nocturne* or one of Chopin's. Or any number of contemporary pieces, as long as they have no lyrics. Whatever you choose, it must be able to achieve its calming effect at the lowest possible volume. Then it can work without distraction, or while being barely noticed by the listener.

Look for these calm solutions:
Listen to http://www.calmcentre.com
Consort with the Calm............page 262
Modelling Calm..................page 260

THE SCENT OF CALM

One of the most sensual ways to spread calm in the workplace is through the use of essential oils. While you need to be sensitive to how different scents perform in different circumstances and conditions – for example, I feel some oils have a heavy effect in humid weather – in the main you can choose your oil combinations from the table on page 204.

Use them in combinations of no more than three. Choose them according to the effects you wish to create, and to their appeal to your nose.

Here are some of the more unusual characteristics of oils you may wish to consider:

- Orange and clary sage are said to improve communications.
- Basil and lemon are said to increase mental clarity for decision-making.
- Ylang ylang is said to relieve anger.
- Pine is as you would expect: it provides a refreshing, inspirational touch for stuffy environments.
- Bergamot is the calming and uplifting scent you will recognise in Earl Grey tea and eau de Cologne.

Your challenge is to determine the combinations that have the correct balance of calming and mood-enhancing. You can afford to trust your instincts on this, because you're dealing with the subtleties of your emotions.

Probably the simplest way to use oils is with a ceramic vaporiser. Fill its shallow dish with warm water, then add a few drops of oil (the better quality the oil, the fewer drops required), place a small candle beneath the dish and light it. Then relax and enjoy the experience.

Burning oils in this way will have a definite calming effect on you and those around you.

Look for these calm solutions:
Using Your Nose .... page 201
The Calm Space .... page 287
Sensuous Stress Reliever .... page 299

A SIP OF CALM

Let me paint you an absurd picture.

Imagine you had a workplace full of stressed individuals, with deadlines encroaching, tensions rising, tempers flaring. At a defined time each day, you are required to take a specific action to ease the tensions and help those around you unwind. But ... the only ingredients you are given to achieve this are:
- processed flour (saps the energy);
- refined sugar (briefly elevates the mood then depresses);
- saturated animal fats (depressing, unhealthy);
- artificial preservatives (have all sorts of negative effects);

- caffeine-intensified beverages (increase tension, promote feelings of unrest); and
- maybe a smattering of nicotine (up, down, addictive) to cap it off.

You wouldn't choose such a silly group of ingredients in a million years, would you? But this is what happens several times in every working day with ... the coffee break.

Here are some calm alternatives which, if you leave them lying about, will quickly supplement the everyday coffee and cookie routine. (As they are non-addictive, their habit-forming ability depends on the effort you put into making them so.)

And, over and above the fact that they substitute for a more harmful product, most have a calming or other benefit as well.

Tension producer	Calm substitute
Coffee	Herbal tea Dandelion 'coffee' Caffeine-free tea Green tea (unsweetened) Water decaffeinated coffee
Tea	Peppermint or any of the herbal teas Chamomile tea Rosehip tea All sorts of new fruit teas Hot water with lemon Cool water
Cookies	Fresh fruit Wholemeal bread Raw vegetables
Commercial snack foods	Fresh fruit Dried fruit Nuts (in moderation)
Cola	Cold spring water Mineral water Pure fruit juices Mostly pure fruit juices
Tobacco	Oxygen

Wherever possible, avoid the quick uplifters: coffee, soft drinks, sugar and fat-laden snack foods. While these may elevate your mood momentarily, you will feel tense and lethargic soon after.

If you need a fast dose of calm, avoid stimulants like the plague. Instead of coffee, have a herbal tea or a glass of water. Instead of throwing yourself into the nearest group or conversation, take a couple of minutes outdoors to unwind.

A word about tea

We tend to lump tea and coffee into the same unwholesome category, but there are some positive health benefits to be had from regular tea. While it does contain significant amounts of caffeine, which is devoid of benefits, it has other properties which are believed to have possible benefits in preventing major diseases like cancer and heart conditions. So, maybe there are worthwhile benefits in substituting tea for coffee (still in moderation, though).

In addition to regular tea there is a blossoming range of herbal teas. I often hear, 'yuk, I can't drink that herbal stuff' – an opinion you can be sure was formulated in the old days when chamomile and peppermint were the only choices. Today your choices grow by the day. (I had a pineapple and coconut tea this morning.)

And a word about water

Your water intake plays a role in the way you react to stress. Consume too little and you will feel lethargic, fatigued and more susceptible to tension.

Consume plenty, on the other hand, and it will help you to remain calm. It also helps in the prevention of hypertension, heart ailments, stroke, respiratory problems, constipation, headache, tooth decay, even the aging process itself.

How much water does it take to keep you feeling healthy and calm? At least eight full glasses a day. Minimum.

- Drink at least eight glasses of water a day.
- Drink two glasses on rising, and one before meals.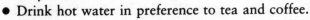
- Drink water (two sips to one) every time you drink alcohol or coffee.
- Keep a jug or bottle of water on your desk.
- Drink water from a quality wine glass so it will taste special.
- Drink cool water in preference to fizzy drinks.
- Drink hot water in preference to tea and coffee.

Make a habit of water drinking, and you'll improve your health and increase your ability to stay calm.

Calm associations

One of the curious long-term manifestations of stress is the way you subconsciously associate it with certain places, or patterns of behaviour.

For example, I always feel nervous when I walk into my dentist's surgery – even though it is a very pleasant place with lots of tropical fish and very calming music (listen to *Deep Calm* on www.calmcentre.com). Remember at school, how you always felt apprehensive when you walked into the principal's office, whether the principal was there or not, and whether you were in trouble or not? In a similar way, you associate certain feelings with certain places or behaviours to do with your work. You may not be conscious of this, but it happens every day of your working life – you unconsciously train yourself to associate stressful behaviour with certain places or events, and a stressful reaction is triggered whenever you encounter that place or event.

I'll give you another example. The owner of a failing business suffers her worst moments every time she opens a spreadsheet on her computer and realises her cashflow problem is slowly dragging her towards bankruptcy. Every week she turns on her computer, revises that spreadsheet, and sees her problem worsen. Within a very short time, this business owner will begin to associate the opening of a spreadsheet on her computer with the despair of seeing her business fail. Soon, every time she opens that program – whether it is to do cashflow analysis or simply to plan the staff holiday roster – she will again suffer those feelings of despair.

This subconscious phenomenon is known as a Programmed Conditioned Response (PCR). In the above case, the PCR had a negative association. It can also be associated with the positive. If, for example, you had your most thrilling sexual experience in the back seat of a Volkswagen, watch out next time someone attractive offers you a ride in a Volkswagen! That is *positive* PCR.

You can create your own *positive* associations, or PCRs, that are good for your mental health and will help you stay calm.

THE CALM SPACE

With little effort and no investment in real estate you can create your very own Calm Space using a PCR. Your Calm Space becomes a special refuge, steeped in positive associations, where you can become calm and at ease simply by moving to that place. If, for example, most of your stressful feelings at work take place at your desk in your office, you might choose to create an alternative place – a Calm Space – in an unused corner of your office. Or in the cafeteria, or the photocopy room, or outside by the fountain (if this doesn't upset your employer).

Whatever the place, your object is to infuse it with relaxed, positive mental associations, so that whenever you go there, you will feel calm, relaxed and powerful.

To transform this space into a calming refuge may take a few weeks, but considering the length of time you stay in a job, this is a minor wait. For the first few days or so, dash to this place whenever you feel particularly calm or happy about something. Physically move there, sit, and savour that positive feeling for as long as you can. Next time you're feeling particularly calm or happy, go back there again. And again, and again.

Do this a minimum of ten times. More if you can.

Within a very short time, you will have created a positive PCR in relation to that place. Your subconscious associations of it will be as a place where you're always calm and happy. This now becomes your Calm Space.

Whenever you feel tense or under pressure, all you have to do is physically move to this Calm Space. The moment you sit, you will begin to feel calm and happy – or at least more so than you did when you arrived.

And the best part of this is yet to come. The more times you use this place to produce feelings of being calm and happy, the more conditioned you become to this feeling, and the more powerful the association. If you use it regularly, it will grow in effectiveness as the days go by.

Look for these calm solutions:
The Sound of Calm .... page 280
The Ions of Calm .... page 276

288

GRIN AND BEAR IT

You can tell instantly whether a person is under pressure just by looking at their face: clenched teeth, furrowed brow, tight jaw, compressed lips. Tension tends to concentrate around the face and neck areas.

There is a powerful physical exercise you can perform that will reverse this tension and help you to relax – at will.

This exercise is so simple and transportable, you can employ it at any time of the day or night, no matter how much pressure you're under, no matter what deadlines you're facing.

It's your humble old wrinkly-eyed, white-toothed smile.

Physically, a smile is the muscular opposite of a tense face. But its real power is psychological. A smile is a PCR, a Programmed Conditioned Response. It is a subconscious trigger that produces an instant neurological stimulation of the pleasure centre of your brain, inducing feelings of happiness and well-being the instant it is flashed. In fact, it is probably the first, or one of the first PCRs you ever learned. You've been practising it, and it has been working for you, since childhood.

If you take it further and break into a laugh, the benefits you will feel are multiplied many times. For one thing, it helps to stabilise your blood pressure and assist your circulation.

So, for the sake of your health, temperament and tension levels, go to any lengths to find something to smile about in your work.

And, while it is in one sense selfish – because it's designed to make you feel good, nothing more – your colleagues will think you're being generous if you perform it in their presence.

You will be able to do it with only a minimum of practice. You just tighten the cheek muscles (A), pull up the mouth corners (B), and guess what – you have a smile (C).

Amazing.

Take it further, and break into a laugh, and the benefits you will feel are multiplied many times.

So, in the workplace, keep on the lookout for

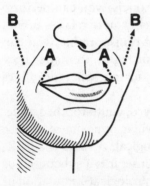
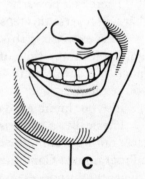

good-humoured laughter opportunities. If none arise, invent them. They will work as much for others' benefit as for your own.

Grin and Bear it

- When you're at work, be constantly on the lookout for things that will amuse you or, better still, make you laugh.
- If nothing makes you laugh, remember something that made you laugh recently. Or pretend you find something amusing, or appealing.
- Then smile. Go on, smile.

A calm mind in a calm body

Now we've established that most stress is a product of what's inside your head, it's time for us to take a look at your body. I've been looking forward to this.

Until now, much of our focus has been on the psychology of the individual, the subconscious and the emotions. By broadening our focus to take in the entire physiology, we not only involve those of you who are more body-conscious, but we add a dynamic new dimension to becoming calm.

Foremost among the physical ways of helping you to become calm is exercise: the most efficient way nature has yet devised to burn off the excess 'stress chemicals' in your system. But there are less strenuous techniques you can employ, that also achieve similar results.

Following are a number of ways that will help you to become calm by doing one of two things: either directly countering the effects of negative stress, or reversing the physical processes that lead to stress.

Enjoy.

STRAIGHT TO CALM

If you perform this technique exactly as I describe it, you will feel calm and uplifted in a matter of minutes.

A stressed person has a very distinct look: slumped shoulders, dropped chin, stooped back, folded arms, clenched fingers, furrowed brow – the muscles contracting, tensing, tightening. A calm person looks like the reverse of that.

You can become a calm person, or at least make yourself feel more relaxed, simply by reversing those tense characteristics – pulling back your shoulders, lifting your chin, straightening your back, loosening your arms, unclasping your fingers.

This understanding is the starting point of Straight to Calm.

You can do the following either seated or standing. If you like, you can stand with your back pressed against a wall the first time you try it. The idea is to sit or stand as straight as you possibly can.

When you start to feel relaxed, take a silver thread and attach it to a hook at the top of your skull. (Yes, it's an imaginary hook, as well as an imaginary silver thread.) Then take that silver thread and extend it all the way to a silver pulley on the ceiling directly above.

Now, gently pull on the silver thread ... bit by bit ... until you feel your body straighten and the kinks begin to unravel from your vertebrae and muscles.

Keep pulling until you feel your whole body begin to lift. Feel it lift a centimetre or so off the floor or the chair.

Your body will now be as straight as you can manage. It will feel lighter than you'll recall having felt before.

Now start Breathing Calm.

> **Look for these calm solutions:**
> Breathing Calm ....page 103
> The Sound of Calm...............page 280
> Basic Visualisation
> Template ....page 118

Straight to Calm

1 Either sit upright or stand, perhaps with your back pressed against the wall. Make your body as straight as you can.

2 Take an imaginary silver thread and attach it to the top of your head.

3 Extend the silver thread all the way to the ceiling and through an imaginary silver pulley.

4 Gently tighten the thread until you feel your body straighten and imagine it lifting a centimetre or so above the ground. Feel your body stretch out – all the way up your backbone.

5 Begin Breathing Calm. Enjoy that calm feeling until the tension has drained from your body and you are entirely relaxed.

CALM AND SWEATY

Strenuous exercise is one of life's proven antidotes to stress. If you run regularly or do aerobics, you'll know this. So, too, if you're a regular walker, cyclist or swimmer.

Physical exercise stimulates those parts of your nervous system that control your 'stress hormones'. This not only calms the nerves, it also enhances your long-term ability to deal with stress and stressful situations.

If you don't have any serious medical conditions (have a checkup if you're unsure), a calming exercise ideal is three to five workouts a week, each at 70 percent of your maximum heart rate (see chart below), lasting for 25 to 30 minutes.

TO CALCULATE YOUR MAXIMUM HEART RATE

Say, for example, you're forty years of age.

	220
Subtract your age from 220.	−40
Maximum heart rate =	180 beats/minute
Exercising heart rate is 70% of	
maximum =	126 beats/minute

(To calculate your heart or pulse rate, place your fingertips on your pulse and count the number of beats in 60 seconds.)

The easiest, and possibly the most relaxing, exercise program I can suggest is walking. Do it three to five times a week, for 30 to 45 minutes. Do it by yourself or with someone else. Do it in a place that gives you pleasure. Use your walk time to plan your day.

Exercise regularly and you'll feel like a new person – becoming calmer and more stress-free by the day.

A word of warning, though: if you push yourself too

hard or are too competitive in your approach, exercise can be stressful in itself. If you want it to be calming, exercise in moderation and enjoy it.

Look for these calm solutions:
The Sound of Calm.............page 280
Park It ....page 220

Calm and Sweaty

Use this as a guide for choosing your exercise program. Do one of the following, three to five times each week. Vary between the different exercises from time to time.
- Walk briskly for 30 to 45 minutes.
- Run for 25 minutes.
- Swim for 25 minutes.
- Cycle (at a reasonable speed) for 45 minutes.
- Perform aerobics for 25 minutes.
- Dance for 30 to 45 minutes.

Strive to maintain 70 percent of your maximum heart rate.

THE JAWS OF CALM

When stress concentrates around the head and the face, tension often comes sharply into focus in the muscles around the jaw. You clench your teeth, and the jaw muscles go rigid. (Watch these muscles pumping when someone tries to contain their anger.)

When your teeth are clenched and your jaw muscles clamped, the tension begins to spread to other parts of your body – leading to stiff back and shoulders, tension headache, lower back pain, and overall feelings of tension. I've heard chiropractors blame clenched jaws for chronic spinal problems.

To date, the treatment for this condition (if it was recognised as a condition) was eclectic, to say the least. A dentist could fit a little prosthetic known as a splint or a de-programmer which was designed to prevent the clenching and grinding of teeth.

Here are a couple of easier, and cheaper, treatments.

Tongue pressing

The first is a simple, but highly effective, way to relax the muscles in your lower jaw (the *masseter* muscles, see point B in the figure below).

To do this, simply press your tongue against the roof of your mouth, lightly, just behind your front teeth. The lightest touch is all that's necessary. It will feel comfortable enough to maintain this action for extended periods of time.

That's all you have to do.

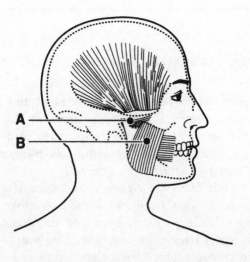

As long as you maintain this light pressure, your jaw muscles will be relaxed, and this will ease further into the muscles around the temples.

The two-fingered way
Another way to relieve the tension in your jaw area is by using two fingers.

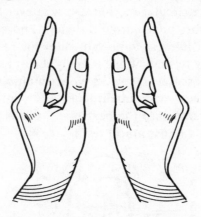

At the jaw muscle between your cheek and the earlobe (point A on the previous figure) you will feel an indentation, which, if you're tense, will be quite tender. Apply a direct inward pressure with the tip of your index fingers until a light pain can be felt. When you breathe out, apply pressure. As you breathe in, let the pressure off.

Repeat this several times until your jaw muscles relax.

FACE UP TO CALM

When you're trapped at work, the place where tension seems to concentrate most is in the shoulders, head and face.

Releasing tension around the shoulders can generally

only be done by one of two ways: through massage (by someone else) or shoulder exercises (see page 304).

You can relieve the tension around your face, however, by accessing a number of acupressure points around the facial area. You do this in one of two ways: either as downward pressure (breathe out, press in; breathe in, release), or as a simple rotary massage action with the fingertips. If you choose the latter, you massage *outwards* in a circular motion. Do whatever feels right.

Acupressure points around the eyes, nose, cheeks and temples are the most important ones for relaxation and are quite easy to find. While initially their precise location may seem obscure, if you let your intuition guide you, you'll find them without difficulty. (If you can't find a point, just move onto the next one – this is meant to be relaxing, not an anatomical test.)

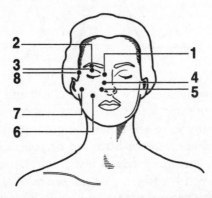

There are three points around the eye socket. The first (1) is where the eyebrow bone meets the bridge of your nose; press gently against the eyebrow bone and you will feel it. The second (2) is in a small indentation beneath your eyebrow bone which you will be able to feel with your thumb. The third (3) is directly behind that point, further into your eye socket. (Treat these last two gently.)

Next we come to two points alongside your nose. The first (4) is in a small groove just below where your eye socket touches your nose. The second (5) is in the indentation between your nostril and cheekbone.

The next point (6) is in the hollow below the front of your cheek, just above your teeth. If you open your mouth wide, you will feel another point (7) on the outer edge of your jaw muscle. It's a sensitive point; you won't miss it.

The last point (8) is one that has a powerful influence on the way you feel – you instinctively reach for it when you're under pressure. It's at your temples. Massaging this point is said to relieve depression as well as feelings of pressure.

Remember, though, that this is meant to be soothing – so take your time and enjoy the experience. When you've finished, sit quietly for 10 minutes and wait for a sense of calm to envelop you.

Look for these calm solutions:

Shoulder Unwind ....page 304

Straight to Calm ....page 292

Grin and Bear It ....page 289

SENSUOUS STRESS RELIEVER

This is a pleasurable little series of exercises that work wonders at wiping away tension, and are deceptively sensuous into the bargain – much more so than they may appear on this page.

You'll recognise some of them from the beauty salon. And, while beauty therapists tend to differ in their massage techniques, you'll find most of them cover the areas I describe.

Perform these exercises for the pleasure of the moment. Let them remind you of those wonderful relaxed moments during a facial. (If you're a man who's never had a facial, abandon any preconceptions of sissiness or 'make-overs', and discover these powerful calming properties in a beauty salon near you – there's probably one in the building next door right now.)

These exercises are meant to be relaxed and sensuous. Don't worry too much about following exactly the 'stroke patterns' I have included: do whatever feels good.

First, spend a couple of minutes Breathing Calm.

While you do this, place the palms of your hands over your eyes, allowing your nose to peek through. Apply a firm pressure for 20 seconds or so, then slowly slide your hands around your face towards your ears, lightly dragging on your facial muscles as you do so.

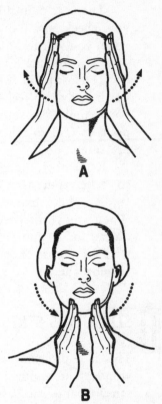

When your hands are at the side of your head, slowly slide them upwards, as shown in figure A, in a 'face lift' action. If you do this slowly, your facial muscles will now feel relaxed.

Then, with your fingertips, softly trace a line down your cheeks – barely caressing your flesh – to beneath your chin, until your fingertips slowly lose contact with your skin, as in figure B.

Your skin will now be tingling lightly. Repeat this action as long as it gives you pleasure, Breathing Calm the whole time. Then sit somewhere quiet and luxuriate in the feeling of calm that surrounds you.

Alternative paths to sensuousness

The figure below is a map of what some believe are the most calming facial massage patterns. To use them, all you have to do is slowly slide the fingers down your face, pausing at each point indicated, to apply a reasonably firm downward pressure. It's not essential that you are 100 percent accurate with either the course or the points – do what *feels* right for you.

The first course (figure A) is designed to remove the tension in your brow and eyes. It covers many of the acupressure points we identified in the preceding section. Start where your eyebrow bone meets the bridge of your nose, then go around the eyebrow indentation, to the temple, to the outer edge of your jaw muscle, to the indentation between your nostril and cheekbone. Use fingertips to trace this arc, pausing at each point to apply a light pressure.

The second course (figure B) is designed to ease the tension in your forehead area. Start at the highest central point of your forehead and trace a line to your temples, arcing above your eyebrows, continue on to your forehead before coming to rest at the acupressure point at the corner of each eyebrow.

The third course (figure C) is designed to ease the tensions in your face and jaw areas. It's a natural-flowing line

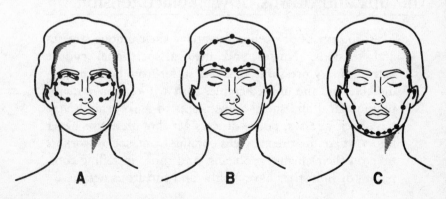

A   **B**   **C**

from the acupressure point at your temples to the top of your cheekbone, to the indentation behind the cheekbone, to the muscle at the corner of the jawbone, to the edge of the chin, through to the point of the chin.

Extract the maximum pleasure from these massages. Put as much tenderness and sensuousness into them as you can. The results will be well worth your effort.

The final sensuous touch

The final touch – or make it the first touch if you'd rather – to all of these facial massage techniques is one that will be familiar to you, but probably one you've never thought of using at work.

It's a hot towel.

Simply take a small face towel, immerse it in warm to hot water, wring it out and drape it over your face.

Then sit back with your eyes closed, Breathing Calm, and feel the tension drain from your body.

Look for these calm solutions:
Standing Up for Calm .... page 308
The Sound of Calm .... page 280
Using Your Nose .... page 202

The ups and downs of workplace tension

Most industries or occupations have their unique stresses and tensions. Nurses and medical personnel endure extraordinary pressures, teachers suffer from both the predictable and the unpredictable, shift workers have major physiological and social adjustments to make, cab drivers have their stresses, police officers get shot at, actors never know where their next role is coming from, social workers take on their clients' problems, and those in failing companies or industries have a slow and torturous decline.

Yet the two *physical* occupational stresses I have singled out are ones you may not have considered all that threatening.

The first relates to keyboard and computer usage because it is fast becoming the most widespread of all work activities. And will become even more so. Moreover, the physical tensions it involves are similar to those encountered by people in other kinds of clerical positions. Most of the physical stresses these people encounter tend to concentrate around the neck and shoulders, before moving *down* into the lower back and legs.

The second area of physical stress we will cover occurs in industries where long periods of standing are required. Such industries include hospitality, health, retail, security and defence. The physical stresses this second group endures tend to concentrate around the feet and legs, before moving *up* into the lower back and shoulders.

So, by addressing the conditions where the tension spreads *downwards*, then the conditions where the tension spreads *upwards*, we should cover the entire body – at least from a musculature point of view.

(There are other common areas of physical stress in the workplace – such as shift work, repetitive strain injury, industrial noise, dust and other pollution – that require specific attention beyond the scope of this book.)

Keyboard calm

So many of us now use computers at work, and suffer a variety of stressful consequences as a result.

The most obvious tension to arise from this activity is the muscular strain that centres around the neck and shoulders. Next comes eye strain. Then comes the generalised feeling of tension that follows extended periods at the keyboard.

I will not buy into the issues of extremely low frequency (ELF) radiation or repetitive strain injury (RSI) other than to make two points. All electric equipment from toasters to computer monitors emits some level of radiation; it is probably wise not to remain *too* close to such equipment for extended periods. It is also worth noting that all repetitive physical activities, from golf to typing, will result in physical strain if you fail to employ the correct techniques (in application as well as rest periods).

Those who sit in front of a monitor will probably be in sorest need, but many of the techniques that follow apply to other clerical functions as well.

THE SHOULDER UNWIND

If you sit working at a computer for long periods of time, the most common problem you'll suffer will be tension in the shoulders, back and neck, which, in turn, lead to stressful feelings. Because your back muscles are extraordinarily strong, they do not always warn you about pain or tension as your other muscles do. Instead, they contract and become progressively tighter, which causes other muscles, such as those in your neck or lower back, to tense.

The easiest way around this is to stop work and perform two sets of exercises – *every 30 minutes*. This is designed to loosen the muscles in your back and shoulders, before the tension spreads to other parts of your body.

You can perform this exercise standing (preferable) or while seated, but it is important that you do it regularly.

Every 30 minutes.

With your back straight, rotate your shoulders backwards (figure A opposite), ten times.

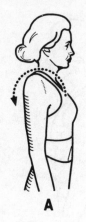 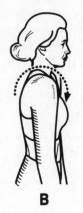 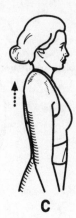

A   B   C

Then, rotate your shoulders forwards (figure B) ten times.

Repeat this exercise until your shoulders feel relaxed.

Next lift your shoulders into an elevated position (figure C) until they feel all tense again, then let them drop, limply.

THE GOOSENECK

The following neck exercise is best performed when no-one's looking, because you can look like a bit of a goose as you do it.

It's called the gooseneck.

This particular exercise is designed to ease the tension in the back of your neck. As with the Shoulder Unwind, it should be performed every 30 minutes when you're working on the computer.

With your back straight, simply pull your chin back into your chest as far as you can. Hold this position for

10 seconds. Then thrust your chin *forward* as far as you can. Hold for 10 seconds.

Repeat this action a few times until your neck feels relaxed.

KICK A PHONE BOOK

Because keyboards and computers are now common tools for people in all different facets of the workforce, the basic ergonomic training which typists used to receive is no longer considered so important.

Typists have long known, for example, of the relaxing effect of having their feet elevated on something as they type. They've also known that this was why phone directories were designed to be as thick as they are: two volumes on top of each other make a perfect footrest for when you're working at a keyboard and monitor.

Put your phone directories to good use. And you'll find they make a relaxing difference to your work.

TAKE A LOOK INTO THE DISTANCE

Computer monitors are seductive things. They keep blinking at you, imploring you to keep watching, to explore their secrets for longer and longer. This is why your eyes tire after only a short period of working.

The way to overcome this is to perform one simple eye exercise every 10 minutes: blink a few times, then allow your eyes to focus on infinity (the horizon). That's all there is to it: blink a few times, then allow your eyes to focus on infinity. If you're in a position that does not permit this luxury, simply allow your eyes to go out of focus instead.

One of the great joys of life is to discover that something so basic can have such immediate, positive results.

> **Look for these calm solutions:**
> Straight to Calm .... page 292
> The Sound of Calm .... page 280
> Calm the Building .... page 274

SAVE YOUR WORK

Here is a simple, two-fingered routine that prevents headache and heartache by eliminating one of the most common stresses a computer user ever experiences: losing your unsaved documents.

The technique is simply to save your documents more often than you think you need to. Every few minutes. And do regular backups of your important work – more than you think you need to.

Sooner or later, this small discipline will save you a lot of headaches and heartache.

STANDING UP FOR CALM

If you work in an industry where long periods of standing are required, you'll be aware of the physical tensions that accompany it. You will also be aware that when these physical tensions occur, emotional tension soon follows.

The stresses tend to begin around the feet and legs. Then the tensions start moving up the body, causing lower back problems and, through referred pain, an aching neck and shoulders.

The first step in avoiding these tensions starts with your footwear and the surface beneath your feet. There is nothing much I can tell you about footwear that common sense would not have already told you – 'practical' out-performs 'fashionable' every time. For the surface beneath your feet, choose carpet, rubber or sprung floorboards over tiles or concrete and you will be well rewarded.

The second step in relaxing the feet and legs is a basic reflexology routine you can perform yourself. According to reflexology principles, the feet are mini-maps of the body and its organs. By applying pressures to specific areas of the 'foot map', therapists claim to relieve problems in other parts of the body.

Whether or not you accept the wider claims about reflexology's healing properties, you can be sure that the one area it is guaranteed to work in is the relief of stress and tension.

Because our feet are protected most of the time, they're particularly sensitive to this subtle treatment. Just massaging your feet stimulates more than seven thousand nerve endings that you wouldn't normally be able to access; this is not only deeply relaxing, but improves circulation as well.

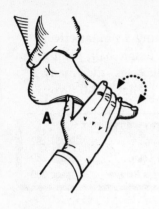

You can use simple reflexology to relieve the tension in your feet, legs and entire body, because these points often relate to other areas.

To begin with, this lunchtime, find a quiet, restful place, remove your shoes and take a minute or so to relax.

Grasp your left ankle in your left hand (see figure A). With your right hand, gently twist your foot backwards and forwards a few times to relax your joints.

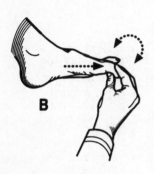

Next, spend a few moments massaging each toe individually. Stretch and rotate each toe from side to side (figure B).

Now, take hold of your foot with your left hand as shown. With your right fist, firmly press up against the underside of your foot (figure C). Press with your right fist, then squeeze with your left hand. Press, squeeze. Do this several times.

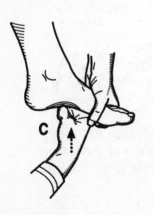

Finally, use the lightest brush of your fingertips – from ankles to toes, tops and bottoms of feet '– to sensitise the nerve endings in your feet.

Repeat with the other foot.

Sit quietly for a few minutes, Breathing Calm, as the relaxed feeling moves up through your legs into the rest of your body.

Relaxing on the ball

A simpler, less structured way of achieving a similar effect is to remove your shoe and stand on a tennis ball, rolling it backwards and forwards as it accesses the many pressure points under your foot. That's all you have to do: press down on the ball and roll it from your toes to your heel. Then repeat with your other foot.

Look for these calm solutions:
Straight to Calm .... page 292
The Sound of Calm .... page 280
Sensuous Stress Reliever .... page 299

PUT YOUR FEET UP

Here's a simple practice to employ at least once a day for relieving the tensions that build up in your legs and feet, as well as your back and neck muscles.

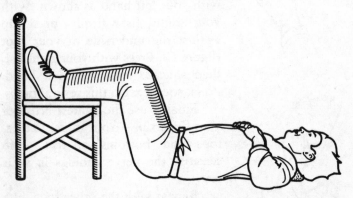

All you have to do is lie on the floor with your feet up on a chair (knees bent). That's all. Not only is it a relaxing break in itself, but it also eases the strain from the legs and lower back.

While you're doing this, you can also relieve tension in the back and neck by using a small rolled towel placed either:

(i) across the back of your neck at the base of your skull; or

(ii) along the upper part of your backbone so a shoulder blade falls on either side of it.

Remain in this reclining position for 10 to 20 minutes, Breathing Calm at the same time.

You may experience a little muscular discomfort from the pressure of the towel – especially if you're really tense – but if you find yourself getting dizzy or nauseous cease the exercise.

Look for these calm solutions:

Breathing Calm ....page 103
The Sound of Calm...............page 280
Self Time...........................page 153
Idling...............................page 216

WHEN THE CAUSE IS YOUR LIFESTYLE

THE LAST CAUSE of work-place stress is something that doesn't directly relate to your work at all: it's

> Becoming calm and relaxed is one of the few disciplines in life that works better the easier you take it.

your lifestyle and habits. Some may argue that things that happen away from your work should have no impact on how you feel or perform while you're there. However, these lifestyle issues have a real bearing, not only on how you feel, but on how you cope at work. Indeed, many people cite personal issues as their main cause of work-place stress.

This is understandable. If you have a stressful life outside of work, chances are you're going to bring stress and tension to work with you.

Changing these habits, or trying to reform you in any way, is not the function of this book. Our purpose is to overcome the *results* of these habits. To do that, you have to first acknowledge these habits exist, then set about compensating for them.

Following are a few suggestions on how you can make *pleasurable* lifestyle improvements – without pain, and without sacrifice. This is really only scratching the surface. After reading these, I'm sure you'll think of many others.

Have fun researching.

PAMPER YOURSELF

Here's a suggestion you won't often see in stress-management books. It's not about altering your lifestyle. It's not about becoming healthy. It's not even about overcoming stress.

It's about having fun.

I have this belief that stress should not be treated as seriously as the 'stress industry' would have us do. Whether stress is driving more and more people to the edge is not the issue. Whether it's more prevalent today than it was up to a hundred years ago is also not important. What is important is that we don't take it too seriously.

Too much talk of stress actually contributes to the problem. It's stressful. This is why, to really become calm, you have to be able to see the lighter side.

It's not easy to feel stressed while you're having fun!

Becoming calm and relaxed is one of the few disciplines in life that works better the easier you take it. Why? Because the more fun you have, the better you feel, the more serotonin (the neurochemical that relieves depression) your brain produces, the more capable you are of enjoying life and being relaxed. When you have fun, you activate this great calm cycle. Hence, the most potent relaxation techniques for you are those that you most enjoying doing.

This is why I advocate treatments like massage. On the surface it may seem remarkably hedonistic. Perhaps it is. But, for half the cost of an evening at a nightclub, you not only receive a pleasurable hour of deep relaxation, but you also receive an extended benefit that will help you go through the week feeling calm and relaxed, instead of tense and hungover.

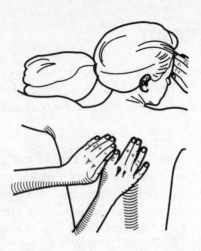

Massage has clear health benefits. It directs the blood flow to various parts of the body, stimulates the heart, encourages more oxygen into the muscles, and helps to eliminate toxins – but it is what massage can do for your spirit that makes it worth the investment. After a massage session, you will enjoy a unique state – a combination of deep relaxation and energy: skin tingling, muscles loose, and your mind at peace.

Try to establish a pattern, because the benefits of massage are cumulative. If you can afford it, enjoy one every week.

INDULGE YOUR APPETITES

You are probably aware that the food you eat affects your emotions and mental state as much as it does your body.

Certain foods have long been known as 'calm foods' because they have a soothing effect on your stress or anxiety levels. Generally, these are not so much individual food items as combinations.

In most diets you'll find two types of foods: acid-forming and alkaline-forming. *The ideal calm diet maintains a ratio of alkalines to acids of about 80:20.* Alkaline foods (80 percent) are things like fruits, vegetables, whole-grain flour and cereals, while the acid-forming foods (20 percent) are things like meat, sugar, coffee, processed foods, white flour and preservatives.

A popular misconception about foods is to view the healthy ones as boring, and the nutritionless ones as fun. Or, to put it another way, big flavours are considered better than subtle ones, taste sensations are more desirable than quality. This is the packaged-goods approach to taste: developed in laboratories, nurtured by supermarkets, and elevated on television. The commercials would have you believe that eating such foods is luxurious or indulgent, but really they amount to little more than unimaginative, portion-controlled snacks.

Real indulgence, on the other hand, not only has sensuality but makes you feel good as well. To most palates, a steaming dish of spaghetti marinara is as tasty as a breast of duck – except it leaves you feeling better afterwards. A great arugula salad is as interesting as french fries, and a mango puree is as seductive as a commercial sorbet – but again, it leaves you feeling better afterwards.

Indulge yourself with the foods that will keep you calm (maintain the ratio of 80:20 between alkaline and acid-forming foods) and your good taste will be rewarded time and time again.

PLAY WITH YOURSELF

Being physically fit brings you many steps closer to calm.

Just as the foods that serve you best can be indulgent and pleasurable so, too, can be the physical routines you employ to keep yourself fit. The concept of 'No pain, no gain' is macho nonsense. Why shouldn't exercise be enjoyable and pleasurable?

Do what makes you feel good. Find an exercise you can get pleasure from, and pursue it. If you can't find one that moves you, go walking. The beauty of walking is that you can do other things that give you pleasure at the same time. You can go watching, golfing, thinking, visiting, talking, listening, planning – any number of things – while you get your exercise.

There is no better start to a calm day than a brisk, 40-minute walk as the sun rises. Walk. Keep your head up. And remember your Breathing Calm.

HIT THE TUB

You won't get away with this at work, but there is a wonderful place you can visit to escape all the tensions and stresses of everyday life.

Often, you'll find this place in your own home. And you can go there – undisturbed – early in the morning, late at night, or any other time you nominate.

It's the bath.

Fill it with warm water. Add bath salts or a few drops of calming aromatic oils. Turn off the lights, maybe light a

Look for these calm solutions:

Sensuous Stress Reliever ....page 299
Breathing Calm ....page 103
The Scent of Calm................page 282
The Sound of Calm...............page 280

candle. Then just sit there, soaking away your tensions as you enjoy Breathing Calm.

HAVE FUN

Lastly, and most important of all, don't take this stress business too seriously. Look for the opportunities to have a laugh, to take the preciousness and pomposity out of life.

If all else fails, remember the advice of the immortal Guru Adrian: 'Having fun is half the fun.'

LONGER-TERM
CALM SOLUTIONS

NOW, FOR THE
SERIOUS STUFF

THE FINAL SECTION of this book is devoted to ways of finding longer-term calm. These recommendations will help you overcome most of the ill effects that arise from lifestyle practices and habits; they do this by substituting new practices and habits.

Remember that man I wrote about earlier – the man with two principles for maintaining calm and perspective in his life? His first principle was: 'I never lose sleep over small issues.' But it was the second that really showed his uniqueness: 'I treat all issues like small issues.'

To be able to react to all situations as if they were small issues is a skill that few possess. But it is one you can easily learn. It won't make you callous or insensitive towards the needs or plight of others. It won't lessen your efforts or dedication to the work you have to do. Nor will it reflect on the importance with which you view your job, your employer, your clients, your employees or your bank manager. It is simply a way of maintaining a sense of calm and perspective, no matter what the world may throw at you.

To achieve this requires an investment of time and effort. And, to be really effective, it will probably require a significant adjustment in lifestyle and attitude.

The six ways to lasting calm

To become a calm person, to find real peace and contentment, it is necessary to pay attention to a number of different aspects of life. I call these the Six Ways to Lasting Calm. They are: Commitment, Meditation, Diet, Exercise, Selflessness and Attitude.

1. Commitment

Not surprisingly, the most important consideration in finding long-term calm is commitment. If you are committed to finding the calm solution to life, you are halfway there.

Assuming you have this commitment, all you have to do is *concentrate on any three of the remaining five areas.* Ideally, you would concentrate on them all.

Follow these solutions and you will become calm, contented and able to cope with anything your job or your workplace can throw at you. Adopt them as part of your everyday routine, and your life will be enriched beyond all expectations.

2. Meditation

Millions believe that meditation is the one essential for a happy, well-balanced, healthy way of life.

If you have read my earlier book, *The Calm Technique*, you will understand how powerful a tool meditation can be. It can transform your life and your attitudes. Use it regularly, and you could reasonably expect to:

- obtain relief from tension, anxiety and fatigue;
- cope better with everyday problems;
- be emotionally stronger;
- have improved concentration;
- be more positive;
- be more tolerant; and
- get more enjoyment out of life.

The meditation technique I refer to is covered in greater depth towards the end of this book (page 325).

It is based on simple understandings and techniques that a large proportion of the world considers commonplace. If you approach these with dedication and sincerity, you will discover the life-transforming powers that meditation can deliver.

3. Diet

Your diet affects your state of mind as much as it does your body. Certain foods can rightfully be described as 'calm foods', and can have a soothing effect on the way you feel, especially in the long term.

Precisely what these foods are is not so important as the principles that underpin their use. Nevertheless, as a simple guide:

Consume more	Consume less
Vegetables, fruits, complex carbohydrates and wholegrains	Alkaline-forming foods like coffee, meat, sugar, white flour, nuts and preservatives
Water (at least eight glasses a day)	Coffee, tea, cola
Vitamins A, C, E and B	Processed foods
Fresh fruit or fruit juice at breakfast	Fats
Vegetable protein	Animal protein

4. Exercise

Regular exercise diminishes the effects of stress on the body.

Regular exercise helps you to cope better.

Regular exercise will make you feel more calm and contented.

5. Selflessness

For a long-term sense of calm and fulfilment, seek out opportunities to help others less fortunate than yourself. When you immerse yourself in the act of helping another individual, you overcome the self-centred nature of your own stresses and anxieties.

Make a habit of helping others.

We are not talking about covering up for inefficient workmates here, or taking on more than your fair share of responsibilities: we're talking about helping others whose needs – emotional as much as physical – are greater than your own.

The benefit to you is something you've probably experienced before: that sense of elation and accomplishment which follows an act of generosity towards someone else. Do this on a regular basis, and your actions will lead to feelings of peace and satisfaction.

6. Attitude

If you can maintain a state of real calm, you will find it easy to maintain a positive, happy outlook on life. The opposite is also true: if you maintain a positive and happy outlook on life, you will find it easy to be calm.

Many say that a positive attitude and a sense of optimism are their own reward. I like to think they are the launching pad to all the wonderful things in life you want for yourself and for others, including a sense of peace and contentedness. They also lead to better health, more effective relationships and vastly improved communications.

Choose four of the six

For long-term peace and contentment, all you have to do is pay attention to 'Commitment' plus any three of the remaining Six Ways to Lasting Calm. They are: Meditation, Diet, Exercise, Selflessness and Attitude.

You will be rewarded many times over if you pay attention to all six.

The calm technique

One of the most powerful skills you will ever learn in life is the ability to meditate. Unfortunately, the mere mention of that

> A free 30-minute massage each morning before you go to work . . . (This is how you should think of 'meditation'.)

word, meditation, frightens many people off. This is understandable, considering the abstruseness of its teaching in many areas.

Let's see if we can make it simpler for you.

A few years ago I wrote a book called *The Calm Technique*. I'm told it is – or was – one of the most widely read books of its type in the world. Part of what that book is about is a simple technique for finding peace and harmony in a restless age.

The meditation style that I call the Calm Technique is a simple exercise that anyone can master and apply. It requires no particular spiritual belief or understanding, and nor does it subscribe to any particular philosophy or way of life. As the title of the original book said, it is 'meditation without magic or mysticism'.

Meditation is the process of stilling the mind – suspending conscious thought, revelling in just being. Once the mind is still, the other benefits flow naturally and of their own accord. You exist purely in the moment. No thoughts to distract you, no worries about the past or concerns for the future; your mind and your emotions in a wonderful, peaceful, effortless neutral. But, unlike when you're asleep, your mind is also wide awake and alert.

The physiological effects

Practised regularly, the Calm Technique induces a series of physiological effects.

While you are in the meditative state, there is a dramatic change in the pattern of your brainwaves. Beta waves are associated with alertness and concentration; alpha with relaxation and visualisation; theta with memory and intuition; delta with sleep and healing. In meditation there is an increase in alpha, theta and delta waves – a combination that exists only in this state!

The Calm Technique also has a direct effect on your metabolism. Your oxygen consumption decreases even further than when you are in a deep sleep. Your heartbeat and blood pressure decrease almost as dramatically. Your blood's lactate level (which increases during stress) decreases up to 50 percent, nearly four times faster than in a state of deep relaxation. These unique physiological states are the *opposite* to those you experience during moments of stress or anxiety.

This is why meditation produces such a profound sense of peace, harmony and well-being.

How to do it

Despite the fact that many organisations devote their existence to teaching it, and despite the fact that I have written books and conducted countless seminars talking about it, meditation is exquisitely simple.

All it requires is for you to still your mind.

You do this by focusing on one thing – to the exclusion of all others. Some meditation techniques would have you focus on a physical object, or on a complex series of actions (as in tai chi). Others require you to concentrate on an image. Yet others suggest a sound. It could be entrancing, meditative music (see Calm Music on page 280), or any sound you choose. More commonly, perhaps, it would be the sound of your own voice speaking a single word – any word – over and over again. In classical meditation parlance, this is known as a 'mantra'. And many schools of meditation will tell you this is a sacred word. If you were to follow this procedure, simply repeating the word over and over again – silently or aloud – for 20 or 30 minutes, you would be meditating.

That's all you have to do. One word repeated (in your mind) over and over again for a period of 20 or 30 minutes. And when your attention strays – which it will – you simply guide it back to that repeated word or sound.

The Calm Technique

1 With low lights, comfortable clothes and temperature, commence Breathing Calm for a minute or so. Close your eyes and listen to your breath.

2 Quietly say one word (for example, 'Calm') to yourself. Listen to yourself speak the word. Choose whatever rhythm you feel comfortable with as you repeat it over and over.

3 Now hear yourself saying it, without actually uttering a sound. Hear the word coming from inside your head, directly behind your eyes.

4 Continue hearing this word, over and over again, for at least 20 minutes. When you discover your attention wandering, gently go back to that word. Don't force yourself; don't worry if you can't do it well, it doesn't matter.

5 After 20 minutes or so, gradually bring your attention back to the present. Sit and wait a few minutes, as you become more alert and awake.

Even as briefly as I have described it, the Calm Technique will work for you provided that you remember four things:

(i) It is meant to be as easy as it appears.

(ii) The experience in itself does not have to be anything special.

(iii) It is not a test of concentration or willpower.

(iv) It is meant to be a restful pleasure.

For a more complete understanding, read my earlier book, *The Calm Technique*. Or, for a more visual interpretation, feel free to log onto the meditation page of our Internet site (http://www.calmcentre.com).

A CALM PROGRAM FOR LEADERS

- Walk or exercise three to five times a week
- One extended planning session a week
- Delegate ruthlessly
- Planning review during walk
- Massage every week
- Do something for others once a week
- Converse with 'ordinary folk', once a week
- 30 minutes Self Time, five days a week
- Self Time on page 153
- Creative Long-Range Planner on page 171
- Pretend to B on page 206
- Idling on page 216
- Information Emancipation on page 149
- Calm and Sweaty on page 293
- Pamper Yourself on page 313
- Look for a Little Stress on page 218

A CALM PROGRAM FOR MANAGERS

- Walk or exercise three to five times a week
- One extended planning session a week
- Planning review during walk
- Delegate
- Massage every month
- Do something for others once a week
- 30 minutes Self Time, five days a week
- Self Time on page 153
- Creative Long-Range Planner on page 171
- Pretend to B on page 206
- Idling on page 216
- Know Your Limits on page 147

- The Power of No on page 145
- Work One Day at a Time on page 156
- Managing Difficult People on page 228
- The Calm Agenda on page 180

A CALM PROGRAM FOR UP-AND-COMINGS

- Walk or exercise three to five times a week
- One long-range planning session a week
- Planning review during walk
- Massage every month
- Do something for others once a week
- 30 minutes Self Time, five days a week
- Self Time on page 153
- Know Your Limits on page 147
- The Art of Negotiation on page 241
- Speaking Your Mind on page 233
- How to Get What You Want on page 232
- The Power of No on page 143
- The Nice Way to No on page 145
- Allocating Time for Calm on page 138
- Work One Day at a Time on page 156

A CALM PROGRAM FOR JUNIORS

- Walk or exercise three to five times a week
- One long-range planning session a week
- Planning review during walk
- Do something for others once a day
- Speaking Your Mind on page 233
- How to Get What You Want on page 232
- Allocating Time for Calm on page 138

- The Power of No on page 143
- The Nice Way to No on page 145
- The 100 Percent Effort on page 159
- The Life Priorities Calculator on page 91
- Assume You're Secure on page 221
- 30-Second Course in Marketing on page 237

HELP!

Calm in a crisis

Despite the seriousness with which you and I view everyday stress-related problems, they usually do not compare with those

There are simple steps you can take that will enable you to remain calm in a crisis, and to move on beyond the crisis.

events of absolute crisis: grief, serious illness, physical or emotional trauma, dismissal, arrest – you will no doubt recognise such events when they occur.

In the event of something like this happening, you may not have the discipline or presence of mind to recall the advice and techniques in this book.

In most cases, the formula that follows will do little to ease the pain, to relieve the grief, or to remedy the situation. What it will enable someone to do, though, is get through to the next step: the *post*-crisis rebuilding.

The steps involved in Calm in a Crisis are simple, perhaps predictable. But they are sensible and effective in getting you through to the next stage.

Calm in a Crisis

- Remove your shoes.
- Stay warm.
- Avoid cigarettes, coffee or alcohol.
- Begin Breathing Calm.
- Listen to each breath, concentrate on your breathing; do it as perfectly as you can manage.
- Seek help.

Who do you turn to for help?

Seeking help is not a sign of weakness. Seek it from a friend, a spiritual adviser, or from one of the many crisis counsellors you will find in the phone book (many do not charge for their services). There are significant, sometimes even life-saving, benefits from establishing this contact. Whether the discussion draws useful advice or not is seldom the issue; the real benefit comes from sharing your experience and in receiving encouragement to continue.

If you are at a loss as to whom you can turn to, look under 'Crisis' in the telephone directory. The directories of most cities have a listing under that heading.

(If you have suggestions as to places that provide help in a crisis, please share your knowledge by adding them to the 'crisis' page on the Calm Centre Internet site at http://www.calmcentre.com)

STAY CALM

The Calm Centre

The Calm Centre has been described as a 'calm think tank' – a loose collaboration of psychologists, natural therapists, writers, artists, film-makers and composers. It was established by the author, Paul Wilson, in 1995.

Above all, the contributors to the Calm Centre share two passions: discovering new ways to induce calm in the individual; and spreading calm through any publishing or broadcasting medium available.

The Calm Centre's philosophy is profoundly simple. It's to be:

(i)   calming;
(ii) focused on solutions;
(iii) as uplifting as possible; and
(iv) creatively worthwhile.

While some of the Calm Centre collaborators work from the United States and Europe, and others work in remote and rather exotic locations within Australia, its headquarters are located in the computer and media-driven heart of North Sydney's business district.

Feel free to visit, and to share your calm experiences, at http://www.calmcentre.com